GW00683449

LESSONS

FOR NEW BELIEVERS

WITNESS LEE

Living Stream Ministry
Anaheim, CA • www.lsm.org

First Edition, September 2005.

ISBN 978-0-7363-2960-6

Published by

Living Stream Ministry
2431 W. La Palma Ave., Anaheim, CA 92801 U.S.A.
P. O. Box 2121, Anaheim, CA 92814 U.S.A.

Printed in Australia

08   09   10   11   12   13   /   9   8   7   6   5   4   3

CONTENTS

PREFACE

This book is a collection of lessons given by Brother Witness Lee in a spiritual training in Taipei in the fall of 1959. The messages have been translated from the original Chinese.

Ephesians 1:4 Even as He chose us in Him before the foundation of the world to be holy and without blemish before Him in love.

1 Peter 1:2 Chosen according to the foreknowledge of God the Father in the sanctification of the Spirit unto the obedience and sprinkling of the blood of Jesus Christ = Grace to you and peace be multiplied.

KNOWING THAT WE ARE SAVED

(1)

In relation to leading new believers, we have the following publications: *Messages for Building Up New Believers* by Watchman Nee and *The Crucial Truths in the Bible* in Chinese. After serious consideration before the Lord, I feel to give some practical material for teaching new believers.

Lesson 1 is "Knowing That We Are Saved." In leading new believers, we need to lay a firm and solid foundation in the matter of salvation. Otherwise, we cannot expect them to grow, to walk the way of the Lord, to consecrate, or to serve the Lord. A person must be clear concerning his salvation, having a firm and solid foundation, in order to grow, walk, consecrate, and serve the Lord properly. Hence, the foundation is very important.

There is no need for me to speak much. I will merely point out the main items. However, when this lesson is presented to new believers, it should involve three or four sessions.

CHOSEN

Ephesians 1:4 says that God chose us in Christ before the foundation of the world. First Peter 1:2 says that the believers were all chosen by God. In helping people to know that they are saved, we must begin with God's choosing before the foundation of the world. We should say to the brothers and sisters, "Your salvation is based on God's choosing you from the beginning. You must not think that your salvation is a coincidence or that you took the initiative to believe in the Lord. No! The beginning, the initiation, rests with God, and it

started even before time began. In eternity past, God chose
you. Before God's hand did anything for you, He already had
a plan in His heart. In His heart He chose you long before His
hand saved you. Because God chose you, you were born in an
age in which the gospel is easily heard, and you live in a
region where it is easy to contact the gospel. His sovereign
authority coordinated the time, space, and environment in
such a way that you were brought to a situation where you
could only respond by believing in the Lord; you had to turn
to Him. Believing in the Lord is the same as being a man. It is
altogether of Him, not of you. You did not initiate it; He
directed it. It did not begin with you; it began with Him
before time began. It was He who chose you in Christ before
the foundation of the world."

PREDESTINATED

God predestinated everyone He chose. Ephesians 1:5 says
that God predestinated us. Romans 8:29 says that those
whom He foreknew, He also predestinated. This predestination is what we call "marking out beforehand." When we
select an object, after we have picked it out, we may put a
mark on it; this is to "mark out" the object. In Greek, *predestination* has the meaning of "marking out." In his translation of
Ephesians 1:5, Darby uses the phrase "having marked...out."
God not only chose the believers in eternity past; He also
marked them out. This is very clear. Once someone is chosen,
he is destined; being chosen comes first, then being destined.
In eternity, God chose us and then marked us out, that is, predestinated us. Therefore, salvation was our destiny.

We should speak in this way concerning selection and predestination only after a person is saved. If, while preaching
the gospel, we say that all those who are saved are predestinated by God, having no way to escape, and that anyone not
predestinated by God cannot be saved, people may then say,
"Fine, I am not predestinated, so forget it."

D. L. Moody encouraged his seminary students to preach
the gospel. A student, who heard Moody's teaching on predestination in class, was impressed and did not dare to preach the
gospel, because he had a problem. He said to Moody, "I dare

not preach the gospel now." Moody asked him why, and he said, "When I am preaching, I look at a person and consider whether he is predestinated; I look at another and consider whether he is chosen. If God has not chosen and predestinated these ones, and they are eventually persuaded by me to believe in the Lord, will I not be making a big mistake?" Moody then replied, "Brother, just do your best to persuade him. As long as you can persuade someone to believe in the Lord, he has been chosen and predestinated by God." Then Moody went on to say, "At the entrance of heaven, the words 'whoever will may come' are written on the outside; this means that whoever believes can be saved. But once a person passes through the entrance and looks back, he will see written on the inside, 'You have been predestinated.' Outside of the entrance is *whoever,* but inside of the gate is *predestinated.*" Thus, when leading those who have passed through the entrance and have been baptized, we should say, "You have been predestinated by God. You believed in the Lord and were saved because God picked you out and marked you out a long time ago."

CALLED

Hebrews 3:1 speaks of the "holy brothers, partakers of a heavenly calling." Every believer is called by God from the heavens.

Romans 8:30 says, "Those whom He [i.e., God] predestinated, these He also called." Once He selected, He predestinated; once He predestinated, He called. If God had not called us, how could we have turned to the Lord? If God had not called us, how could we have heard the gospel? The gospel is the voice of God calling us. Thus, there is a hymn that says, "The Lord is calling you today." Today God is calling with the voice of the gospel.

Romans 1:7 speaks of the "called saints." Some Bible versions render this phrase as *called to be saints;* this is an incorrect translation. The proper translation is "called saints." All believers are called saints. We can be saved and sanctified, thus becoming saints because God has called us.

Ephesians 1:18 says, "That you may know what is the hope

of His calling." God's calling is a calling of grace, in which is the greatest hope. The first step in God's saving, after His choosing and predestination, is His calling us.

Ephesians 4:1 says, "Walk worthily of the calling with which you were called." Therefore, God's calling is a great thing, not a small matter. We need to let all the new believers know that they were saved unto the Lord because they received God's calling.

SPRINKLED BY THE BLOOD

After God calls us, there is repentance and belief. Once we believe, God sprinkles us with the blood shed on the cross by His Son. Without the sprinkling of the blood, God has no way to do the subsequent steps of the work of salvation in us. This is because we were filthy and sinful.

First Peter 1:2 refers to the "sprinkling of the blood of Jesus Christ." The sprinkling of the blood of the Lord Jesus upon us is its application. We were evil, filthy, and full of transgressions, God's condemnation was upon us, and there was no way for the record of our sins to be annulled. But when the redeeming blood of the Lord Jesus was sprinkled upon us, it solved all these problems. The blood not only covered our sins; it also purged them away. The sprinkling of the blood upon us enables God to continue with many works of grace within us.

REDEEMED

As soon as the blood is sprinkled upon us, we are redeemed. The blood is for redemption.

Ephesians 1:7 says, "In whom we have redemption through His blood." The emphasis in redemption is on being redeemed, not on being saved. Although there is the connotation of being saved, being saved does not come first; redemption does. After we sinned, we came under the condemnation of God's righteous law. We needed to pay the price of the righteous requirement of God's law in order to be freed from the law. We were bound by the law and were under the condemnation of the righteous requirement of the law. However, the Lord Jesus shed His blood on the cross, satisfying the righteous requirement of the law and paying that price for us. Hence, as soon as the blood was sprinkled upon us, we were delivered from the law and freed from the condemnation of the law. This is redemption from the law through the blood of the Lord Jesus.

The price of redemption is the precious blood of the Lord Jesus. First Peter 1:19 says that we were redeemed "with precious blood, as of a Lamb without blemish and without spot, the blood of Christ." To be redeemed is to be bought. We were redeemed by the Lord's precious blood as the ransom. This is our being purchased by God. Therefore, Acts 20:28 says that God obtained the believers through His own blood. Because the blood had been sprinkled upon us, we were redeemed and freed from the law unto God.

FORGIVEN

Surely, a redeemed person's sins have been forgiven. Acts 10:43, 1 John 2:12, and Colossians 2:13 show that as soon as we believe in the Lord and are redeemed, God forgives us of all our sins, and the record of our sins is completely settled before God. All the sins that we committed before God are forgiven and dealt with once and for all, and we are no longer condemned. Since we have been sprinkled by the blood and have thus been redeemed, our sins, regardless of how great, how numerous, how deep, and how serious, are forgiven by God.

WASHED

We are not only forgiven; we are also washed. Being forgiven means that the liability for sins is gone. Being washed means that the record of sins is gone. For example, any debt I owe is recorded in an account book. If you relieve me of my debt, I will no longer be responsible to repay it. However, my account book will still have a record of the debt I owed you. If we could use a chemical solution to completely remove this record from the account book, there would no longer be any trace of the record. God not only forgives us, but He also washes us, washing away the traces of our sins. This is clearly shown in Revelation 1:5 and 1 Corinthians 6:11. He used His blood to wash away our sins. God has washed us in Christ because we believed in the Lord.

SANCTIFIED

The emphasis of being sanctified is not on becoming holy and pure. The word *sanctified* in the original text, whether in the Old or New Testament, means being separated. To be sanctified is to be separated. A person who has been called by God, sprinkled with the blood, redeemed, forgiven, and washed has spontaneously been separated unto God. Previously, he was among the worldly people, but now he has been separated unto God. Formerly, he was with sinners and in a crowd of sinners. Now he has been separated unto God. This separation unto God is to be sanctified.

First Corinthians 6:11, 1:2, and Romans 1:7 show that once a person is saved, God separates him unto Himself; he belongs to God and is thereby sanctified.

When we eat, the food on the table is sanctified through our prayer (1 Tim. 4:5). Formerly, the food was common and was intended for worldly people, but our prayer separates the food unto God for His use, thereby making it holy. This is what sanctification means. Likewise, we were once the descendants of Adam, the people of the world; we were in a crowd of sinners and were for the world and sin. One day, however, God called us, sprinkled us with His blood, and separated us unto the name of the Lord. Once separated in this way, we became sanctified.

JUSTIFIED

Some people think that a person is first justified and then sanctified. According to experience, we need to be justified before we can have a sanctified living. Thus, it can be said that sanctification follows justification. However, as a matter of fact and position, we are sanctified and then justified. When 1 Corinthians 6:11 speaks of being sanctified and justified, the sequence is that we are washed, sanctified, and justified.

Unless a person is sprinkled with the blood, redeemed, forgiven, washed, and sanctified by God, God has no way to justify him. In order to be justified by God, a person must be sprinkled with the blood of the Son of God, redeemed by God, forgiven by God, washed by God, and sanctified by God unto God. Such a person is no longer condemned by God or by God's law. Hence, God can justify him. This is not by a person's works but by Christ and His redemption. This is presented in 1 Corinthians 6:11 and Romans 5:1.

RECONCILED TO GOD

Once a person is justified, he is reconciled to God. In the past we were God's enemies because of sin, but now by the blood we are forgiven, washed, separated unto God, in harmony with God, and justified by God. Consequently, we are reconciled to God. This reconciliation includes acceptance. As soon as we are reconciled to God, God accepts our very person.

Colossians 1:20-22 shows that we, God's enemies, have been reconciled to God by the blood the Lord Jesus shed on the cross. Romans 5:9-11 says that since we have been justified because of the Lord Jesus, we are also reconciled to God because of Him, or through Him. Now we no longer have any problems before God and are accepted by Him. Since all enmity between God and us has been removed, we have been completely reconciled to God and are in harmony with Him; we are acceptable and pleasing to God.

REGENERATED

We are now thoroughly cleansed outwardly and have no more problems with God. However, this is not enough, because our life within is still natural and of the old creation. Thus, we need another life; we need regeneration.

God's salvation has two aspects: inward and outward. The outward aspect can be compared to putting on clothes, and the inward aspect, to eating. For a person to exist, he needs to put on clothes in order to look proper and he needs to eat in order to survive. He needs to take care of both these inward and outward aspects. Likewise, God's salvation also takes care of both our inward and outward needs.

In Luke 15 there are two aspects to what the prodigal son obtained from the father when he returned home. The first thing the father did was outward; he gave his son a robe, a ring, and sandals to wear. When the son returned, he was like a beggar, exceedingly ragged and filthy in his appearance. There was no way for him to enter into the father's house in such a condition because the father's house was grand and beautiful, and his beggar-like appearance did not match the father's house. Thus, while he was still outside the house, the father changed his clothes and put a robe, ring, and sandals on him. He now looked proper, matching the condition of the father's house; consequently, he could enter the father's house. This, however, is merely outward redemption, not inward salvation. Therefore, after he entered the father's house, the father said, "Bring the fattened calf; slaughter it, and let us eat and be merry" (v. 23).

This parable is a type of salvation. It shows that the Lord Jesus in His redemption has become our outward robe of righteousness in order that we may be redeemed and accepted by God. It also shows that He is like a slaughtered calf, giving us His life so that we can take Him in as our life supply, satisfying us within and making us merry.

Hence, everything that God does in the first ten items is outside of us. He chose us, predestinated us, called us, sprinkled us with His blood, redeemed us, forgave us, washed us, sanctified us, justified us, and reconciled us to Himself, accepted us; all of these items are outward. These items are very precious, and there is no doubt that we are saved persons. We have no more problems before God, before the law, and before His righteousness. We have the basis, the proof, and the assurance that we are saved. However, God's salvation does not stop here. God's salvation must go one step further so that we can receive His life within, so that we can be regenerated.

Regeneration means to be born of God. This is to be begotten of God, to have God Himself enter into us as life, and to be born of Him.

We need to realize that if man had not fallen, he would have only needed to receive life within him; this is the story of the garden of Eden in Genesis 2. There, man did not have the problem of needing clothing; he had no need of being redeemed outwardly. It was not until the fall of man in

Genesis 3 that clothing became a necessity. As soon as man fell, he felt ashamed and sewed leaves to make an apron to cover his body. Eventually, God made a coat of lamb's skin to clothe him. The coat of skin refers to Christ being our righteousness that we may be accepted by God outwardly. This is the outward aspect of redemption, which is due to man's fall. If man had not fallen, the story between man and God would only have an inward aspect related to life. However, we are all under the effects of the fall. Like prodigal sons, we have returned to God's presence; hence, we must first be dealt with outwardly. We must be justified and accepted by God in Christ. Only then can God come into us to enliven us, causing us to be regenerated to have God's life.

First Peter 1:3 says that God has regenerated us unto a living hope through the resurrection of Jesus Christ from the dead. First Peter 1:23 says that we have been regenerated through the living word of God. First John 5:1 says that we have been begotten of God. Furthermore, John 1:12-13 says that we, who have received the Lord, were all begotten of God. There are also two additional verses concerning regeneration. John 3:3 says, "Unless one is born anew, he cannot see the kingdom of God," and verse 5 says, "Unless one is born of water and the Spirit, he cannot enter into the kingdom of God."

Regeneration is having God enter into us as life—having the life of God in addition to our human life. This is the second life, the second birth; hence, it is called regeneration. In man's first birth he is born of his parents, thereby receiving Adam's life. In his second birth he is born of the Spirit and of God, thereby obtaining God's life. Regeneration is to be born of God.

PASSED OUT OF DEATH INTO LIFE

Once we are regenerated, we pass out of death into life; we are made alive. The Bible shows that formerly we were not only sinners; we were also dead. Therefore, it is not enough for our sins to be washed away by the blood of His Son. We also need to be regenerated by His life so that we can pass out of death into life and be made alive.

If God only cleanses us outwardly without regenerating us

inwardly, His salvation would be like the work of a mortician. A mortician may clean a dead person outwardly, but the person is still dead even though he is clean. This is not the ultimate goal of God's salvation. In His salvation God not only wants to cleanse us, to take away our sins; He also wants to regenerate us, to make us alive. Because we were dead in our sins, we needed God's forgiveness and God's regeneration in order that we may be made alive (Eph. 2:5). As soon as we are regenerated, we pass out of death into life; we are made alive.

John 5:24 says that he who believes "has passed out of death into life." Ephesians 2:5 says that God "made us alive together with Christ." Originally, we were dead in our offenses and sins, but now God has made us alive together with Christ. Colossians 2:13 says that God made us alive, having forgiven us all our offenses.

Being made alive is a crucial point in God's salvation. If we do not have life and are not made alive, we can never walk, grow, or serve God. We can walk, grow, act, and serve God on the basis of having the life of God and being regenerated and made alive.

RESURRECTED

Those who have been made alive still need to be resurrected. To be resurrected is to rise up, to transcend. In John 11 Lazarus was not only made alive in the tomb, but he rose up and left the tomb. Ephesians 2:5 says that God "made us alive together with Christ," and verse 6 says that God "raised us up together with Him," Christ. In the original text, to be resurrected is to be raised. A believer who does not walk or serve the Lord has merely been made alive; he has not been raised. In John 5:8 the Lord Jesus said to the paralyzed man, "Rise, take up your mat and walk." This is resurrection. We are saved not only to the extent of being made alive but also to the extent of being resurrected. This is similar to the lame man at the door of the temple who was healed in Acts 3:8; he was "walking and leaping and praising God." After receiving the Lord's healing, he did not sit in one place, saying, "Halle-lujah, praise God, I am made alive; I am made alive." He did not do this. He walked, leaped, and praised God. This is resurrection. God's salvation is to save us to the extent that we are not only made alive but are resurrected, raised up, and able to act and live.

ASCENDED

The moment we believe in the Lord and are saved, we ascend to the heavens and become heavenly people. We are transcendent. Ephesians 2:6 says, "Raised us up together with Him and seated us together with Him in the heavenlies in Christ Jesus." We have not only been raised up; we have also ascended. This is God's salvation, and we should say, "Hallelujah!" We may not have any feeling when we hear this, but we need to rejoice and say, "We are all in the heavens! We have not only been raised up; today we are all in the heavens!"

SEATED IN THE HEAVENLIES

Ephesians 2:6 not only says that we have ascended but that we are sitting in the heavenlies. We were formerly lying in a tomb, but we have been made alive, raised up, ascended, and seated in another place—in the heavenlies; this is salvation. If we do not know of our being seated in the heavenlies, we cannot walk properly on earth. In order to walk the path on earth, we need to be seated in the heavenlies. This is to be saved; this is God's salvation. Someone may ask, "How can we go to the heavenlies to be seated there?" This is not superstition, nor is it foolish talk. Consider a lamp in a building that is unconnected to a power plant. However, if the electricity in the power plant is connected to the lamp, the lamp becomes connected to the power plant. Likewise, we have ascended and are sitting in the heavenlies because the Lord who is sitting in the heavenlies has been connected to us. It is not that we have ascended and are now sitting in the heavenlies; rather, we have ascended and are sitting in the heavenlies in Christ.

RENEWED

Once we are in the heavenlies, we are renewed inside and

out. If anyone is in Christ, he is a new creation. The old things have passed away; they have become new. We are altogether new from inside to outside. In the heavenlies everything is new. These points can be seen in Titus 3:5 and 2 Corinthians 5:17.

RECOVERED TO SIGHT

When we are saved, our eyes are opened to see. Acts 26:18 says that God opens our eyes. The Lord's gospel and His life have illuminated our eyes. In the past we were blind, but now we are saved, and our eyes have been opened and illuminated so that we can see. Seeing does not only require life within, but it also requires a position. Although I may be living, I can still be in darkness if I am in a basement. But, praise God, today we have ascended, and we are in God's light. We not only have life inwardly; we are also in the light outwardly. We are altogether an illuminated person in God's salvation.

SET FREE

At this point we are completely free; nothing can bind us, and nothing can control us. Formerly, we had sin, death, Satan, the world, the old creation, and the law. We were blind; everything was controlling and binding us. Before we were saved, we were not free; we were slaves of sin and under the authority of Satan. But now that we have been saved in the many aspects mentioned above, we have indeed been set free! This is the freedom spoken of in Galatians 5:1 and 13 and in John 8:36.

SAVED

This does not mean that we are saved only when we reach this point; rather, it means that being saved includes so much and is so rich. This is what it means to be saved in 2 Timothy 1:9, Titus 3:5, and Romans 5:9-10. In these verses salvation does not merely refer to being forgiven outwardly; it also refers to being regenerated inwardly, and includes the rich content of being in ascension, being seated in the heavens, being renewed, having our sight recovered, and being set free.

KNOWING THAT WE ARE SAVED

(2)

In lesson 1 we considered nineteen aspects of our salvation. Some of these aspects include being forgiven, reconciled to God, made alive, set free, and being saved. But our salvation does not consist of merely these aspects. We also need to help new believers know the kind of persons we have become after being saved. There are at least eight points related to this matter of our salvation.

THE NEW CREATION

Second Corinthians 5:17 says that if anyone is in Christ, he is a new creation. We know that the universe is the old creation of God. Although there are many different items in the old creation, they do not have God's element within. Even though they were created by God, they are not mingled or united with God. They were created by God, not begotten of God. They have been created by God's power, not begotten of God's life. They were out of God's hand, not out of His nature.

But the new creation is completely different. Within the new creation there is the element of God because the new creation comes from the union and mingling of God with the created ones. The new creation was created by God and also begotten of God. Whereas the old creation was based on God's power, the new creation is based on God's life. God created the old creation with His infinite power, but He begot the new creation with His eternal life. The old creation is old because it did not have the element of God. It was defiled by sin and corrupted by Satan, thereby becoming old. The new creation is new because God's element of newness has been added to it. Everything of God is new and eternally fresh. Therefore, in eternity future the *New* Jerusalem will exist forever and ever.

Every believer has God's element mingled with him and, therefore, is a new creation. Although the new creation has the element of God's power, the emphasis is on God's life, not on His power. God regenerated us with the life of His resurrection power, thereby causing us to become the new creation. Therefore, the old things in us have passed away and have become new.

CHILDREN OF GOD

Since we are begotten of God, we are surely the children of God. John 1:12 says, "As many as received Him, to them He gave the authority to become children of God." Everyone who receives the Lord Jesus is not only saved; he also receives authority from the Lord, and this authority is of life. We have received a life from the Lord, and this life becomes the authority for us to become the children of God.

First John 3:1 says, "Behold what manner of love the Father has given to us, that we should be called children of God; and we are." We are all children of our natural parents, and at the same time, many of us also have children. We know that the relationship between children and parents is altogether a relationship of life. This relationship gives unlimited rights to the children. The rights that the children enjoy before their parents are unlimited. As long as it is within the ability of the parents, there is nothing they will not do for their children. Not only so, the character, natural disposition, and life of the parents are in their children. This means all that the parents are and all that the parents have belong to the children. This also applies to the children of God. As those who have been saved and have become the children of God, we have received all that God is and all that God has as our inheritance. We have inherited what God is, and also we have inherited what God has. God Himself and all that He has are our portion.

Once we are saved, we become this kind of person. Previously we were God's enemies, but now we are God's children.

In the past we had nothing to do with God and could not receive an inheritance from Him. All we could do was accept His judgment and His condemnation. But now we have become God's children. We have not only escaped His judgment and condemnation, but we have also received God Himself and all that God has as our inheritance.

MEMBERS OF GOD'S HOUSEHOLD

A child is a member of a family. We who have been saved are not only children begotten of God but also members of God's household. Ephesians 2:19 says that we are "members of the household of God."

However, this is not the experience of many believers. Many times when a person is brought to salvation to become a child of God, he does not have a home in reality. This can be compared to people who give birth to a child but who have no home for the child. Therefore, the child is taken to a child-care center or to an orphanage. The result of our bringing people to salvation may also be the same as sending them to a "child-care center" or to an "orphanage."

This result is because the ones who preach the gospel do not have the church as their home. Since they do not have such a home, the children they beget cannot be taken to a home. If they had a home in reality, when the child was born, he would be born into a home and spontaneously become a member of a family.

Everyone admits that the household of God spoken of in Ephesians 2:19 is the church of God. First Timothy 3:15 says, "The house of God, which is the church of the living God." We should never think that after a person is saved, the church is a small matter. Those who are not properly living in the church are not in the house of God, even though they have the life of God and have become God's children. Therefore, once we are saved, we should properly live in the church as members of God's household.

It is truly a blessing for a child to have a home. The children in a home are often the most blessed. The riches of the home are their portion. Because it is their home, they can even enjoy things that their parents would not use for themselves. It is truly a pitiful situation if a child does not have a home. It is especially a blessing for little children to have a home. This also applies to God's children. We should never be those who are saved, have become God's children, and yet are a homeless people.

CITIZENS OF GOD'S KINGDOM

Believers are not only members of God's household; they are also citizens of God's kingdom. This is seen in Ephesians 2:19. Furthermore, Revelation 1:6; 5:10; and Philippians 3:20 show that we are the heavenly citizens of God's kingdom. Titus 2:14 says that we are God's particular people. After we are saved, we become citizens in God's kingdom; hence, we are heavenly, particular, and different from others.

The emphasis of a home is enjoyment, but the emphasis of a kingdom is obligation. In the physical realm there are homes and nations. Even though there are obligations in a home, the emphasis is on enjoyment. With respect to a nation, even though there is enjoyment, obligations surpass enjoyment. As believers, we also have a spiritual home and a spiritual kingdom. Our spiritual home is God's house, and our spiritual nation is God's kingdom. In God's house, we have more enjoyment than we have obligations. In God's kingdom, we have more obligations than we have enjoyment. So once we are saved, we should not only have full enjoyment in the house of God, but we should also fulfill our obligations in the kingdom of God.

We need to remember that we are members of God's household and citizens of His kingdom. In the household, we enjoy the Father's care and provision, but in the kingdom, we are under the Lord's ruling and are subject to His authority. There is no citizen of a country who is not under the protection of that country. Since we are citizens of God's kingdom, we are also under the protection of God's kingdom. This protection is stronger than the protection of a house.

However, we must know that today we are citizens of God's kingdom, but ultimately we will reign in the kingdom of God. In the end, we will all be kings in the kingdom of God.

Revelation 1:6 and 5:10 say that God has made us a kingdom. This means that, as citizens of God's kingdom, we allow Him to reign, and we reign for Him. Today it seems as if we are citizens in God's kingdom, but we are actually being trained to be kings.

Brothers and sisters, have we considered that as citizens in God's kingdom we are actually being trained to be kings? This can be compared to a prince who grows up in a royal palace as a son but is actually being trained to one day reign as a king. Have we ever thought that as believers, we are citizens of God's kingdom for the purpose of being trained to reign for God? Revelation 20 tells us that one day the overcomers of Christ will be co-kings with Christ to reign with Him.

PRIESTS OF GOD

Revelation 1:6 and 5:10 speak of us being priests. In God's household we are children, and in God's kingdom we are citizens being trained to reign. We are also priests of God serving before Him. As soon as we are saved, we should serve God as priests. But today in degraded Christianity only a small number of saved ones are separated to be priests. Today the so-called fathers in the Catholic Church are called priests. Even in Protestantism, the pastors in the Episcopalian Church are sometimes called priests. But according to the Bible, every Christian is a priest. Every believer should be a priest and should be one who serves God.

The brothers and sisters have referred to me as a person who serves God. My question to them is this: "Whom do you serve? I serve God, but what about you? Whom do you serve?" Once a brother even said to me that he had the liberty to do many things that I could not do because he was not serving God like I am. I immediately responded, "Brother, yes I serve God. But whom do you serve? Do you not realize that if you do not serve God, you are serving the world, and you are serving mammon?"

Every believer must be a priest who serves God. Our specific duty, our primary occupation, is to serve God. All other things are side jobs. Being a teacher is a side job, taking care of family is a side job, doing business is a side job, farming is a side job, and working in an office is a side job. Whatever we do is a side job. Our primary occupation is to serve God as a priest. The priests and Levites in the Old Testament farmed and had household chores, but these were their side jobs. Their primary occupation was to serve God. This applies to Christians. Every believer should serve God as his primary occupation. Everything else is a side job.

GOD'S INHERITANCE

Ephesians 1:11 and 14 speak of being God's inheritance. It is difficult to see in the Bible any inheritance in the universe for God, other than His saints. In a broad sense, all things in the universe belong to God, but God does not consider them as His treasure and His inheritance. In the Old Testament God said repeatedly that His people, the Israelites, were His inheritance. However, the Israelites are merely the earthly people of God, and the believers are the heavenly people of God. So we are all the more God's inheritance, all the more God's possession.

We are God's possession. We are His precious inheritance. We are in God's hands and under His protection. Even though we are still in the old creation, Ephesians 1:13 says that as God's inheritance we have been sealed with the Holy Spirit. This can be compared to buying things at a factory. Once we have bought them, we need to put our seal on the items because we have not taken them from the factory. We need to seal the items, to separate them from everything else in the factory. Then at the appropriate time we take the sealed items home. In the same manner, even though we have not been raptured to be with the Lord, the Lord has already placed His Holy Spirit in us to mark us out, confirming that we are of God and that we are His inheritance.

GOD'S TEMPLE

First Corinthians 3:16 and 6:19 say that we are God's temple. God is in us; the Spirit of God is living in our spirit. Once a person is saved, he is not only begotten of God, having God's life; he is also God's dwelling place, God's resting place.

God lives in him, and God can completely entrust Himself to him. This is the high status of a believer.

In the Old Testament a priest was a priest, and the temple was the temple. But in the New Testament a spiritual priest is the spiritual temple because the priest and the temple are the same. We, the saved ones, are God's priests and His temple. We are, on the one hand, those who serve God, and on the other hand, the temple in which God dwells. These are all very great things.

MEMBERS OF CHRIST

Ephesians 5:30 and Romans 12:5 say that we are also members of Christ. This means that once we are saved and have the life of Christ, we are a part of Christ, just as our hands and feet are our members and a part of us. If we cut off our feet, we would immediately be incomplete. We praise the Lord that once we are saved, we enter into a high status of being a part of Christ and being indispensable to Christ. Our salvation is eternally secure.

There was a black slave girl who was saved and very happy. One day a highly educated friend of her master saw that she was very happy. She was happy while she washed clothes and swept the floor. She was smiling so much that it seemed as if she could not close her mouth. Out of curiosity, he asked her, "Why are you so happy today?" She said, "Oh, I am saved! I am saved! I am in the hands of the Lord Jesus!" Based on John 10:28-29 she added, "We are the Lord's sheep. He gave us eternal life, and we will not perish. No one can snatch us out of His hand." She explained that the Lord Jesus' hand was big and powerful, and that, being in His hand, she could not be snatched out by anyone. She was eternally saved. Her master's friend was not saved, but having some knowledge of Christianity, he made fun of her. He said, "Don't you see that our hands have spaces between the fingers? You must know that since our hands are small, the spaces also are small. But because the hands of the Lord Jesus are big, the spaces also are big. A small child like you must be careful in His hands. Do not be too happy; otherwise, you may slip between His fingers!" But this child was so clear.

She said, "Sir, the hands of the Lord Jesus are big; that is absolutely correct. I am small, and that is also correct. Let me tell you, I am not only in the hands of the Lord Jesus, but I am also His little finger. So I will never slip out of His hands."

This shows that she knew she was a member of Christ and could not slip through His fingers and perish. Our salvation is firm and secure. The Lord has not only made us citizens of His kingdom, priests who serve Him, and His temple and His dwelling place, but He has also made us part of Him, His members. Our salvation is secure to this extent.

A member is not only secure, but it also has a function. In relation to God, we are priests to serve Him, and in relation to Christ, we are members with a function to express Him. On the one hand, we are God's dwelling place for God's rest and His priests to serve Him, and on the other hand, we are members of Christ with living functions to express Him.

In order to manifest our function as members, we need to grow in life and to exercise. On the one hand, we need the Holy Spirit in us to cause us to grow and mature in life gradually, and on the other hand, we need to exercise much in the church. We cannot be lacking in either of these aspects.

For example, all children have life and can grow. But a child in a Chinese family will learn to speak Chinese, and a child in a Japanese family will learn to speak Japanese. As a result, they will speak different languages and their functions and skills will differ, even though their life and growth are the same. This shows the importance of the church. The leading and training by the church to new believers shapes the functions they can manifest in the future.

In order for a member to manifest his function, he must have inner growth by the Holy Spirit and outward exercise. It is regrettable that some people repudiate and condemn outward exercise and put too much emphasis on the inward growth in life. However, our example clearly shows that although both children grow, the one in the Japanese family does not speak Chinese, and the one in the Chinese family does not speak Japanese. Therefore, we cannot underestimate outward exercise, just as we cannot underestimate the inward growth in life.

BELONGING TO GOD

We have considered eight "beings." Let us now consider the matter of belonging. We belong to God, that is, we are of God (2 Tim. 3:17). Since we are the children of God, we are of God; since we are God's household, we are of God; since we are citizens of God's kingdom, we are of God; since we are priests of God, we are of God; since we are God's temple, we are of God; since we are God's inheritance, we are all the more of God. We belong to God because we are God's.

Since we are of God, we belong to Him. We are not without the Lord. Even the most educated person in the world does not know whom he belongs to, but we know that we belong to God. As soon as we are saved, we belong to God. In other words, He is our Lord, and He has sovereign right over us. Thus, we do not need to be afraid of perdition. Every person is careful with his precious items and keeps them safe out of a sense of responsibility. In the same way, since we belong to God and are under His sovereign right, He eternally bears full responsibility for us. We can forget God, but He cannot forget us. Even if we want to stay away from God, because we are His possessions and He is our Lord, He will never let us go. The sovereignty over us is in God's hands. We are of God.

BELONGING TO CHRIST

Romans 8:9 shows that the believers belong to Christ also. Since we are members of Christ, we are of Christ. Once we are saved, we are eternally saved. Furthermore, once we are of Christ, we are of Him eternally. He will never change, and in the same way, our being of Christ will never change.

BELONGING TO HEAVEN

First Corinthians 15:48 says that we are heavenly, that we are of heaven. We were originally in Adam, who was made of clay and earthy. But now we are saved, and we are in Christ. We are heavenly because we have the heavenly life and nature within us. We are on the earth but not of the earth, for within us are the heavenly life and nature.

Because we are heavenly, our taste is often heavenly. The more earthly desires we have, the more we suffer within. Whenever we taste the heavenly flavor and touch the heavenly reality, we feel very comfortable, sweet, and happy. This is because our nature is heavenly. Christians are special people. Our inner nature is heavenly; hence, we often cannot follow people in the world. Outwardly we have the same appearance as people in the world; we all have four limbs and five senses. We have wives, husbands, and children, and we all eat, wear clothes, study, and work. Outwardly there is no difference between the people in the world and us, but inwardly our nature is different. They are earthy, while we are heavenly. This difference is because we belong to heaven, not earth. For this reason, those who are of heaven and those who are of earth often cannot go together.

GOD ABIDING WITHIN

We also have a few things. First, we have God. In preaching the gospel, we often say that if man does not have God, he feels empty, but if man has God, he no longer feels empty. We do not feel empty because we have God. We do not merely have God objectively, but we have Him subjectively. God is abiding in us. First John 4:13 and 15 say that God abides in us. Verse 15 says that God abides in us because the Lord Jesus became our Savior. Verse 13 says that God abides in us because God has given us the Holy Spirit. This means that the Lord Jesus came to be our Savior and that the Holy Spirit entered into us in order to bring God into us so that He may abide in us. Today we not only have God as our Lord, bearing full responsibility for us in the heavens, but we also have God abiding in us to be our everything.

First John 4:4 says that He who is in us is greater than he who is in the world. The greatest one in the world is Satan, but the One who abides in us is greater than Satan. Outwardly speaking, we are insignificant and unimportant because we have no position in the world. But inwardly speaking, we are great because the God who is greater than anyone in the world abides within us.

CHRIST LIVING WITHIN

First, we have God abiding within; second, we have Christ living within. This is mentioned in the New Testament numerous times. The clearest verse is 2 Corinthians 13:5, which says, "Do you not realize about yourselves that Jesus Christ is in you, unless you are disapproved?" Regardless of how weak we are or how little faith we have, as long as we are saved, we have Christ in us. Christ being in us does not depend on the amount of our faith but on whether we have faith. Our faith can be so small that it seems as if it cannot be any smaller. But even if our faith is as small as a mustard seed, we are not disapproved. We have Christ in us. Not only did He die on the cross for us, but He is even inside of us, living for us. From our perspective, we may consider ourselves to be weak, but from His perspective, we are strong.

We must see that once we are saved, the God who is above all and greater than all abides in us. At the same time, we have Christ in us. Even though we are weak, Christ in us is strong. Thus, we must learn not to look at ourselves but to look only at Christ. We should not be concerned that we are weak or that we have only a little faith, but rather, we should simply believe that the Christ who abides in us is strong. If we do this, we will become strong. This is our salvation.

THE HOLY SPIRIT LIVING WITHIN

We have God and Christ, and we also have the Holy Spirit. This is spoken of in the New Testament many times. It is sufficient, however, for us to refer to just two portions. In John 14:16-17 the Lord Jesus said that when the Holy Spirit comes, He will be with us forever and shall be in us. Romans 8:9 also says that whoever is of Christ has the Spirit of Christ within him. Since we have God and Christ, we also have the Holy Spirit indwelling us. Regardless of how dead, dry, down, or bored we may feel, the Holy Spirit in us is living, fresh, and uplifting. Thus, we should not look at ourselves, but instead, we should believe in, pay attention to, and follow the Holy Spirit within.

Our salvation not only includes being accepted by God,

belonging to God, and becoming heavenly objectively, but it also includes gaining the Triune God subjectively. God, Christ, and the Holy Spirit—the Father, the Son, and the Spirit—the Triune God—are all in us. From the standpoint of the Father, God is in us. From the standpoint of the Son, God is in us. And also from the standpoint of the Spirit, God is in us. The entire Triune God is in us. What we believers have is great, full, rich, and high.

THE ETERNAL LIFE OF GOD

When we have the Triune God, we have the eternal life of God. John 3:15 and 1 John 5:12 state this clearly. God in us is life. We should not separate the eternal life of God from God Himself; instead, we must see that God is life. The phrase *life of God* is spoken of once in the New Testament in Ephesians 4:18. Apart from this verse, the Bible speaks only of God being life or God as life. We often speak of "the life of God," and people may understand this to mean the life in God coming out to become our life. This, however, is not completely accurate. God Himself comes into us to be our life. The life of God is God Himself. Therefore, the New Testament rarely refers to the "life of God"; rather, it speaks of God being life or God as life.

The Triune God who indwells us is the eternal life that we receive. As the Father, the indwelling Triune God is great; as Christ, powerful; and as the Holy Spirit, full of vitality and living. The Triune God within us is our life, enabling us to live, walk, and work.

A person's living, activities, and work all depend on his life. The kind of life a person has determines the kind of man he is, the living he has, and the work he does. The Triune God is in us to be our life. What a transcendent life this is! Therefore, we can also be transcendent men, living a transcendent life, and doing a transcendent work!

The importance of eternal life is not related to receiving eternal blessings in the future but in being our life today, in leading us in our conduct, living, work, and walk. Once we are saved, the eternal life lives in us, enabling us to live the life of God in heaven on earth today. This is real, and it is for us today. Concerning this point, we are not afraid of speaking too strongly or too much, for the more we stress this point, the better. We must impress new believers that the Triune God within them is glorious and great; He is very great, very strong, and very living. He is great because He is God, He is strong because He is Christ, and He is living because He is the Holy Spirit. He is great, strong, and living. He is in us as our life, living for us and enabling us to live on earth the life of God in heaven. Oh, this is such a glorious matter! This is what it means to be a Christian!

Hence, no Christian should have a sad face. We do not need to wait until we "go to heaven" in the future to enjoy the eternal blessings. This is the concept in Catholicism and degraded Christianity. No! While we are still on this earth, we can enjoy the glorious God within us as the glorious life. Even though we are in a body of humiliation, we can live a glorious life and be a glorious people. On the one hand, Christians are lowly and insignificant, as if they are the scum of all things (1 Cor. 4:13). Yet on the other hand, Christians are great. We have the Triune God in us as life, we can live a glorious life, and we are a glorious people.

Is this a theory and doctrine to us? Praise God that this is true in our experience. We are higher than the people in society who have the highest positions. We are not lower than them. Outwardly, our clothing may not match theirs, our position may be lower than theirs, we may not be as well known as they are, and our wealth may not match theirs, but inwardly they cannot match us. Therefore, Christians are weighty. We should not be proud, but God lives in us as our life. This is glorious and honorable. If we realize this, we will spontaneously express this weightiness in our living.

GOD'S NATURE

Second Peter 1:4 says that as believers, we are partakers of the divine nature. Since we have the life of God, we also have the nature of God. The emphasis on life is on the capacity to live, and the emphasis on nature is on the inclination of our living. We desire to be heavenly because the nature of God, the inclination of God, is heavenly. We desire to be holy because God's nature and inclination are holy. We feel uneasy when we are proud and comfortable when we are humble because this is the nature and inclination of God. We feel uneasy when we take advantage of others and very happy when we share with others because this is God's nature and inclination. These are all matters of nature and inclination. The life of God within us is the capacity to live, and the nature of God within us has become the inclination of our living.

Some people like to eat sour things. They feel good when they eat sour oranges, sour grapes, or sour vinegar. I, however, cannot eat sour food; for me, sweet things are better. Therefore, I will readily eat something sweet, but something that is sour I will eat only with difficulty. This is a matter of taste. Brothers and sisters, if we realize that the divine nature within us has a particular taste, we will see that it is easy to be freed from the world and not love sin and evil. God is in us not only as our life but also as our nature. Within us He is the capacity to live, and He has also become our taste in our living. His life and nature in us make it very easy for us not to love the world and to overcome sins and evil.

THE LAW OF LIFE

Hebrews 8:10-11 and Romans 8:2 reveal that in addition to having the capacity to live and having a taste in our living, we also have a natural law. The law of life in us enables us to spontaneously know what is wrong and what is right. We spontaneously know what is of God and what is not of God. We have a spontaneous ability to stay away from wrong and draw near to what is right, to choose what is of God and forsake what is not of God. This is a natural law.

All laws are related to some natural ability. For example, according to the natural law of gravity, an object thrown up into the air will fall down. We do not need to bring an object down from the air; it will come down by itself. Here is another example: if we wave our hand in front of a person's eyes, he will blink. This is in response to a natural law. A law is a natural ability that causes a person to spontaneously feel or behave in a certain way. Every believer has the Triune God,

God's life, God's nature, and the law of life within him. This law is the life and nature of God, and God's life and nature are the Triune God. No matter how we say it, God Himself, the Triune God, is in us as our life, nature, and law of life.

THE ANOINTING

The anointing involves more than just the Holy Spirit, because there is not only ointment but anointing. First John 2:27 says that we have an anointing. According to the original text, the word *anointing* is a verbal form of the word *ointment*. This means that the ointment is moving. Therefore, this verse does not merely say that the Holy Spirit is in us but that the operating, the moving, of the Holy Spirit is in us. Every believer not only has God's life, nature, and the law of life within him; he also has the continuous operating of the anointing. The law in us spontaneously regulates and empowers, and the anointing constantly enables us to know how God is leading and teaching us. We are so blessed! We have seven items in us—God, Christ, the Holy Spirit, life, nature, the law of life, and the anointing, but these seven items are just one. God is Christ, Christ is the Spirit, the Spirit is life, life is nature, and nature is the law of life. When the law operates within us, it is the anointing. These are all the working of God in us.

IN CHRIST

Romans 8:1 says, "There is now then no condemnation to those who are in Christ Jesus." Second Corinthians 5:17 says, "If anyone is in Christ, he is a new creation." As a result of the eight "beings," three "belongings," and seven "havings," we are *in* Christ as soon as we are saved. A thorough knowledge of the thirty-eight points in this and the previous lesson form a firm foundation for our salvation. We will know clearly and solidly that we are saved.

LESSON THREE

TERMINATING THE PAST

After a person is saved, his old way of living and his old conduct should come to an end. Before he was saved, he was a sinner living a life in sin. He was also a man of the old creation, conducting himself in the old creation. But now that he is saved, he should terminate the things of the past because he is a new person, having the life of the new creation.

THE NEED FOR TERMINATION

Once a person is saved, there is a change in his being. Consequently, it is natural that he should have a new beginning. Therefore, he must terminate his former life and conduct.

In the Old Testament, immediately after the Israelites were saved by keeping the passover, they left Egypt. They forsook all the Egyptian ways of living and fully terminated the Egyptian things. From that day forward they lived a new life and walked a new way; everything they did was new. The things of the past and their former way of living came to a complete end. This is a very clear type.

After we are saved, we need to be baptized. Baptism, which is a burial, shows that we need to be terminated. A burial is the biggest termination. As soon as a person has died and is buried, everything of his past is over. A person who has been buried cannot continue his old life and the things he once did. Whether one is ready to be baptized or has already been baptized, he should know that baptism is a termination. What we bury in the tomb is everything of our past and our old way of living. Baptism is like the crossing of the Red Sea. In baptism we go into the water on one side and come out on the other side. The water signifies the termination of all the things in our past. Therefore, now that we have been saved and baptized, we should follow the leading of the Holy Spirit to practically terminate all the things of our past and our former manner of living. Every person who is saved and wishes to follow the Lord must take this step.

If a person does not terminate his past after he is saved, he will be unable to advance as he should as a Christian. Although he desires to go forward, he will still long for the things of Egypt. On the one hand, he wants to be a Christian, and on the other hand, he still lives the life of the old creation. He wants to follow the Lord, but he still holds on to old sinful things. Such a person seems as if he is both a Christian and a person in the world. He seems to be both a child of God and a person belonging to the devil. This is wrong.

We must realize that once a person is saved, he is completely changed. Therefore, all aspects of his living, including the things in his living, should be completely changed. Everything of his past should come to an end.

NOT NEEDING TO SEARCH THE PAST

When we terminate the past, we should never try to search through and examine all the things of our past. We should not do this. Our past is under the precious blood of the Lord; God has forgiven us. It is finished. There is no need to expose and examine what the precious blood has covered. This is a common practice in many revival meetings. Some revival meetings place special emphasis on a believer's need to search through all the things of his past, even to the point of asking a person to openly confess his past mistakes and sins, revealing them to everyone.

Some people were touched by the Holy Spirit and confessed their sins before men (Acts 19:18). However, it is not a rule that every person must do this when they are saved. This is not a principle. To take this as a principle is rather dangerous and extreme. When we were in northern China, some in the Pentecostal movement were always promoting such an open confession. They encouraged Christians to speak concerning all their offenses before men. Some of the confessions sounded ridiculous, and those who made these confessions often ended up in trouble. We cannot do this, and the Bible does not require us to do this. There is no portion in the Bible that teaches a person to search through all the things of his past after he repents and is saved. Receiving this as a teaching or principle, to search through the things that happened prior to our salvation in order to deal with each one of them, is beyond the teaching of the Bible. It is also incompatible with the focus of the gospel. The focus of the gospel is that everything in our living, including the things of our past, has been forgiven by God and has been placed under the precious blood of the Lord Jesus.

There is no verse in the entire Bible that says to search through our past. The Bible, however, does present numerous examples of things that believers did after they were saved. For example, some serving in the military and tax collectors went to ask John the Baptist what they should do (Luke 3:12-14). Before hearing John's preaching on repentance, they had taken things from others by false accusation and had cheated others. However, John the Baptist did not tell them to repay what they had taken. He did not care about their past; he only cared about what they did from that point onward. He told them to be content with their wages and not to collect more tax than was required. John told them only what they should do from that point forward. This is the gospel. We do not need to add anything to the gospel of God. All our previous failures and sins are under the precious blood. God does not want us to uncover and examine the things that have been covered by the precious blood. These things have been forgiven, washed away, and covered. What is over is over!

Since they are over, why do they still need to be terminated? Termination is not searching the past. Termination is putting an end to the things in front of us. We should leave the things of the past in the past but conclude anything related to our present involvements. Even though the offense of a person who worshipped idols in the past is washed away by the blood of the Lord once he believes in the Lord, he may presently still have an idol in his home. We should tell him that he needs to remove the idol. The sin of worshipping idols in the past is over. No matter how much he worshipped idols in the past, there is no need to speak of these experiences. We should not even repeat the name of the idol. However, from the day of his salvation, the idol in his home and in his life must be removed and terminated. This is the meaning of termination. Termination is not searching through the past. It is to put an end to the things of the past that remain with us. No matter how bad or wicked we were, no matter how much we offended God and how many filthy things we did in the past, everything has been taken care of by the precious blood. However, if certain things of the past remain with us, we need to terminate them and stop their further influence. This is what we call termination.

Thus, the first thing we need to realize is that God's salvation is complete, and no matter how serious, how deep, how numerous, or how gross our sins were, they were all taken care of under the precious blood. We do not need to do anything additional to take care of our past sins. In order to obtain God's forgiveness, we do not need to search our past and deal with each item in a thorough way. The gospel is the gospel of grace. Searching through all the items of our past is against the focus of the gospel and offends the grace of God. We do not need to do what the grace of God has already done. God in His grace has completely forgotten our past. God's forgiving is the same as His forgetting (Heb. 8:12). We should not remember what God has forgotten. We should not expose and examine what God has terminated. This is not right. This is not termination. Termination involves ending the living of the old man. We should put an end to everything in our life that is a continuation from the past. It is critical that we do not allow these things to continue.

ONLY TERMINATING THE THINGS OF THE PAST

A believer who desires to witness for the Lord and to walk the way of the Lord in a pure manner must fully terminate the things of his past. For example, if a casino operator is saved, his sin of operating a casino has been forgiven by God. All the dark things he may have done in operating the casino are forgiven by God. However, if he desires to be a proper Christian and follow the Lord, he must stop operating the casino. The casino must be closed. He will not lose his salvation if he does not close the casino, but there will be no way for him to be a proper Christian. If he wants to walk the way of the Lord, he must close the casino. The closing of the casino is a termination.

Another example is a person's clothing, especially women's clothing. Some clothing overexposes the body, and other clothing looks strange; they are unbecoming. When a person wearing such clothing is saved, God forgives her for the way she dressed in the past, and the matter is over. However, the clothing must be terminated. She will not lose her salvation if she continues to wear this clothing, nor will she break a "law." But it will be difficult for her to be a proper Christian if she continues to wear such clothing. She should terminate, that is, no longer wear, strange clothes and clothes that expose her body. This will enable her to follow the Lord properly and walk on His way.

In order to follow the Lord and bear witness for the Lord, we need to terminate everything that is improper. How can a believer bring people to the Lord if he does not close his casino or nightclub after he is saved? He will be unable to witness for the Lord. The same applies to a sister who still wears strange clothing and exposes her body. Even if she desires to bear witness for the Lord, it is unlikely that people will be saved. If we desire to walk on the right path and to bear a proper testimony, we must terminate the things of our past life. The more seriously we address this point, the better. This is not a requirement of the law, and there is no regulation regarding how we should terminate the past. However, if we want to follow the Lord properly and bear witness for Him, we must terminate our former manner of living. However, this is a conclusion of the past, not a searching through our past. In order to follow the Lord and bear witness for the Lord, we need to conclude our past, but we do not need to search through our past. Terminating the past is necessary; searching through the past is unnecessary and even can be harmful.

EXAMPLES OF TERMINATION

All the actions of a person who is saved by grace depend

upon the moving of the Holy Spirit, not on regulations. There is no explicit teaching in the Bible regarding how a person should terminate the past after he repents and is saved. However, the New Testament has clear examples that show the work of the Holy Spirit within a believer in regard to terminating the things of his past and dealing with the improper items. There is no direct teaching in the Scriptures concerning terminating the past; there are only examples.

Abandoning Idolatrous Things

In 1 Thessalonians 1:9 Paul said that when the Thessalonians believed in the Lord, they turned away from idols. Most unbelievers in places like China and Japan have idols and things pertaining to idols in their homes. Thus, once a person is saved, he should completely remove idolatrous things from his life without waiting to be baptized. It may not be necessary to act immediately in regard to other matters, but we should be quick to terminate things related to idols. If we feel that we do not have the strength, we can ask a few brothers to pray with us for our strengthening and encouragement. However, we should not allow them to remove the idols for us. We need to terminate the idols ourselves.

We should realize that it is possible for there to be a union between men and demons. Those who worship idols often develop an emotional attachment to them. After they are saved, they are reluctant to abandon the idol. They may even hide it in a certain spot so that they may bring it out and admire it at a later time. This is the real experience of some saints. Therefore, in order for a believer to close the door, he must thoroughly deal with idols. God absolutely detests idols! God is a jealous God. He will not allow men to worship gods other than Himself. All believers must abandon every idolatrous and superstitious thing.

The brothers and sisters know what items pertain to idolatry. These include physical idols, shrines, candlesticks, and books on Buddhism. Anything that pertains to idolatry must be removed.

Some Chinese practice reading facial features, some practice fortune telling, others use horoscopes, and still others practice divination. These practices are related to idolatry. Therefore, they must be thoroughly terminated. There should no longer be any idols or items pertaining to superstition in a believer's home, especially after he is baptized. Everything pertaining to idols must be abandoned. The more we abandon and terminate these things from our past, the better.

The presence of idols in the home of a new believer can cause a family member who is sick not to recover. The presence of idols may cause another new believer to be confused and in darkness concerning spiritual matters. Yet another new believer can be lacking in any manifestation of the gift of the Holy Spirit. However, once they remove the idols from their homes, a sick family member can recover, confusion and darkness can be dissipated, and the manifestation of the gift of the Holy Spirit can occur. God detests idols. Therefore, we must abandon and terminate idols at all costs.

We must even abandon things that do not apparently seem to be idols. Portraits or statues of false gods must be abandoned, including portraits and images of "Jesus." Every portrait of "Jesus" is false. The Bible says that when the Lord Jesus was on earth, he had no attracting form or beautiful appearance (Isa. 53:2). However, every portrait of "Jesus" presents Him as being beautiful. This shows that they are false even though they were painted by the best artists. It is pitiful that Christians, not just Catholics, have such portraits in their homes. Many Christian books also contain such superstitious portraits. In God's eyes such portraits are blasphemous and should be discarded.

The reason we should not have any pictures of Jesus is not simply because such pictures are fake. We should not keep even an original picture of Jesus. God does not allow images (Exo. 20:4). Every image is an idol. We can use only our spirit to worship the pneumatic Christ. Our physical body should not be the focus of our worship of a visible image. This, however, is the principle of the Catholic Church. The Catholic Church teaches that we should physically worship a visible image rather than use our spirit to worship the invisible God. This is a heretical teaching of the Catholic Church.

Statues of Mary in the Catholic Church are a great idol.

They must be dealt with and abandoned. We should abandon any idols that are associated with an image of Jesus or Mary. I have met brothers and sisters who abandoned all portraits and statues but still kept a portrait of Jesus in their room. This is forbidden. Every portrait and image is forbidden by God. We should worship God only in spirit. We should not have any physical portraits or images.

Destroying Demonic and Filthy Things

In Acts 19:19 the believers in Ephesus who practiced magic brought their books together and burned them. The value of the books was fifty thousand pieces of silver. We have used this example as a basis for helping others to have a burning of demonic, filthy, and improper things. Some people have mah-jongg sets, dice, Chinese dominos, and poker cards in their homes, and others have wine vessels, pipes for smoking, pictures of movie stars, and other things in their homes. Pictures of movie stars are filthy things that corrupt many people. There are also filthy books and pictures. Some believers have indecent and pornographic pictures in their homes. These are demonic and filthy. New believers should follow the leading of the Holy Spirit to remove any such demonic and filthy thing from their lives and their homes.

In 1941, I went to Weihaiwei in Shangtung Province to preach the gospel. Some believed in the Lord, were saved, and wanted to terminate the things of the past in their homes. Every household willingly brought their mah-jongg sets, which were of the best quality, and put them in a huge pile. Some brothers suggested that we sell the mah-jongg sets because they were so nice and expensive, saying that it would be a pity to burn them. I said, "We can sell many things, but we cannot sell the mah-jongg sets. We must burn them." On that day we piled up some wood, poured gasoline on top, and burned the mah-jongg sets. During the burning, some of these brothers and sisters, no doubt, felt some pain in their hearts. However, they were not compelled to burn their sets; rather, they brought them voluntarily. Every new believer should have this type of clearance. Unbecoming clothing that is demonic and filthy should also be burned. Sleeveless clothing or items with low necklines can be altered. How we deal with our clothing should be according to the Holy Spirit's inward touch. The Holy Spirit will inwardly speak to people about the need to burn some of their clothing, even if it is expensive. If the Holy Spirit touches us inwardly to burn an item, we should obey, no matter the value of the item.

Furthermore, some luxurious cosmetics should also be burned. These are all classified as demonic and filthy. We should neither use nor give to others what is improper, indecent, demonic, or filthy in nature. We should not sell such things to others; we should burn them. The biblical principle is burning. In Acts 19:19 the Bible specifically states the value of the things burned, showing that the believers in those days burned expensive items. Fifty thousand pieces of silver in those days is considerably more than fifty thousand dollars today, but all these were still burned. When we abandon demonic and filthy things, we should not consider the cost or the loss.

Making Restitution

The salvation of Zaccheus presents the matter of making restitution (Luke 19:2-8). As soon as Zaccheus was saved, he said to the Lord that if he had taken anything from anyone by false accusation, he would restore four times as much. This is to deal with unrighteous gain. Restoring four times as much is neither a law nor a principle; it was according to the Holy Spirit's moving and the inner urging of Zaccheus's conscience. It may not be necessary to restore four times as much; perhaps slightly more than the original amount is enough. We should be careful about putting too heavy a burden on the conscience of the new believers.

It is not necessary to dig into our past to find out whom we owe in order to repay them. However, if the Holy Spirit touches us, making us conscious of the fact that we owe others material things, we should follow the leading of the Holy Spirit to properly restore what we owe.

There are several matters that need to be considered when restoring our debt to others. First, a person may not have sufficient financial means to take care of this matter. A person who stole ten thousand dollars in the past may not presently have one thousand dollars. He does not have the financial means to repay his debt. In this circumstance, if he feels that the Holy Spirit wants him to deal with this matter, he should repay as much as he can and confess this sin before the person whom he owes, even though his money is limited.

Second, there are times when we should let the person we owe know that we are repaying them, but there are times when it is wise to not let the person know. We need to seriously consider the situation so that others are not implicated. If we will cause problems by implicating others, we should repay secretly. If someone knows that we stole something from him, we should make an open restitution to him. However, if he does not know that we have stolen something from him, and if by informing him we will implicate others, our restitution should be done in secret. We should repay secretly so that others do not suffer material loss. This requires wisdom because our repayment may give rise to disputes and create an injustice for others.

Third, if the person whom we owe has passed away, in principle, we should give what we owe to his closest relative. If his wife is alive, we should repay his wife. If his children are living and his wife is not, we should repay his children. We should repay the person who is beneficially entitled to his estate. If we cannot find such a person, it is best to give what we owe to the poor.

Fourth, it may be difficult for the conscience of a new believer to set an amount to repay, whether the exact amount, double the amount, or more. Consequently, such ones should fellowship with the more mature believers in the church. Basically, a new believer should neither repay so little that his conscience condemns him nor repay so much that his conscience cannot bear the burden. There is no fixed rule. We must consider all circumstances, follow the leading of the Holy Spirit, and do what is appropriate.

We should be very careful in making restitution because others are often involved. Some situations may involve the government, others may involve private parties, and still others may affect the relationship between a husband and wife. Therefore, we should not simply consider the peace in our conscience and our innocence before the Lord without considering others. We must not involve others in dealing with these matters. Some people have caused discord between husbands and wives and even caused family disputes in dealing with these matters. This, in fact, can increase one's indebtedness to others. Therefore, we need to be wise and deal with this matter appropriately so that those whom we owe are compensated without causing others to suffer. This will glorify the Lord and be profitable to others as well as ourselves. The principle in making restitution is to glorify the Lord. This profits others as well as ourselves. We need to deal with this matter according to this principle so that no one suffers loss.

Terminating the Past Living

Before the Lord we should terminate our past living. Although the Bible does not have a definite example concerning this point, the revelation of the New Testament shows that God desires us to bring our past living before Him in order to terminate it. Should we continue to parent as we did in the past, or study in the way we did in the past? Should we continue to live our lives as we did in the past, having the same type of relationship between husband and wife, the same type of friendships, dressing in the same way, and even spending money in the same way? Should the furniture, decorations, and other items in our homes remain as they were in the past? This dealing needs to include everything.

This is not a written requirement. However, since we are saved and are a new man, our living and daily walk should have a new beginning. After we are saved, we should turn to the Lord to see whether any person, thing, or matter in our living should remain the same.

If we are willing to go before the Lord in this way, many things will need to be terminated. This does not mean, for example, that we will cease to be husbands. Rather, it simply means we will no longer be the same type of husband that we were in the past. We cannot continue to be the same type of parents as we were in the past. We cannot continue to study the same way we did in the past. The decorations in our homes should not be the same as in the past. This is the meaning of terminating our former manner of living.

Once again, there is no need to search through our past. Termination of the past does not involve asking which items of our past are wrong. Rather, as children of God, we should ask whether we should be the same as in the past. A dynamic salvation will often cause a person to immediately inspect his home, change his clothing, and even change the decorations in his house. This indicates that termination of the past is not a teaching but a work of the Holy Spirit that brings an end to our former manner of living and brings in the living of a new life. This is terminating the past.

Four matters need to be brought before God for termination: idolatrous things, demonic and filthy things, indebtedness to others, and the former manner of living. If a believer does not allow the Holy Spirit to work in him regarding these matters, he cannot go on. Although this is not a teaching, law, or regulation, all of the above will occur spontaneously in a person who lives in the Holy Spirit and allows the Holy Spirit to work in him.

Not Regulating according to Teaching but by the Moving of the Holy Spirit

Terminating and dealing with these items is a matter of following the moving of the Holy Spirit, not of following any regulation or doctrine. As believers we have the moving of the Holy Spirit within us. Our responsibility is to give ground to the Holy Spirit when He touches us. We do not need to focus on removing item after item. This is not a matter of outward regulation. Instead, the Holy Spirit will touch us concerning these matters. When He does, we should respond. We should not be concerned about price, position, reputation, face, or material loss. If we care for these things, we will quench the moving of the Holy Spirit and not experience a full salvation. Thus, we will be unable to seriously follow the Lord.

The Spirit of God is working within us, and the life of the Lord within us is powerful. If we allow the Holy Spirit to work, not caring for our position, reputation, face, or personal interest, the Holy Spirit will certainly lead us to terminate and deal with these items by the power of the life within us. The Holy Spirit is doing a renewing work not only in our life inwardly but also in our living outwardly. He wants to renew us inwardly and outwardly, to make us a new man living a new life and walking on a new path. He wants to renew us completely from center to circumference.

Let me repeat, this is not a regulation or doctrine. We want all believers to give the Holy Spirit complete freedom to do a renewing work. The Holy Spirit will not only renew our mind, perception, emotion, and will but also renew everything in our outward living. This termination and dealing is absolutely not a legality in the church. This is not a rule or requirement in the church. However, the life we have received is holy, and the Holy Spirit within us is working. Through this holy life, the Holy Spirit will persist in requiring us to abandon demonic and unclean things and to terminate our old manner of living. Our responsibility is to follow the leading of the Holy Spirit and let the Holy Spirit gain ground in us through His moving.

Caring for the Conscience

We should care for the feeling of the conscience in terminating and dealing with these items. We cannot ask others concerning the extent to which we should deal with each matter. We must ask our own conscience. We need to deal with everything to the extent that we have peace in our conscience. Others cannot determine this for us. We should follow our conscience.

A believer who wants to follow the Lord must ensure that his conscience is void of offense. No one with an offense in his conscience can be a good Christian. No one with an offense in his conscience can have genuine growth in life. No one with an offense in his conscience can have faith before God and be enlightened by God. Therefore, we need to take care of our conscience so that it will be void of offense and at peace.

We must also be careful. We should not let our conscience become overly sensitive. An overly sensitive conscience will become weak and more easily deceived by Satan. Therefore, we should use common sense to balance the feeling of our conscience. For example, Satan often deceives us related to making restitution. Our conscience may feel that we should repay one and a half times the amount. However, when we repay this amount, Satan may tell us that we should have repaid twice the original amount. Agreeing with him, we repay twice the amount. However, Satan immediately comes again and says that we should have repaid three or even four times the original amount. This has happened to people. They have an overly sensitive conscience, which becomes weak, thereby inviting Satan's attack. If this happens, we need to use common sense to balance our overly sensitive conscience. Common sense tells us that since we have repaid one and half times the original amount, it is sufficient. We should not be governed by an overly sensitive conscience. We should use common sense to balance us.

However, we should not annul the feeling of the conscience simply because we are afraid of repaying a certain amount. We should not reduce the amount we repay because we think that it is too great of a financial loss. This will cause an offense to continue to remain in our conscience, and we will be unable to walk properly on the Lord's way.

It is, therefore, important to maintain a balanced feeling in our conscience. We should not annul the feeling of the conscience; neither should we foster it. If our conscience is not sensitive enough, we cannot be strong. If it is overly sensitive, it will become weak, and we will still be unable to be strong before the Lord. We need to do what is appropriate. We should not annul any sensitive feelings in our conscience; neither should we foster any overly sensitive ones to the extent that our conscience becomes weak. We need to care for our conscience so that it can be void of offense and strong. Only in this way can we live properly before the Lord.

It is not easy to practice these points. Many practical matters need to be considered. Therefore, we should not rush into dealing with the past simply because we have repented and are zealous. Rather, dealing with the past requires us to walk continually before the Lord. We need to be careful, balanced, and appropriate, doing neither too little nor too much so that we can be delivered from every improper situation and stand properly. In this way, we can advance and make progress in life, in testimony, and in spiritual knowledge. This is a step every believer should take.

CONSECRATION

This lesson is concerning consecration. Every person should enter through the gate of consecration as soon as he is saved in order to walk the way of consecration. We will consider seven aspects of consecration.

THE CONTINUATION OF SALVATION

Salvation is the beginning of a person's spiritual life, not the conclusion. When a person is saved, he is saved once and for all; his salvation is eternal. However, being saved is merely a spiritual birth, a person's spiritual beginning.

In the Old Testament, when the Israelites held the passover in Egypt, God told them to count that month as the first month, the beginning of the year. Even though it was not the first month of the year, they changed their calendar because God wanted them to consider the passover month as the beginning of the year. Once a person is saved, he has a new beginning before God. This is a new day in life. A person's physical birth is the day on which he was begotten by his parents. His spiritual birth is the day he was saved and regenerated. Therefore, salvation is a beginning, not a conclusion.

After a beginning, there should be a continuation. This continuation is to present oneself to the Lord. Consecrating oneself to the Lord is the continuation of salvation.

There is a clear type of this step in the Old Testament. Exodus 12 is a record of the Israelites keeping the passover. In chapter 13 God required the children of Israel to sanctify their firstborn unto Him because they were saved through the passover. Whoever is saved by God should belong to Him.

In other words, a person should offer himself to God as soon as he is saved. We should never think that our initial salvation is a conclusion. We should be clear that it is only a beginning. After being saved, we need to go on step by step. The first step is offering oneself to God.

THE NEED FOR GROWTH

A believer who wants to walk the way of the Lord, grow in life, and allow God to work thoroughly in him needs to offer himself to God. He needs to offer himself to God in order to enjoy all the riches in God's salvation.

Walking the Way of the Lord Needing Consecration

As soon as we are saved, God places us on His way so that we can follow Him. In order to follow Him we need to give ourselves entirely to Him. We should say, "From now on I want to be led by You. I will no longer walk my own way; instead, I want to walk Your way. I will no longer decide for myself in any matter; I want You to lead me in everything. I put myself completely in Your hands to let You plan and determine every step of my way. I do not want to choose my own way. I put myself in Your hands; take me and lead me on." In order to receive God's leading, we need to have a definite consecration. The Lord cannot guide us if we do not entrust ourselves into His hands.

Growth in Life Needing Consecration

Once we are saved, there is another life in us that needs to grow. We need to give this life the opportunity to develop so that it can grow daily. Therefore, our emotion must be handed over to the Lord, our mind must be touched by the Lord, and our will must surrender to Him. Then the life in us will have an opportunity to develop. Every living organism needs a good environment in order to grow properly. Suppose we place one baby chicken in a good environment and another in a poor environment. The one in the good environment will grow to be big and strong, and the other will be small and weak. This also applies to plant life. If two trees are planted at the same time in different environments, the one in the good environment will grow tall, and the one in the poor environment will be stunted. The difference in their growth is mainly due to the environment.

All believers receive the same life of God. However, some experience much growth in life even though they have only been saved for one or two years. There are also those who have been saved for many years but who have little growth in life; rather, they seem to be withered and old. This is because some people consecrated themselves to the Lord immediately after they were saved. Thus, the life within them had an opportunity to develop. The others kept themselves in their own hands instead of offering themselves to the Lord. They did not give the Lord's life an opportunity to develop in them. A thorough consecration to the Lord activates the function of the life within us, making it lively and strong and causing the sense of life to become sensitive. Before consecrating ourselves, we did not feel it was wrong to do certain things. After consecrating ourselves, however, the sense of life causes us to feel that these same things are wrong. Before our consecration we were confused, unable to discern what was of God. But after a thorough consecration, the function of the inner law of life is immediately manifested. Whenever we touch anything that is not of God, the law of life within us operates to give us the feeling that this is not of God; it is apart from God. Similarly, when we touch something of God, this law of life manifests its function, giving us the deep feeling that we have touched something that is pleasing to God. Therefore, the manifestation of the law of life and the growth of the sense of life enable the life in us to grow gradually.

God's Work in Us Needing Consecration

A person who wants God to work in him must be consecrated. God has much work to do in us. Although we are saved, we still need God to work in us. The Bible says that we, the believers, are living stones. God desires to use these living stones to build His spiritual house, His dwelling place. These stones need to be dealt with by God. Ephesians 2:10 says that we are God's masterpiece, a very special part of God's work in the universe. God desires to work His nature, disposition, thinking, desires, wisdom, and all of His virtues into our being. God works in us so that we can be conformed to the image of His Son (Rom. 8:29).

Since we are not dead material, like wood or stone, God needs to have our consent before He can work in us. We are living. God will not have a way to work in us if we do not agree. God will never force us. He is a patient God; He can wait. Although He is willing to work in us, He will not proceed if we do not give our consent. He will wait until we are willing. It is true that He desires to break us, but He first needs to obtain our consent. If we say, "God, I am here, willing to be broken by You," He can begin to break us. It is a pity that many believers have never consecrated themselves or agreed to let God work in them. They may have been saved for five, ten, twenty, or even thirty years, but there is very little of God's work in them because they do not allow God to work. In order for God to work in us, we need to come before Him on our knees and say, "I know that You chose me and saved me because You want me to become good material for Your building. You want to do Your good works in me so that I can be conformed to the image of Your Son for the accomplishment of Your masterpiece in the universe (2 Tim. 3:17; Eph. 2:10). I agree with Your work in me. I welcome You to work in me. I offer myself to You and commit myself into Your hands. My consecration is not only for You to lead me but also for You to do a thorough work in me." Brothers and sisters, this is a thorough consecration. Consecration is, in fact, our consent.

Enjoying the Riches of God's Salvation Needing Consecration

The blessings that we enjoy in God's salvation are so rich! God Himself, Christ, and the Holy Spirit are our portion. Christ's death and resurrection, His glorification, His obtaining authority over all things in heaven and on earth, and His transcending over all enemies are our portion. We gained all these at the time we were saved. However, in order to enjoy these blessings, we must be consecrated.

If we have never offered ourselves to the Lord, we have no way to enjoy the Triune God even though He dwells in us. We will also be unable to experience the Lord's mysterious death and glorious resurrection, and the Holy Spirit will have no way of leading us into these experiences. Although we have ascended with Him and are seated together with Him in the heavenlies, we will still be earthy people in our practical living if we are not consecrated. Although the Lord's victory is our portion, we will remain in our failures if we do not offer ourselves to Him. The Lord has received authority over all things in heaven and on earth, and this authority has also been given to us. However, in order to enjoy and experience this authority, we must be consecrated. If we do not give ourselves to the Lord and stand together with Him, we will have His authority in position but not in experience or reality. Everything that the Lord accomplished for us is ours; however, in order to experience them, we must be consecrated.

Throughout the ages those who have spoken concerning spiritual experience paid much attention to the matter of consecration. Brother Andrew Murray, who mainly spoke concerning abiding in the Lord and fellowshipping with the Lord, said that in order to experience abiding in the Lord and fellowshipping with the Lord, one must be consecrated. In *The Christian's Secret of a Happy Life,* Hannah Whitall Smith said that if a believer wants to lead a happy life, he must be consecrated. George Müller, who spoke concerning faith, said that if one wants to have a living faith, he must consecrate himself to the Lord. There are others, who advocated gaining the power of Pentecost, who said that a person must consecrate himself in order to gain the power of Pentecost. There are also people who said that learning how to pray and becoming praying persons require consecration.

These statements are all true because consecration is a gate, a door. If we do not enter through this gate, we will remain outside; we will be unable to see and partake of the rich contents inside. When we go to a hospital, a school, or even our own home, we must enter through a door. Wherever we go, we need to enter through a door. Consecration is the gate to experiencing all the riches in God's salvation. Whoever has

not entered through this gate cannot practically experience
the riches of God's salvation.

A RESPONSE TO GOD'S LOVE

Every believer has received God's love, which is great.
Romans 5:5 says that the love of God has been poured out in
our hearts through the Holy Spirit. Second Corinthians 5:14
says that the love of Christ constrains us. We deserved to die
and perish. However, the Lord died for us. The love that
caused the Lord to die for us constrains us. It would be difficult for any Christian who meditates on this love not to be
touched or constrained by this great love of the Lord. We
cannot but respond to this moving and constraining love. Our
response is spontaneous. The love of God constrains us inwardly
when He requires something of us. The love of God leads us to
answer God's requirement, saying, "I am willing to offer myself
to You. Even though I have nothing but my dreadful self, all I
can do is offer myself entirely to You." Presenting ourselves to
God in this way is a response to His love.

Romans 12:1 says, "I exhort you therefore, brothers, through
the compassions of God to present your bodies a living sacrifice." This is the constraining of God's love and His requirement
on us. With this love, we should respond to God and say, "I
have no way to repay Your love; any repayment is beyond me.
I can only present myself to You." When someone expresses
his love for us, how can we not respond? Dear saints, we have
received such a great love from God. How can we not respond
to God's love?

THE RIGHT THAT GOD DESERVES

Offering ourselves to God is also to grant Him the right
that He deserves in regard to us. First Corinthians 6:19-20
says that we are not our own because we have been bought
with a price. This price is the precious blood shed by the Lord
on the cross. The Lord has bought us with His blood. Since the
Lord has purchased us, He has authority over us and we
belong to Him, just as we own whatever we pay for.

Questions of use are never a factor in regard to the material things we own. This, however, is not the case with those

who have received grace. Although God has purchased us, He can be prevented from enjoying His right over us if we disagree with His use of us. Therefore, it is necessary for us to consecrate ourselves. Consecration is our allowing God to have the right that He deserves. We need to say, "Lord, since You bought me with a price, I do not belong to myself; I am Yours. I yield all authority to You. I am Your bondslave. From now on, You have authority over me and I give myself to You forever. I do not want to run away or be unlawful, just as Onesimus was unlawful when he ran away from his master (Philem. 15-16). Therefore, I present myself to You; I give myself to You."

Romans 14:7-8 says, "None of us lives to himself, and none dies to himself; for whether we live, we live to the Lord, and whether we die, we die to the Lord. Therefore whether we live or we die, we are the Lord's." We each belong to God. We belong to God not only while we are living but also after we die. We need to consecrate ourselves to God as an acknowledgment of His authority over us and as an indication that we allow Him to have the right that He deserves. Our consent to God's authority over us is because of His constraining love and because of the price He paid to purchase us. Every new believer should indicate such willingness before the Lord.

A BURNT OFFERING FOR GOD

Although our consecration to the Lord is for Him to use us to satisfy His wishes, we must first become a sacrifice before we can be for God. We cannot be for God unless we have first become a sacrifice. Becoming a sacrifice is a major step in consecration. It is possible for us to appear consecrated yet not be a sacrifice. There are three important points to being a sacrifice.

A Change in Position

Once an offering is presented as a sacrifice, its position is changed. It has lost its former position and is now on the altar. No matter if it is a lamb or a bull, once it is offered as a sacrifice, its position is changed. It was formerly with the flock or the herd; it is now on the altar.

A Change in Use

Once an offering is presented as a sacrifice, its function or use is also changed. Formerly, a lamb or bull was used by people in the world, but once it is placed on the altar, it can no longer be used by them. It is now for God's enjoyment. Therefore, an offering that is presented as a sacrifice experiences not only a change in position but also a change in use. Hence, consecration is not merely a matter of uttering a few sentences of prayer; consecration is to present oneself as a sacrifice. The result of this kind of consecration is that our position and use are changed. Formerly, we were in the world; now we are on God's altar. Formerly, we lived for our family, wife, husband, children, parents, and the world; now we live for God.

We all know that a sacrifice is not something common. Before being offered as a sacrifice, any object is common. Once it is offered as a sacrifice, however, it is separated. Thus, once a person consecrates himself, he is separated unto God; he is a living sacrifice presented to God. His position is changed, and his use is changed as well.

A Change in Appearance

Everything that is presented as a sacrifice must pass through the process of God's dealings, especially if it is presented as a burnt offering. The sacrifice spoken of in Romans 12:1 focuses on the burnt offering. In order for a bull or a lamb to be presented as a burnt offering, it must be slaughtered, flayed, cut into pieces, washed, laid on the altar, and consumed by fire until it becomes a heap of ashes. A sacrifice that is burnt to ashes has been thoroughly dealt with; even if there are further dealings, it will remain a heap of ashes. At this point the sacrifice is a sweet savor for God's enjoyment.

It is a pity that many Christians are "willing" to consecrate themselves to God but are unwilling to be dealt with by Him. They are like bulls or lambs that have not been slaughtered, flayed, cut into pieces, washed, or consumed by fire. They remain untouched and unchanged; they remain entirely natural. Only those who have been dealt with by God are for

God. Only after God has dealt with us in this way can our service be in resurrection, no longer a natural service. Only after we have been dealt with by God in this way can our work be in resurrection and a sweet savor unto Him. Many people today love the Lord zealously. Although they have consecrated themselves to God, they still have a very strong natural flavor. This is because they are unwilling to be stripped by God; they have not allowed God to consume them. They cannot be used by God because their self is unchanged. God cannot use their bad qualities nor even their good qualities because these qualities are still natural. A person can be used by God only when he has been dealt with by God, just as a sacrifice must be slaughtered, flayed, cut into pieces, washed, and burned to ashes until its appearance is completely changed. At this point his position, use, and appearance have all changed, and he has become a heap of ashes. In the eyes of men these ashes are nothing, but to God they are a sweet savor. Only this kind of person can be for God and can be used by God to satisfy His wishes.

THE PRACTICE

We now need to consider the practice of consecration, that is, how to practice consecration.

Consecrating Ourselves Once and for All

Consecration is a gate, and we must be determined to enter through this gate. Consecration is entering through a gate. We cannot regard this as a doctrine. A person who has not consecrated himself is outside of the gate. Only a person who has consecrated himself is inside of the gate. Therefore, we need to enter through this gate with determination.

We need to have thorough prayer in which we confess our sins and hand ourselves over to God. The sins, mistakes, contamination, and corruption that we sense before God need to be confessed one by one. All that we are, all that we have, and our everything then need to be handed over to God. We cannot casually and generally say, "God, I consecrate everything to You." This is insufficient. We need to thoroughly hand everything over, item by item. We need to hand ourselves over to the Lord. We need to hand over our wife, husband, and children to the Lord. We also need to hand over our education, career, future, and everything to the Lord. This is similar to a merchant selling his business. He hands over everything of his business, including furniture and stock, to the buyer. We should have this type of prayer alone before God. For some Christians, consecration is like a second salvation. Therefore, the more thorough it is, the better.

Constantly Renewing Our Consecration

Consecration is not only a gate but also a path. In all spiritual matters, we must first step inside the gate and then walk on the path. The principle in the Bible is not to walk on the path and then enter through the gate. The biblical principle is that we first enter through the gate and then walk on the path (Matt. 7:13-14). This is the God-ordained order. Therefore, after we enter through the gate of consecration, we must continue to walk on the path of consecration. Although entering through the gate is once and for all, walking on the path requires a continual renewing, a daily consecration. Numbers 28 through 29 show a type of consecration. God charged the Israelites to offer the burnt offering daily. They had to daily offer the burnt offering in the morning and in the evening. They could not say that they had offered a sacrifice yesterday and therefore did not need to offer one today. Consecration, like eating, is a daily matter. Furthermore, the Israelites had to present burnt offerings on every Sabbath, at the beginning of every month, and during every feast. They also had to present an offering at other important times. This shows that after we have entered through the gate of consecration, we need to consecrate ourselves before God every morning. The first thing we should say after we get up every morning is, "Lord, I place myself in Your hands again this morning." At night when the day is over, we should go before Him again and say, "I give myself to You again." When we need to do specific things, we need to say, "Lord, I present myself to You once again." Whether we are going to study, teach, take up a post in the government, give a message, or visit the brothers, we should first present a burnt offering, consecrating ourselves to God. Even if we want to see a movie, we should first kneel down before the Lord and say, "Lord, I am a consecrated person. I want to see a movie, but I acknowledge my consecration to You!" Once we acknowledge our consecration in this way, we will be clear whether we should go to see the movie or not. When we are about to quarrel with our spouse, we should acknowledge our consecration first. Once we do this, we will know whether we should quarrel or not. Therefore, we need to live a life of consecration practically. Consecration is not only a gate but also a path. After entering through the gate, we need to walk on the path.

BELIEVING

God Accepting Our Consecration

God accepts every sacrifice that is presented to Him. He even accepts a sacrifice presented to Him by mistake. God burns every sacrifice that is placed on the altar. To accept is to burn. Therefore, we should not be concerned with whether God will accept our sacrifice but only with whether we are consecrated. God accepts every consecration. Even if our consecration is not completely sincere, it will eventually become real; a partial consecration will become a full consecration. Whoever puts himself on the altar cannot run away from it. God accepts whatever we put on the altar. Therefore, we should believe that our consecration has been accepted by God. We will be accepted as long as we consecrate ourselves to God. We also need to be aware of Satan's cunningness. He either tries to hold people back so that they will not consecrate themselves, or he causes those who have consecrated themselves to doubt God's acceptance of their consecration. Once a person consecrates himself to God, Satan always whispers in his ear, "Your consecration is not solid, not thorough, not pleasing to God; it has no value and is insignificant. Your consecration is meaningless." Satan makes us doubt our consecration. He always works in these two ways. Therefore, we need to guard against his schemes and reject his words. We must stand on the ground of our consecration and say to him, "Even if our consecration is not thorough, and even if it is not fully genuine, God has accepted it. God does not question the things placed on the altar. God accepts them all."

The experiences of many Christians confirm this. Many people consecrated themselves to the Lord when they were young. Afterward, they began to love the world and became prosperous. After ten or twenty years God still called them back to the ground of the consecration they made in their youth. Even though they had long forgotten the consecration made in their youth, God did not.

Jacob's consecration in Genesis 28 was a kind of bargaining. He said to God, "If You will be with me and keep me in this way that I go and give me bread to eat and garments to put on, so that I return to my father's house in peace, then You will be my God." In other words, if God would not keep him, not give him food, not give him clothing, and not bring him back to his father's house in peace, he would not take Him as his God. Jacob's consecration had conditions. When Jacob went to Paddan-aram and stayed there for twenty years, he completely forgot his consecration. God, however, not only took care of his food and clothing but also gave him two large camps. Although he returned home in an imposing manner with two large camps of wives, children, cattle, rams, and servants, he had forgotten about his consecration. But God had not forgotten. When Jacob was living in Shechem, God came to him and told him to arise and return to Bethel. God wanted him to return to Bethel, the place of his consecration. Man can forget his consecration, but God never forgets. Jacob's consecration in Genesis 28 was not completely sincere and proper. Our consecration is probably much better than his. His consecration was an attempt to bargain with God! Nevertheless, God did not reject Jacob's consecration. God remembered it. Thus, once we consecrate ourselves, God counts it and accepts it.

Once a man presents himself to God, he is in the hands of God. God can wait ten, twenty, or even fifty years for him. In God's eyes, ten years are about the same as twenty years. Eventually, God will gain him. After more than twenty years, God told Jacob, "Go back to Bethel to set up an altar for Me. I am the One who appeared to you when you were running away from your brother. You made a vow and consecrated yourself to Me there. You need to go back to the ground where you first consecrated yourself." Therefore, the Bible and the experiences of the saints show that God always accepts a person's consecration.

Our Consecration Being Irrevocable

No one can revoke his consecration. Anything that has been presented on the altar cannot be taken back. Leviticus 27 reveals that any offering a man presents to Jehovah is holy. He may not exchange or substitute either a good one for a bad one or a bad one for a good one, but if he attempts to substitute an animal for an animal, then both it and its substitute are holy (v. 10). Whatever is offered on the altar cannot be taken back or exchanged because God has accepted it forever. Likewise, when a person consecrates himself to God, the consecration is irrevocable.

A person who has consecrated himself is different from a person who has never consecrated himself, just as a person who is married is different from a person who has never been married. Even a person who is divorced has no way to annul the fact that he has been married. Similarly, a person who has consecrated himself is still consecrated, even if he falls, fails, or stumbles. Such a person is still different from someone who has never consecrated himself. Likewise, a consecrated person who has fallen and failed is different from an unconsecrated person who has fallen and failed. Our first experience of receiving God's grace is salvation; our second experience is consecration. A sinner needs to be saved, and a saved person needs to be consecrated. A person in the world needs to be saved to become a Christian. After becoming a Christian, he needs to consecrate himself in order to walk the way of the Lord, to live the life of the Lord, to let the Lord work in him, and to enjoy the riches of God's salvation. Only in this way can he be a proper Christian to enjoy the blessings that God has prepared in Christ.

Dear brothers and sisters, consecration is a gate. We need to enter through this gate with determination. Consecration is also a path. After we enter through the gate of consecration, we need to walk on the path of consecration, renewing our consecration daily and continually. Moreover, once we consecrate ourselves, we need to believe that our consecration has been accepted by God and can neither be revoked nor altered.

WALKING ACCORDING TO THE SPIRIT

After consecration, a believer needs to learn to walk according to the spirit.

In general, Christians do not know what *spirit* refers to in the phrase *walking according to the spirit*. They think that *spirit* refers to the Holy Spirit, the Spirit of God. Hence, with regard to walking according to the spirit, they have a common but inaccurate understanding: they think that this means to obey the Holy Spirit. Strictly speaking, walking according to the spirit and obeying the Holy Spirit are not exactly the same. Although they are very similar, they are also quite different. The expression *obeying the Holy Spirit* is neither clear nor accurate. People understand this teaching to mean that they need to obey the Holy Spirit when He touches them. However, how does the Holy Spirit touch us? And how do we obey Him? Even those who speak of obeying the Holy Spirit are not clear concerning this.

When we speak of walking according to the spirit, we are referring to the regenerated human spirit. This is a very practical lesson. If we do not know how to walk according to the spirit once we have been saved, have terminated the past, and have consecrated ourselves to the Lord, it will not be easy for us to grow properly. Every Christian needs to know the simple way to grow in life. We will divide this lesson into ten points.

THE POSITION OF THE SPIRIT

Most people divide man into two parts: an outward part, which is the body, and an inward part, which is the "spirit-soul." Psychologists also divide man into two parts: a physical part and a metaphysical part. But the revelation in the Bible shows that man is of three parts: a visible body outwardly, an invisible spirit inwardly, and a soul between the body and the spirit.

In Chinese, the term *ling-hun,* literally, "spirit-soul," refers to one thing. However, in the original text of the Bible, *spirit* and *soul* are two separate words that refer to two different things (1 Thes. 5:23). Hence, the soul is one thing, and the spirit is another. The soul is man's personality, man's self, including the mind, emotion, and will. Thoughts and considerations, joy and anger, preferences and decisions are all matters related to the soul, not the spirit. There is another part within us that is deeper than our mind, emotion, and will. This is our spirit. The spirit is the deepest part within man. The outermost part of man is the body, within the body is the soul, and deeper than the soul is the spirit.

When a believer wants to do something, he often considers whether or not it is right to do it. If his emotion feels happy doing it, his will often decides to do it. But at that moment, in the deepest part of his being there may be some resistance, disagreeing with the action and disapproving of it. This protest from deep within comes from his spirit. Our spirit is the deepest part of our being. Walking according to the spirit is walking according to the deepest part within us.

THE CONSCIENCE IN THE SPIRIT

The spirit within man has three parts: conscience, intuition, and fellowship. Fellowship governs our communion with God. Intuition is a sense that is not based on the reasonings of the mind. For example, when a person wants to do something, he thinks about it, searching for a reason to do it. If he feels happy about it, he decides to do it. The feeling of resistance, however, which comes from his deepest part, is not based on any reason; hence, it is intuition.

In the spirit there is also the conscience. The conscience is a major part of the spirit. The Chinese people often say that the conscience has been discovered. This means that the function of the conscience has been activated. They also say that we need to act according to the conscience, which means acting according to the feeling of the conscience. The feeling of the conscience is often contrary to the mind's reasonings, to the emotion's likes and dislikes, and to the will's decisions. Often when a person is about to do something, there is a protesting in the deepest part of his being, even though his mind, emotion, and will approve of the action. This protest within most probably comes from the conscience. This function of the conscience is a function of the spirit. The feeling of the conscience is also the feeling of the spirit. The reason the conscience is most commonly associated with the spirit is that it is a major part of the spirit. Once we know the function of the conscience, we will have some understanding concerning spiritual matters.

THE SPIRIT BEING MADE ALIVE AND RENEWED

When God created man, He created a spirit in man so that man can commune and fellowship with God, intuitively know God's desire, and determine whether a matter is proper or improper. At the time of man's creation, the spirit was living and functioning. However, because man sinned, the human spirit was damaged, and the function of the spirit was nearly lost. Consequently, sinners do not like to contact God and cannot contact God because their organ for contacting God has been damaged. Our ears are for hearing, but we will be unable to hear any sound if our ears are damaged, and we are deaf. Likewise, the capacity of our human spirit to contact God was damaged, and the function of our spirit was therefore lost because of sin. Even though unbelievers say that they act according to their conscience, their conscience is actually insensitive, and the feeling of their conscience is inaccurate. According to the Bible, they are dead in relation to the function of their spirit (Eph. 2:1).

Confucius taught that the highest principle involves learning to develop the "bright virtue." The bright virtue actually refers to the function of the conscience in the spirit. This is what Wang Yang-ming, a Chinese philosopher, called "innate knowledge and ability." They taught that a man's bright virtue needs to be cultivated and that his innate knowledge and ability need to be developed. These teachings prove that the spirit within fallen man has problems because it is not bright.

However, at the moment we were saved, our spirit was made alive and renewed. As we were listening to the gospel, the Holy Spirit moved us and touched our conscience. He caused the truth of the gospel to penetrate our mind and enlighten our spirit, particularly our conscience, enabling us to realize that we were sinners before God. After the Holy Spirit touched, enlightened, and condemned us, we condemned ourselves, and the conscience began to function properly (Rom. 2:15). Then we confessed and repented before God and received the Lord Jesus as our Savior according to the feeling in our conscience, which is the feeling from the moving of the Holy Spirit. As a result of our confession and repentance, God forgave us and cleansed us by the blood of the Lord Jesus, and the Holy Spirit entered into our spirit, regenerating us. Our deadened spirit was made alive. Our spirit was renewed once it was made alive.

Salvation is twofold. First, a person's sins are forgiven before God, and the record of his sins is annulled. Second, he is regenerated within, and his spirit is made alive and renewed. Therefore, a person's salvation is not merely a matter of his position before God, but it is also a matter of receiving life within him and having his spirit enlivened and renewed. If salvation is only a matter of man's position before God, there could be no change in the life and living of a believer. Believers experience a change in their life and living because their spirit has been made alive and renewed. This results in a change in the deepest part of their being. The Spirit of God enters into their deepest part, transforming them in their spirit. The Spirit of God brings the life and nature of God, that is, God Himself, into our spirit. He brings an additional element into our spirit. This element causes our spirit to be enlivened and renewed. Hence, we have a conscience that is fresh, living, and much stronger than the conscience of unbelievers. The conscience of unbelievers is dead, but our conscience is living; the conscience of unbelievers is old, but our conscience is renewed. When we were saved, the Holy Spirit brought the life of God and God

Himself into our spirit so that our spirit was made alive and renewed.

THE HOLY SPIRIT BEING WITH OUR SPIRIT

After the enlivening and renewing of our spirit, the Holy Spirit dwells in our spirit and lives in our spirit. The Holy Spirit is now mingled with our spirit, which is one spirit (1 Cor. 6:17). Romans 8:16 says, "The Spirit Himself witnesses with our spirit." This indicates that the Holy Spirit dwells in our spirit and also is mingled with our spirit as one spirit. Therefore, not only is our spirit, including the conscience, made alive and renewed, but the life and nature of God Himself dwells within our spirit, which is mingled with the Holy Spirit as one spirit. The Holy Spirit who indwells us is always operating within us and anointing us. Our spirit is no longer merely a human spirit because something new has been added into it.

For example, grape juice, sugar, and a little fruit syrup can be added to a glass of pure water. Once these ingredients are added to the water, it becomes a delicious drink. Likewise, there are new "ingredients" in the spirit of a believer. The spirit that is frequently referred to in the New Testament Epistles, such as the spirit according to which we should walk in Romans 8:4, is a spirit with these new "ingredients." In the Chinese Union Version of the Bible, small dots are often placed beside the word *Holy* when the words *Holy Spirit* are used in the Epistles. This indicates that the word *Holy* is not in the original text. The word *spirit* in many of these places refers not only to the Holy Spirit of God but also to the mingled spirit—the Holy Spirit mingled with our spirit as one spirit.

Ephesians 6:18 speaks of praying at every time in spirit. In this verse the Chinese Union Version translates *spirit* as "Holy Spirit," even though the word *Holy* is not in the original text. *Spirit* in this verse actually refers to our mingled spirit with its new "ingredients." The apostle exhorted us to pray in such a spirit.

Romans 8:4-6 says, "That the righteous requirement of the law might be fulfilled in us, who do not walk according to the flesh but according to the spirit. For those who are according to the flesh mind the things of the flesh; but those who are according to the spirit, the things of the Spirit. For the mind set on the flesh is death, but the mind set on the spirit is life and peace." In these verses, the Chinese Union Version again translates the word *spirit* as "Holy Spirit." There are small dots beside the word *Holy,* indicating that the original text does not have this word. Therefore, the spirit in these three verses is not simply the Holy Spirit but the spirit that is mingled with the Spirit as one spirit. Our spirit which is mingled with the Spirit is versus the flesh. As Christians, we should not walk according to the flesh but walk according to the spirit, that is, the mingled spirit. Romans 8:2 speaks of the law of the Spirit of life. The Chinese Union Version translates this as "the law of the Holy Spirit who gives life." However, the words *Holy* and *gives* are not in the original text. Hence, the literal translation is simply "the law of the Spirit of life." The Spirit of life is also the spirit that is the mingling of the Spirit with our spirit.

Galatians 5:16 says, "Walk by the Spirit and you shall by no means fulfill the lust of the flesh." Verse 25 says, "If we live by the Spirit, let us also walk by the Spirit." The Chinese Union Version uses *Holy Spirit* in both verses, but it should simply be the Spirit, which is the mingled spirit. In the Bible there are many such examples. Walking according to the Spirit is to walk according to our enlivened and renewed spirit, which is the issue of the mingling of the Spirit with our spirit.

THE SENSE OF THE SPIRIT

Since our spirit has been enlivened and renewed, the function of our conscience has been restored, the life of God, even God Himself, is moving in us, and the Spirit of God is anointing us. Therefore, our spirit is full of feelings. Our human spirit has been made alive and is fresh, our conscience has been enlightened, the life of God, even God Himself, is moving within us, and the Holy Spirit is anointing us within. It is difficult to comprehend just how living and how full of feelings we are within!

WALKING ACCORDING TO THE SENSE OF THE SPIRIT

To walk according to the spirit is to walk according to the sense of the spirit. Whether we should speak, how we should speak, how much we should speak, to whom we should speak, and where we should speak should all be according to the sense in our spirit. Whether we should do a certain thing, go to a certain place, or contact a certain person should all be according to the sense in our spirit. Whether we should use a certain thing, buy a certain thing, speak a certain message, or pray for a certain matter should be according to the sense in our spirit. Whenever we walk according to the sense in the spirit, we are following the spirit.

If someone asks us whether he can go to a movie or wear certain clothing, we should direct him to his sense within. We should not ask others whether we should do something; we should check the sense in our spirit. Our living and walk as Christians are not according to the teachings we hear in sermons or the opinions and suggestions of other people. We should reject not only our flesh and lust but also the common, traditional teachings and general concepts of Christianity. We should put aside all of man's views, ideas, and opinions and turn to our deepest part to walk according to the sense of our spirit. Whenever we follow our flesh, indulge our lust, or live according to our preference, we are defeated Christians. Whenever we follow our concepts and walk according to our opinions, we are natural Christians. Neither of these walks is acceptable to God. God desires Christians who are simple, direct, and single, caring only for the sense of the spirit and walking according to the sense of the spirit before Him. This is to walk according to the spirit.

After a person is saved and is genuinely open before the Lord, having consecrated himself to the Lord, the Holy Spirit within him has the ground to operate and anoint him. As a result, there is much feeling in his spirit, and he will have a sense concerning all matters. When he is about to speak, a sense within may tell him not to speak. When he wants to say something additional, the sense in his spirit may tell him that enough has been said. When he wants to criticize someone, his spirit will feel uneasy. The sense in his spirit even guides him in the things that he buys. When he wants to contact his friends, the sense in his spirit will indicate whether it is appropriate. All these senses come from the spirit. Sometimes it is from the conscience, but most of the time it is from the intuition, a sense that comes directly from the spirit.

When I was young and newly saved, my heart was burning for the Lord. At the time, the Chinese New Year was coming, but I had not thought much about it. Early in the morning, on the day of the New Year, I knelt down to pray and read the Bible and was full of the Lord's presence. I had no thought or feeling in regard to the Chinese New Year. After praying, I saw my mother, and she said, "Son, have you forgotten the Chinese New Year? You have not put on your new clothes." She then took out a new robe, which I put on. After finishing breakfast, I went back to my room to pray. However, my spirit was uneasy, and I could not touch the Lord in my prayers. When I asked the Lord about this, I only had a sense that the problem was related to the New Year robe. I immediately took off the robe, changed back to my old clothes, and knelt down to pray again. Immediately, the spirit within was alive. This shows the intuition of the spirit. It was my first clear experience of the sense of the spirit.

This shows that being a Christian is not a matter of following numerous regulations involving what we should and should not do. Within Christians is a wonderful mingled spirit. From the day of our salvation, the Holy Spirit lives in our spirit and is mingled with our spirit as one spirit. This Holy Spirit is constantly operating in our spirit and anointing us. He gives us feelings in everything so that we may know how to conduct ourselves.

The sense given to us in the operation of the Holy Spirit often seems like it is our feeling, because this function comes out of our spirit. This feeling of the Holy Spirit is the feeling of the Spirit that is mingled with our spirit.

Many Christians expect the Holy Spirit to knock them over like a violent wind when they pray, causing them to be greatly moved and to repent in tears. Although I dare not say that this is not good, I can say that this is not very precious. The most precious thing about being a Christian is that in our spirit there is a constant speaking, a constant sense; it is a sense and a speaking at the same time. Often we think a reaction is simply a thought, but actually it is the feeling of our spirit. This kind of feeling continues unceasingly even though it is gentle and does not compel. We should treasure, focus on, and take care of this feeling. We should immediately obey this feeling; we do not need a strong wind to blow upon us. Waiting for the Holy Spirit to blow upon us as a strong wind is not normal. A powerful "moving" of the Holy Spirit can be Satan in disguise and thus not reliable. The most reliable and proper feeling is often a gentle sense that does not compel. It is like a voice but not a voice; it is a sense that prompts but does not compel. This most precious sense is the operating and anointing of the Holy Spirit within our spirit.

When the Bible speaks of the work of the Holy Spirit within the human spirit, it speaks of operation and anointing. Although this operation and anointing is powerful, it is not violent. It can be compared to applying ointment to one's skin. No one violently applies ointment to his skin, as if he were beating his skin. The applying of ointment is always gentle, tender, and full of feeling. The operation of the Holy Spirit within our spirit is also gentle and tender. The Holy Spirit is not like a tiger; rather, He is like a dove. He is not rough but gentle. When we are rough, a dove will often fly away. The operation of the Holy Spirit within us is tender yet powerful. He never stops operating within us, even when we reject Him. If we ignore the sense He gives us in the morning, He will still operate during the night. If we ignore His operation during the night, He will still anoint us in the morning, because He continually operates within us. This is the work of the Holy Spirit within our spirit.

We should not think that this moving of the Holy Spirit is something extraordinary. Some people have an inaccurate concept regarding the moving of the Holy Spirit. When they pray, they anticipate something extraordinary, thinking that the moving of the Holy Spirit will rush upon them. They prepare themselves for a powerful move of the Holy Spirit. But the moving of the Holy Spirit is not like this. From the day we were saved, the Holy Spirit lives in us and mingles with our spirit as one spirit. Like an ointment, He operates and anoints us within. It is impossible to distinguish between the feeling of our spirit and the feeling of the Holy Spirit. We should not even try. Whenever there is a sense in our deepest part, in principle, we should pay attention to it and take care of it. We should walk before God according to the sense in our spirit. This is to walk according to the spirit.

WALKING ACCORDING TO THE SPIRIT BEING TO OBEY GOD

In a Christian's living, the most important thing is to obey God. However, these words seem very abstract and are not easily realized. Obeying God really means to walk according to the spirit. To obey God is not merely to walk according to the letter of the Bible nor according to the teachings in the Bible. To obey God is deeper than following the letter and teachings of the Bible. It is so deep that it involves the feelings of the spirit, the deepest part of our being. When we walk according to the sense of our spirit, we are obeying God. Hence, in principle, a Christian's living, walk, motives, thoughts, speaking, and attitude must absolutely follow the sense in our spirit. If we walk in this way, we will be persons who obey God.

THE ISSUE OF WALKING ACCORDING TO THE SPIRIT

Romans 8:6 says that the issue of walking according to the spirit is life and peace. The issue of not walking according to the spirit is death, which often involves the sense of restlessness. In contrast, peace involves calm, comfort, and a sense of rest. This is easy to understand and comprehend. If we follow the spirit, we will have peace. For example, we may want to watch a movie, even though there is a sense in our spirit not to do this. In such a case, we should follow the sense in our spirit and acknowledge that we are consecrated persons and, therefore, obey the sense in our spirit. If we do this, we will immediately sense the peace within. If, however, we do not follow the sense in our spirit and insist on watching the movie, we will lose our sense of peace. On the way to the movie we will sense an inward restlessness that deprives us of our peace. Once we are in the theater, this sense of uneasiness and restlessness will grow stronger. This feeling of unease will not dissipate once the movie is over. Even as we sleep, there will not be peace. Peace is the issue of following the spirit; having no peace is the issue of not following the spirit.

Let us consider another example. A sister may see an inexpensive piece of fabric that she wants to buy. However, because she has already designated the money in her pocket as an offering to the Lord, there is a struggle within her. She may say to herself, "This piece of fabric is so cheap that I should not miss this opportunity to buy it!" However, she also has a sense that she should not use this money because it has already been designated as an offering. If she follows her logical judgment and buys the piece of fabric, she will lose the peace within. She will have no peace on her way home. Even at home, she will still have no peace and be unable to pray. This struggle may continue for a couple of days. After fellowshipping with a sister, she may have a sense to sell the fabric and offer the proceeds to the Lord according to the original plan. Then the inward peace, which she lost by not walking according to the feeling in her spirit, will be restored. Peace always returns when we deal with our disobedience, either through action, as in the case of the sister, or repentance, as in the case of watching the movie.

It is easy to understand the sense of peace, but what about the sense of life? The sense of life involves a sense of satisfaction. It also involves strength as opposed to weakness, and light as opposed to darkness. The sense of life involves satisfaction, strength, and light. If we want to watch a movie but have no sense to do so, we will feel satisfied, strong, and full of light if we follow this feeling. On the contrary, if we disobey this feeling and go to the movie, we will feel empty, dissatisfied, weak, and full of darkness within. The absence of life is death. The issue of obeying the sense in our spirit is satisfaction, strength, light, comfort, peace, and rest. The issue of not obeying the sense in our spirit is emptiness, weakness, darkness, uneasiness, and restlessness. These are the issue of not walking according to the spirit and disobeying the sense in our spirit.

WALKING ONLY ACCORDING TO THE SPIRIT

As Christians, it is unnecessary for us to exercise our will to do good, to strive and struggle, or to determine to please God because to will to do good is present with us but to work it out is not (Rom. 7:18). To will, to strive, to determine, and to struggle is the philosophy of moralists and religionists. Being a Christian does not require all these things. A Christian needs only one thing, that is, to constantly walk according to the spirit. We do not need to determine to be humble, to obey our parents, and to love others; all these determinations are futile. Even if we succeed according to our determination, God will not approve of our success because it is not God living out of us.

To be a Christian does not require anything except that one learns to turn to the spirit and walk according to the feeling of the spirit. Day by day he needs to take heed to the inward feeling, and in everything he does, he needs to obey the feeling of the spirit. If we obey the feeling of our spirit in this way, we will not need to make up our mind to be humble; we will spontaneously be humble. We will not need to make a determination to honor our parents; we will do so spontaneously. We will not need to struggle and pursue to love; we will spontaneously be loving. Moreover, this kind of humility, honor, and love surpasses human humility, honor, and love, because they do not come out of us; rather, they are God living out of us.

In the New Testament there are many commands, such as husbands loving their wives, wives submitting to their husbands, and children honoring their parents. These demands are not meant to be fulfilled by our own efforts. Rather, they require us to obey the feeling of the spirit within so that God may be lived out of us. When we walk according to the spirit within, husbands will spontaneously love their wives, wives will submit to their husbands, and children will surely honor their parents. This is not our doing; it is God living out through us. As a result, we live out Christ. In this way Christ not only lives in us, but He is expressed through us.

After salvation, almost every believer determines to do good, to improve himself, to try his best to be humble, meek, and patient, to honor his parents, and to love his neighbors as himself. He does not realize that all these determinations are to no avail. Although these commandments are in the New Testament, we need to realize that they are for man to live out in Christ and in the Holy Spirit. God never requires us to do all these things by ourselves. Rather, He wants us to turn inwardly. He wants us to take care of and obey the feeling of the spirit in our living, our actions, and our walk. When we walk according to the spirit in this way, all the virtues of Christ will be lived out from us. Therefore, to be a Christian requires nothing other than walking according to the spirit.

OVERCOMING BY WALKING ACCORDING TO THE SPIRIT

When a person is willing to walk according to the spirit, he will overcome sin, the flesh, the world, and Satan. If we walk according to the spirit, we will spontaneously overcome sin, the flesh, the world, and Satan with no effort. On the contrary, those who constantly focus on how to overcome sin and the world will easily fall into sin and are bound and entangled by the world. Likewise, the more a person pays attention to overcoming Satan, the easier it is for Satan to attack him. Hence, the secret to living an overcoming life is to walk according to the spirit. As long as we live in the spirit and walk according to the spirit, we will overcome. *Restlessness comes from Satan*

We praise the Lord that there is only this one matter in being a Christian. Whether in giving messages, praying, staying at home, doing business, being parents or children, being husbands or wives, being employers or employees, and in relation to our clothing, food, lodging, and transportation, in big things and small things, all we need is to walk according to the spirit. There is no need to will, to run, to determine, or to strive. If we walk according to the spirit, we will overcome sin, the flesh, the world, and Satan; we will be filled with life and peace inwardly. Day by day the life of Christ within us will gradually grow unto maturity. Ultimately, we will be full of the measure of the stature of Christ.

READING THE BIBLE

This lesson is to aid new believers in reading the Bible. The points in this lesson will be presented in a simple and practical way.

THE BIBLE BEING THE WORD OF GOD

New believers must know that the Bible is the word of God. Second Timothy 3:16 says, "All Scripture is God-breathed." Second Peter 1:21 says that the words in the Scriptures were written by men who were borne by the Holy Spirit. Since the Bible is the breathing of God Himself and is written by the prophets and apostles who were moved by the Spirit of God, it is the word of God.

Containing Life

The Bible contains life. John 5:39 says that there is eternal life in the Bible. John 6:63 says that the Lord's words are spirit and life. The Bible is full of the life of God; hence, it can supply us with life. The Bible even says that we can eat the words in the Scripture as food. Jeremiah 15:16 says, "Your words were found and I ate them." In Matthew 4:4 the Lord Jesus said, "Man shall not live on bread alone, but on every word that proceeds out through the mouth of God." These verses indicate that the Bible is full of the life supply, the bread of life, that nourishes us. These words not only nourish our spirit directly but also supply our soul and our body indirectly.

We should never consider the Bible to be a book of knowledge for study. Instead, we should regard the Bible as a book that is full of the life of God. When we read the Bible, we should obtain the life supply in it.

Containing Light

The Bible not only contains life but also light. Life is for supplying; light is for revealing and enlightening. Hence, we should not regard the Bible as a common religious classic for the study of religious doctrine. The Bible is full of God's light. We read the Bible to be enlightened by God and to receive His revelation so that we may understand His intention and purpose toward us.

If we see that the Bible is a book of life, we will not receive it as a book of knowledge for learning. If we see that the Bible is a book of light, we will not receive it as a common religious classic. These concepts need to be adjusted. We should take the Bible as a book that is full of life and full of light. The Word of God supplies us with the bread of life that nourishes our whole being because it contains life. The Word of God is also able to enlighten us concerning the will of God, the mystery of God, and the eternal plan of God because it is full of light. It can also manifest our true condition and enlighten us concerning the way that we should take, the things we should do, the work we should carry out, and the conduct we should have. This is a matter of enlightenment, not teaching; it is a matter of God's revelation in light, not religious doctrine.

One must have a clear understanding of these two characteristics of the Bible. Otherwise, he will spontaneously think that it contains teachings and knowledge. People inevitably consider the Bible as a classic teaching, a book of knowledge. Only those who have received revelation realize that this book is different from all other books. It is not an ordinary book; it is the book of books. This book is the word of God; it is the breathing of God through the Holy Spirit and was written by godly men in human language. Its content is altogether life and light. From this book, we obtain the life supply as nourishment for our entire being. We also obtain revelation in the light in order that we may know God's intention, our own condition, and how we should live and walk. Thus, we must adjust our concept concerning the Bible.

THE ATTITUDE IN READING THE BIBLE

We need a proper attitude in reading the Bible. This attitude is based on our knowledge of the Bible. We know that the Bible is the word of God, containing life that surpasses knowledge and containing light that surpasses doctrine. Therefore, we should have a serious attitude when we read the Bible.

Contacting God Himself

When we read the Bible, we should have an attitude of contacting God Himself. The Bible is the word of God, and the word of God is the embodiment of God. It is God Himself, the breath of God, that is, the breathing out of God. Hence, each time we come to read the Bible, we should be inwardly prepared to meet God, to contact God Himself.

We should not read the Bible merely with our mind. We must seek God with our spirit and our heart. We must have a sincere heart to draw near to God and a quiet and open spirit to fellowship with Him. This attitude is completely different from the attitude we have when reading newspapers and magazines or secular books. When we read secular publications, we need only a focused mind. However, when we read the Bible, we are contacting God, who is Spirit. Thus, we must have a heart that is true and sincere toward God and a spirit that is quiet and open to Him. In this way, we may be reading the Bible, but inwardly we are actually contacting God Himself. This is the attitude we should have when reading the Bible.

Receiving the Life Supply

We should also have an attitude of coming to receive the life supply. We should never come to the Bible to seek knowledge or study facts. This can be compared to studying the rice, meat, and vegetables on the table instead of eating them so that we can be nourished and supplied. The Bible is a treasure store of the spiritual bread of life. Thus, we should always have the attitude of taking the bread of life from this treasure store for our supply. This is not merely a matter of understanding or comprehending with our mind; it is a matter of receiving the life supply from the Bible with our spirit. This point must be emphasized. We must change our concept. We should not say in our heart, "I come to the Bible in order to study it." The proper attitude is to regard the Bible as a treasure store of the bread of life from which we draw the bread of life and are supplied. We read the Bible in order to obtain the life supply.

Receiving Enlightenment

We should also have an attitude of coming to receive enlightenment and not to study the truth. To study the truth is one attitude, and to receive enlightenment is another. In studying the truth we need only our mind, but to receive enlightenment, we need our heart and our spirit. We need to come before God and say, "I want to touch the light in Your Word. My heart and my spirit are open to You. Lord, enlighten me through Your Word. As I read, grant me not only the understanding, but even more, shine Your light through Your Spirit on the letters. Enlighten me concerning Your heart's desire and expose my true condition. I do not want merely to comprehend, but even more I want to see. I want enlightenment and revelation."

We should also learn to pray when we read the Bible. We should spontaneously have a prayer deep within us, saying, "Lord, I come to Your Word to contact You, not merely to read. Cause my heart to incline toward You and my spirit to open to You. Cause me to love You more than knowledge and doctrine. May my inner being be nourished and enlightened by Your Word." We should have this kind of prayer, intention, and attitude.

Those who read the Bible must realize what the Word of God is and have a proper attitude toward the Word of God. Many do not read the Bible properly because they lack this preparation. If we are well prepared with regard to these two points, it will be much easier for us to read the Bible in a proper way. We will immediately be on the proper path to touch life, to come to the light, and to fellowship with God in life and light. In other words, we will contact God, and in Him

and through His Word, receive the life supply and the revelation in light. Only then can we gain the real benefit from the
Bible. This is not a matter of knowledge or a matter of truth.
A person who obtains nourishment and receives revelation
will spontaneously have understanding. However, the nourishment and revelation he receives is above and beyond
understanding. We must have such an attitude in reading the
Bible.

THE WAYS TO READ THE BIBLE

We have been studying different ways to read the Bible for
many years. We have even published books such as *How to
Study the Bible*. But what we would speak of today is the simplest and most practical way to read the Bible. There are many
ways to read the Bible that either require too much time or
are too demanding for new believers. We should give new
believers a simple way to read the Bible. The Bible can be
read when one is at work or at school. Even if a person is very
busy, it is still possible to read a short portion of the Bible.
This is a very convenient way of reading the Bible.

Reading Sequentially

First, we should read the books of the Bible sequentially.
Some new believers read the Bible randomly. When they rise
in the morning, they shut their eyes and open to any page in
the Bible. If they happen to open to the book of Psalms, they
read a psalm, and if they open to the book of Revelation,
they read Revelation; they simply read whatever page they
open to. If the page they open to contains a difficult portion,
they may avoid it and go to another page. If they come to an
easy portion, they may read for a short period of time. This is
not acceptable. The Bible must be read consecutively and not
randomly. Having a responsibility before God, believers
should not randomly approach the Bible. We need to read
the easy portions as well as the difficult ones. Even if we do
not understand a portion in the Bible, we still need to read
it. Hence, we should always read in sequence. For example,
we should even read all the names in the genealogy in
Matthew 1:1-17.

We should read the Old Testament and the New Testament simultaneously. We should not wait until we finish reading the Old Testament before reading the New Testament. We should read the Old Testament consecutively beginning with the book of Genesis and at the same time read the New Testament consecutively beginning with the book of Matthew.

Every Christian should allocate two different times to daily read the Bible. One time should be in the morning, and the other can also be in the morning or in the afternoon or evening. According to the experience of many Christians, it is best to read the New Testament in the morning and the Old Testament during the other time. We should read a consecutive portion during both times.

Reading Only One Chapter Each Time

Second, we should not read too much each time; at the most, one chapter should be read at a time. Some suggest reading one chapter of the New Testament in the morning and three chapters of the Old Testament during the second time. In this way one can read through the entire Bible once a year. Although I formerly agreed with such a practice, I now feel that it may not be so beneficial. Some people are limited in their time and mental capacity. If they rigidly read one chapter of the New Testament and three chapters of the Old Testament each day, they may be reading the Bible simply for the sake of reading. Eventually, they may not even know what they have read. Thus, our experience tells us that it may be more beneficial to read one chapter of the Old Testament each day and finish it in three years.

This is similar to studying; we cannot be thorough in our studies if we are fast. If we read a book slowly, sentence by sentence, we will be clear when we finish the book. After three years of reading three chapters in the Old Testament every day, we may not know what we have read, even though we would have read it three times. It is better to read one chapter of the Old Testament every day and finish the Old Testament in three years. By doing so, we will gain a deeper impression.

This is not a fixed rule; each person should consider his own situation. Nevertheless, experience shows that it is better not to read more than one chapter at a time. It may not even be necessary to read through the New Testament once a year. It would be just as good to spend two years reading the New Testament. We can read half a chapter or even less than half a chapter daily. We may even read one chapter in three days. In this way we will spend one year to finish reading the four Gospels and the book of Acts and then another year to finish reading the Epistles and the book of Revelation. At the end of two years we will have a clear impression of the New Testament.

We should not desire to be fast. Previously I encouraged others to read the Bible once a year. Gradually I realized, from my experience and from the experience of others, that speed is not necessarily beneficial. We should not be too fast, and we should not be too impatient. It is sufficient for a new believer to read half a chapter of the New Testament and no more than one chapter of the Old Testament daily. In this way it will take three years to finish reading the Old Testament and two years to finish reading the New Testament. This will leave a deep and clear impression.

Therefore, we need not hurry. The most important thing is to be persistent and avoid impulsive reading. We should read a short portion of the Bible daily. If we read too much each time, it will not be easy for us to enjoy reading. Moreover, it will become a burden to us. This is not necessary. We should daily have two separate times for reading the Bible. The morning should be spent reading no more than one chapter of the New Testament. The other time should be spent reading no more than one chapter of the Old Testament. This is an excellent way to read the Bible.

Remembering the Main Points

Third, we should learn to remember the main points when reading the Bible. When we read Genesis 1, we should remember the order of the six days of creation. We should be able to say that on the first day, light and darkness were separated; on the second day, the water above was separated from the expanse below; on the third day, the land and waters were separated, and plants were brought forth; on the fourth day, the sun, moon, and stars appeared; on the fifth day, God created fish in the sea and birds in the sky; and on the sixth day, God created the animals on the earth, and He created man in His image and gave him dominion over all creation. These are the main points of Genesis 1. It is helpful to remember the main points when reading a chapter or a passage.

Receiving Inspiration and Turning It into Prayer

Fourth, in reading the Bible, we should receive inspiration and turn it into prayer. This is to blend the reading of the Word with prayer—reading and praying, praying and reading. It is rare not to receive any inspiration after reading a chapter or a portion of the Bible. We should always receive inspiration, regardless of which chapter or portion of the Bible we read. We should grasp the inspiration we receive and not let it go. The moment we receive inspiration, we should stop reading and turn the inspiration into prayer. This is to turn our reading of the Bible into prayer.

However, there is no need to pray for a long time. We should simply pray briefly and then resume our reading, continuing to read and pray. We should read for a while, then pray when there is inspiration. After a few prayers we should resume our reading. In this way we will no longer be aware of whether we are reading the Word or praying because our reading and praying have become one. This is the most beneficial way to obtain nourishment from reading the Word.

For example, after reading through Genesis 1 and remembering the main ideas, we will spontaneously have some inspiration. Perhaps we sense that our inward being is also in a state of waste, emptiness, and darkness and that we need the Spirit of God to work in us and the light of God to shine in us. We should turn this feeling into prayer, saying, "Lord, the condition of my inner being is waste, empty, and dark. I desperately need Your Spirit to operate in me and Your light to shine in me." After such a prayer we can continue reading. We may read the portion we have just prayed over again and then continue reading. Once we receive inspiration, we should receive it and turn it into prayer. After praying, we can continue to read. When we receive more inspiration, we should again turn it into prayer. We should read and pray in this way.

Memorizing the Precious Verses

Fifth, we should also learn to memorize the precious verses in the Bible. There are precious verses in almost every chapter or portion in the Bible. Whenever we come across these portions, whether it is a verse or a sentence, we should memorize it. Even if we are unable to accurately memorize every word, we should memorize the main idea. For example, the most precious portion in Genesis 1 is verse 26: "God said, Let Us make man in Our image, according to Our likeness." We should memorize this portion or at least memorize the main idea. Verse 1 is also very precious and is worth memorizing: "In the beginning God created the heavens and the earth." Words that are negative can also be memorized. For example, "But the earth became waste and emptiness, and darkness was on the surface of the deep, and the Spirit of God was brooding upon the surface of the waters. And God said, Let there be light; and there was light" (vv. 2-3). All these verses are very precious and should be memorized.

Every new believer should memorize these precious verses. If we do not memorize them as a new believer, it will be difficult for us to memorize them later. For example, Psalm 1:1 reads, "Blessed is the man / Who does not walk / In the counsel of the wicked, / Nor stand on the path of sinners, / Nor sit in the seat of mockers." Even though I have read this verse many times, I always forget the sequence of this verse whenever I quote it. This is because I did not memorize it properly at an early stage. Therefore, new believers should form the habit of memorizing important verses once they begin reading the Bible. This practice is very beneficial.

Underlining

Sixth, we should learn to underline. This is also an important aspect of reading the Bible. One should underline precious verses and portions that impress him. If one uses only one color for underlining, there is no problem in using red. However, it is better for new brothers and sisters to use several colors. It is best to use seven different colors.

The first color, red, should be used for the Lord Jesus and His redemption. We should underline all the important verses in the Bible that are related to the Lord Jesus and His redemption in red. Of course, this is not a regulation but simply a suggestion.

The second color, blue, should be used to underline all the heavenly things. Everything that is heavenly should be underlined in blue.

The third color, golden yellow, should be used to underline everything that is of God. In the Bible, gold symbolizes God's nature. Hence, it is best to underline God Himself and all things pertaining to God in golden yellow.

The fourth color, green, should be used to underline all things that are related to the Spirit and to life. Green is the color of life. For example, Genesis 1:2 says, "The Spirit of God was brooding upon the surface of the waters." This can be underlined in green. Another example is John 1:4, which says, "The life was the light of men." This verse should also be underlined in green. Anything that is related to the Spirit and to life should be underlined in green.

The fifth color is pink. This color should be used to underline important things that are not related to the Lord, heaven, God, or the Spirit.

The sixth color, black, should be used for Satan. The preceding five colors represent positive things; black is reserved for Satan. Whenever we come across things related to Satan, such as the serpent, the great dragon, the devil, and so forth, we should underline them in black.

The seventh color, dark purple, is very close to black but has a tinge of red. This should be used to indicate sinfulness, the flesh, the world, darkness, etc. Anything that is not Satan himself but is something bad should be underlined with this color.

It is good to use these seven colors for underlining. Reading and underlining the Bible every day is very profitable. After reading the Bible through and underlining it, it will be much easier to read it a second time.

We should underline the Bible as we read it, but this is not compulsory. It is also not necessary to underline everything the first time we read through the Bible. We would be remarkable people if we could identify all of these seven items the first time we read through the Bible. This is not even possible. However, as we read the Bible, we may see Christ in a portion and underline it. A year or two later, we may see something more in the same portion and underline it. This type of reading is spontaneous and beneficial.

Let me repeat that underlining is not obligatory, and we should not be distracted by it. Mere underlining without prayer, reading, or pray-reading will simply be an exercise in underlining and not a reading of the Bible. We must realize that underlining is merely to help our reading of the Bible.

We should not underline in a careless and untidy way. It is best to use a ruler and underline in a neat and orderly manner.

If some prefer not to use seven different colors at present, it is right to use only four colors. There should be black to represent Satan, and the remaining three colors can be red, yellow, and blue. In any case, it is entirely up to the individual's convenience. It is always useful to have some markings in the Bible.

Not Seeking a Thorough Understanding

Seventh, we should not seek a thorough understanding when reading the Bible. It is necessary to understand what we are reading, but to seek too much understanding may turn out to be harmful because it causes us to be preoccupied with matters that we are not prepared to understand. We should simply understand what we can of what we read and lay aside whatever we cannot understand. We should simply let them go because it is important that we read a portion of the Bible daily.

For example, the first half of Matthew 1 has many names, such as "Abraham begot Isaac, and Isaac begot Jacob." There is no way to understand the significance of these names the first time a person reads the Bible. For this reason, we should read this portion without even trying to understand the significance. There will be some understanding because even though we do not know who Abraham is, we will know that Abraham begot a son named Isaac. Verse 17 reads, "Thus all the generations from Abraham until David are fourteen generations, and from David until the deportation to Babylon, fourteen generations, and from the deportation to Babylon until the Christ, fourteen generations." After reading this verse we will at least understand, at a minimum, that there are three sets of fourteen generations even though we may not understand the events related to the deportation to Babylon. We should not insist on seeking profound understanding when reading the Bible. This will delay our effort and often ruin our practice of reading the Bible. In the end, we still may not be able to understand.

We should not be concerned if we do not have a thorough understanding of the Bible because it is impossible to understand everything when reading the Bible. Regardless of how experienced and how thorough we are, it is impossible to understand everything in reading the Bible. We should read according to our level, receive as much as we can understand, and let go of the things that we cannot understand. This is the simplest and most spontaneous way to read the Bible. This is the same as eating a meal. When there is a piece of bone with our chicken, we simply put the bone aside. It would be terrible to think that we must chew a bone to pieces in order to deal with it. Before we can "deal with" the bone, our teeth will have been broken and our mouth bruised. This can only bring us harm. Some people read the Bible in this way. They do not eat the meat but instead chew on the bones. Eventually they not only harm themselves but also suffer from hunger since they have not eaten anything. Our reading of the Bible must never be like this. Although everything that is presented in the Bible is meant for us to eat, there are some things that we cannot eat now; they must be saved for later. We should not waste our effort; we should eat whatever is edible and put aside what we cannot eat until later.

Musing on the Word

Eighth, if time permits, we should also muse on the Word.

This includes comparing portions and making cross-references. We should do this as we read through the Old and New Testaments. For example, we may remember the point concerning the seed of the woman in Genesis 3 when we come across the portion in Galatians 4 that says the Lord Jesus was born of a woman. At this moment, we may spontaneously muse on the fact that since the Lord Jesus was born of a woman, He must be this seed of a woman. In comparing Christ, who was born of the woman in Galatians 4 with the seed of the woman in Genesis 3, there will surely be some light.

Such musing does not need to take place while we are reading the Bible. We may read the Bible in the morning and muse on what we read on the way to work. Some people have half an hour or one hour to spare during the day, and during this time they recall and muse on the Word that they have read in the morning. They may recall what they have read and consider it with a portion they read in the past. This is very beneficial. We can do this kind of recalling, musing, and comparing during our free time apart from the time allocated for reading the Bible. It can even be done when sightseeing. All these are included in the reading of the Bible.

It is sufficient to read the Bible according to these eight points. There are many books in Christianity that offer many suggestions on reading the Bible. We have considered them and have practiced some of them, but our experience shows that the ways presented in these books should be simplified. In particular, it should be very simplified for new believers. It will be very good if all of these eight points can be practiced.

THE TIME FOR READING THE BIBLE

The Best Time Being in the Morning

Anything that we do requires time. The best time to read the Bible is in the morning. This is based on Psalm 119:147-148, which says, "I anticipated the dawn and cried out; / I hoped in Your words. / My eyes anticipated the night watches, / That I might muse upon Your word." This reveals that in ancient times, those who sought God hoped in the word of God before dawn and before the exchange of the night watch. Exodus 16 speaks of the Israelites gathering manna in the wilderness. The manna had to be gathered in the morning before the sun appeared, because once the sun appeared the manna would melt away. Manna is compared to the bread of life in John 6:33 and 35. Like the Israelites, we are walking in the wilderness, and every day we need a supply of spiritual food. Thus, we need to rise up every morning to gather manna from the Bible. Our Lord Jesus is the Word of God, and the content of the Word of God is the Lord Jesus. When we come to the Bible every morning to gather manna, we are actually seeking to touch the Lord and to receive Him as our bread of life.

This manna will melt away when the sun appears. If we do not take advantage of the quiet time in the morning to read the Word of God but instead, wait until the children wake up, the newspaper is delivered, and those selling vegetables have arrived, it will be impossible for us to read the Bible and receive benefit because of the appearance of all of these "suns." Hence, before dawn, before the sun appears, we should spend time in the Word of God to gather manna, to gather Christ as our nourishing food for the day.

If for certain reasons some people are unable to read the Word in the morning, other times will do. However, these are exceptional cases. It is best to read the Word in the morning.

Apart from reading the New Testament every morning, we should also find another time during the day to read the Old Testament. We should allocate a certain amount of time every day for this. This time may be after dinner or before going to bed at night. We should find time to sit down to read the Word of God. It is best to have these two times every day for reading the Bible.

Spending at Least Twenty Minutes to Read

If possible, we should spend at least twenty minutes to read the Bible, and it is better to spend even more time. Spending thirty minutes to an hour is very good. If we are unable to spend twenty minutes, we should at least spend ten minutes. We should never spend only five minutes; we should at least spend ten minutes. This applies to our reading of the Bible in the morning as well as at other times. It is best to spend about twenty to thirty minutes each time we read the Bible.

Setting Aside Extra Time

We should also set aside extra time, apart from our daily reading schedule, to study the Bible. We may spend half a day just to study an important truth. We may even spend a few weeks to study the Bible in the morning, in the afternoon, and again in the evening when on vacation. This is an additional reading of the Bible. It is to study important and deep matters in the Bible. This is not part of our usual routine but is an additional reading.

I believe enough has been spoken on the new believers' reading of the Bible. May the brothers and sisters establish such a practice in reading the Bible as soon as they are saved.

PRAYER

Let us briefly consider twenty-one points concerning prayer.

THE SIGNIFICANCE OF PRAYER

The significance of prayer is to contact God in our spirit and to absorb God Himself. Prayer is the human spirit contacting the Spirit of God, through which man absorbs God. Therefore, the significance of prayer lies not in asking God for things but in contacting and absorbing God.

THE ORGAN FOR PRAYER

Man needs to use the proper organ in whatever he does. He needs eyes to see and ears to hear. Likewise, he needs to use the proper organ to pray. The organ for prayer is the human spirit.

John 4:24 says, "God is Spirit, and those who worship Him must worship in spirit and truthfulness." Jude 20 says, "Praying in the Holy Spirit." Ephesians 6:18 says, "By means of all prayer and petition, praying at every time in spirit." These verses show that God is Spirit and that for man to contact God, he must use his spirit.

The human spirit is the deepest part of man's being. A person who prays with his spirit contacts God with his innermost part. When a person does not contact God with his innermost part, his prayer is ineffective. Therefore, we need to learn to reject our mind when we pray. If we think too much in our mind, our prayer will be hindered. The faculty for prayer is not the mind but the spirit.

THE MEANS OF PRAYER

The means of prayer is the blood of the Lord and His name. It is by means of the Lord's blood and the Lord's name that we can contact and absorb God.

The Lord's blood is versus our behavior, and His name is versus our person. As far as our behavior is concerned, we are filthy and altogether evil. Even our righteous deeds are like a soiled garment in God's eyes (Isa. 64:6). Therefore, we can never rely on our good works and our virtues in order to draw near to God. If we rely on our good works and virtues when we pray, there will be problems in our fellowship with God, and our petition will seldom be heard. We can rely only on the Lord's blood when we come before God in prayer. The Lord's blood redeemed us from our sins before God, satisfied the righteous requirement of God, and speaks something better for us. Hebrews 10:19 says that we have boldness to enter the Holy of Holies in the blood of Jesus. We must rely on the Lord's blood when we pray.

We cannot rely on ourselves when we come before God in prayer because our being is unacceptable to God. We must depend on the Lord's name. In the parting words of the Lord in John 14 through 16, the Lord said that if we ask anything in His name, He will do it (14:14; 15:16; 16:24). To pray by means of the Lord's name is to pray in the Lord's name, that is, to pray in the Lord's person. This is to pray by being clothed with the Lord, as if the Lord Himself is coming before God to pray. Such prayers are acceptable to God.

WHAT TO PRAY ACCORDING TO

Our prayer should be according to our inner sense. We must learn to pray according to the inner sense when we come before God. We should never pray according to what we have previously decided or according to our thoughts. If we put aside what we have decided, forget our thoughts, and open our spirit with a sincere heart to draw near to God, we will definitely have an inner sense. We should pray according to this sense. If the sense tells us to weep, we should weep; if it tells us to rejoice, we should rejoice; if it tells us to praise, we should praise; or if it tells us to confess our sins, we should confess our sins. We should follow the inner sense and pray according to it.

PRAYING WITHOUT HINDRANCE

Praying without hindrance requires a conscience void of offense. Once there is offense or condemnation in our conscience, our prayers will be immediately hindered. This is because the spirit is needed in prayer, and the conscience is the most important part of the spirit. If there is condemnation or offense in our conscience, our spirit will collapse, and we will be unable to pray. Offenses and condemnation in our conscience are a barrier between us and God, also making us unable to pray. Therefore, in order to pray without hindrance, we must deal with our conscience so that it is void of offense and without condemnation.

The only way we can have a conscience that is void of offense is by the cleansing of the precious blood of Jesus. Hebrews 10:22 says, "Let us come forward to the Holy of Holies...having our hearts sprinkled from an evil conscience." This is the reason we must pray by means of the precious blood. Without the precious blood of the Lord Jesus, our conscience will always accuse and condemn us, making us aware of our offenses and unable to draw near to God with boldness. However, whenever we rely on and apply the precious blood of the Lord, the offenses and condemnation in our conscience are removed, and there is no hindrance in our prayer. Therefore, we need to always keep our conscience void of offense. Whenever there is a sense of sin, a sense of accusation and offense in our conscience, we should immediately confess our sins before God and be cleansed by the Lord's blood.

DEALING WITH SINS FOR PRAYER

The dealing for prayer is the confession of sins. A person who knows how to pray spends much of his prayer time confessing his sins. This is because there are many inward and outward problems in our being when we come before God. If we draw near to God with a sincere heart and an open spirit, He will shine in us as light. When He shines in us, exposing our real self and true condition, we must confess our sins. After confessing our sin in this way, we often sense another. When the Lord shines in us, we may spend the initial time in our prayer just confessing our sins.

When we do not deal with our sins by confessing them in God's light, but rather come hastily before God, abruptly asking for different things, our prayer will not touch God because there is still a barrier. Such prayer and supplication are like beating the air. We must, therefore, have a sincere heart and an open spirit when we come before God in prayer. We need to rely on the Lord's blood and allow Him to shine in us. Then we need to confess our sins one by one according to God's shining and the inward sense. This kind of confession is the dealing for prayer. A good prayer is often preceded by dealing with sins through confession. If we know how to pray, we will never neglect dealing with our sins by confessing when we come before God in prayer.

The Old Testament presents a very clear type of this. When a priest entered the tabernacle to minister and serve God, he first had to pass through the altar. This is a type of dealing with sins. In order for a sinful man to draw near to God, he had to pass through the altar. This also applies to us in the New Testament age. When we draw near to God in prayer, we must first receive the shining of God and then confess our sins one by one according to the inner sense until we are transparent within, until there is a clear way between God and us. It is at this time that we can entreat God according to the inward sense. Therefore, in a good prayer, confession always precedes supplication.

THE UTTERANCE OF PRAYER

There is much to be considered related to our utterance in prayer. It should never be regarded lightly. Even in our daily living and in our relationships with others, our speaking is very important. For example, if a child asks his parents for something in a proper way, his parents will be happy to give it to him. If he asks in a wrong way, his parents may give it to him, but not be so happy. Some children are pleasant when they speak. Once they open their mouths, their parents have no alternative but to oblige. On the contrary, some children provoke their parents when they speak with them. The difference is in their utterance. Another example is that all diplomats pay much attention to their words. We need to give much consideration to our utterance when we come before God to pray.

We should not think that since God is omniscient, He knows what we need. This is the reason some regard prayer lightly, referring to Matthew 6:8, which says, "Your Father knows the things that you have need of before you ask Him." This is true. However, the Bible also says that the Canaanite woman cried out to the Lord, saying, "Have mercy on me, Lord, Son of David!" (15:22). She prayed desperately but was rejected. The Lord Jesus did not answer her. Then His disciples came and said to the Lord, "Send her away, for she is crying out after us" (v. 23). The Lord said, "It is not good to take the children's bread and throw it to the little dogs." The woman immediately changed her utterance and said, "Yes, Lord, for even the little dogs eat of the crumbs which fall from their masters' table" (vv. 26-27). She used expressions such as *little dogs, crumbs,* and *fall from their masters' table* to force the Lord Jesus to respond to her need. She used the Lord's own words as leverage against Him in her speaking. She used the expression *little dogs,* which came out of the Lord's mouth, and placed herself in the position of a dog. It is as if she was saying to the Lord, "You are right. I am a dog, so You cannot ignore me." Her words caused the Lord not only to give her grace but also to praise her faith. This shows that praying is similar to negotiation. We need to learn the utterance of prayer.

It is important for the utterance of prayer to be concise and to the point, not repetitive. The Lord Jesus said, "In praying do not babble empty words as the Gentiles do" (6:7). When words are repeated, they become redundant. We must exercise to use words that are concise and to the point in prayer and avoid superfluous words.

PRAYING AUDIBLY

During our personal prayer time, we should pray audibly.

This can be considered as a principle of prayer. Audible prayer will prevent our mind from being distracted. In silent prayer we may pray for this and that, and wander in our prayer. It is difficult to pray silently for fifteen minutes; silent prayer cannot last long. For prayer to be sustained, we must pray audibly. However, we should not shout or scream. This is not refined and can damage our prayer. This refers to personal prayer or prayer with a few people. This does not refer to prayer in the meetings.

THE POSTURE IN PRAYER

Should we stand, sit, or kneel down when we pray? This concerns our posture in prayer. In the Bible people always knelt down when they offered good, devout, and earnest prayers. There are examples of this in both the Old Testament and the New Testament. Kneeling down to pray shows a devout attitude toward God, and once we kneel down, our entire being is settled. It is not easy for our inner being to be settled when we are standing. When we sit down, we are more settled than when standing. When we kneel down, we are even more settled than when sitting down. But if we lie down, we will become dead within. Except in cases of illness, our spirit will be unable to rise if we lie down to pray. Therefore, our posture in prayer also needs to be carefully considered.

There is no law that says we must kneel down to pray. Often the environment does not allow us to kneel down. So we should train ourselves to be able to pray in every situation. We need to be trained to the point that whether we are talking to others or riding a bus or a bicycle, we still can pray within. Those who minister the word must also learn to look to the Lord in prayer as they speak.

THE BURDEN OF PRAYER

Every person who comes before God in prayer should not utter casual and empty words; rather, he should pray according to the burden and inward sense. However, the burden of prayer should not be so broad that it covers eight or ten points all at once. Some people pray as if they are reciting a book or taking attendance. This kind of prayer is very light. In order for our prayer to be weighty, our burden should not be too broad. At the most, good prayer should comprise three or four items. The best is to pray for one or two items. If there are several items, it is better to pray for a few items and pray for the rest at a different time. This can be compared to moving five boxes. If we overestimate ourselves and try to move all five at once, we will be unable to move them and may even drop them. We should first move two boxes, then another two, and the last one at the end. In this way we can move all the boxes. This is the way to pray.

WAITING IN PRAYER

Everyone who prays should learn to wait on God. We should never initiate anything by ourselves when we pray. We need to be calm and wait before God for His instructions and initiation in our prayer. All good prayers are initiated by God, not by us. When we pray, we must first stop ourselves. Our stopping is to wait on God.

There are many who have difficulties in the matter of waiting. Once they cease all activity in the midst of their prayer, their mind becomes more active. We need much exercise in this matter. We need to exercise to the extent that once we kneel down before God, our whole being is calm and able to wait for His instructions. When we have God's instruction and initiation, there will be a sense within and a word of burden. We can then start praying according to His inward burden.

INQUIRING IN PRAYER

When coming before God, many people immediately begin to ask God for things and never inquire of Him. We should not ask God for things, but rather we should inquire of Him. Even if we want to pray for the church, we should first inquire of the Lord, saying, "Lord, I have a feeling to pray for the church. Is this Your will? Do You want me to pray for the church at this moment? How should I pray?" Prayer that is preceded by inquiring is the best prayer.

Inquiring in prayer and waiting in prayer are two sides of one thing. One who waits is one who inquires. Similarly, a person who inquires is a person who waits. Abraham's prayer in Genesis 18 was very good; there was an aspect of waiting in his prayer. The Bible says that when the two angels turned and went toward Sodom, Abraham remained standing before God. This is waiting. While waiting, he began to intercede. He was not telling or begging; he was inquiring. He said, "Will you indeed destroy the righteous with the wicked? Suppose there are fifty righteous within the city; will You indeed destroy and not spare the place for the sake of the fifty righteous who are in it?" (vv. 23-24). He was inquiring. To inquire is to acknowledge the sovereign authority of God, that is, to acknowledge that He is Lord.

Those who know how to pray always inquire. Listen to the prayer of one of the psalmists in Psalm 27:4. He says, "One thing I have asked from Jehovah; / That do I seek: / To dwell in the house of Jehovah / All the days of my life, / To behold the beauty of Jehovah, / And to inquire in His temple." He was inquiring in the temple of God. Furthermore, in the books of Samuel, David had several prayers in which he inquired of Jehovah. Asking for things does not require any learning, but inquiring requires a great deal of learning.

TELLING

There is the need of telling in our prayer in addition to asking. To tell is to speak to God concerning our feelings; to ask is to request from God. There are these different aspects of prayer that require our exercise.

FAITH IN PRAYER

We need to learn to have faith in inquiring, telling, and even asking. The most crucial thing in order to have faith is to be simple. Do not analyze, but simply believe in God's word. God's word is precious. After prayer, we may sometimes have a word within from the Bible that clearly tells us that God has heard us. There are also other times when we pray to the extent that our inner sense tells us that God has heard our prayer, although there is not an explicit word. When we sense that the burden within has been discharged, and there is no further problem in the matter of our request, we should believe.

We should not analyze, doubt, or worry, because this will only cause us to lose faith.

If a burden is still present after we pray, we should pray again. We should pray until the burden has been lifted and is no longer with us, until we have peace within and no longer feel the need to pray. In such a condition, we should believe that God has heard our prayer. We need to learn to simply believe in God's word and in the feeling within.

GIVING THANKS IN PRAYER

Those who know how to pray always give a considerable amount of thanks in their prayer. It is unreasonable to ask without thanking. We always thank someone who agrees to do something for us. We not only thank him when he has accomplished the task, but we even thank him when he merely agrees to do the task. Consequently, there should be thanksgiving in every prayer. Once we have peace within and the burden has been lifted, we should give thanks. We should say, "Thank You, Lord, that I can tell You what concerns me. I have peace within. I believe You have heard my prayer and answered my petition. I thank You." We should not wait until our prayer is fulfilled to give thanks; we should begin giving thanks even before it is fulfilled. Each time we sense peace within as we pray, we should give thanks.

PRAISING IN PRAYER

The emphasis in giving thanks is to thank God for His grace, and the emphasis in praising is to praise God for His acts. Through prayer, we not only touch God's grace but also witness God's acts. God's grace requires thanksgiving, and His acts require praises. We can praise by saying, "Lord, I praise You. You are the wonderful Lord who does wonderful things. Even as I tell You of my difficulties, I sense that You have already taken care of this matter. Your promise is sufficient for me. Praise You!" With respect to the grace of God, we need to give thanks, and with respect to the acts of God, we need to offer praises.

WORSHIPPING IN PRAYER

There should also be worship in our prayers. Worship is toward God Himself. We should thank God for His grace, praise Him for His acts, and simply worship Him. Each prayer that is heard and fulfilled enables us to experience God. Experiencing God issues in worshipping God. The Bible shows that worship of God is derived from man's experience of God. The best and the most evident worship of God was rendered by Jacob as he was dying, leaning on his staff. Jacob's staff was the symbol of his sojourning on the earth. Because of his many experiences of God, he was able to worship God. This also applies to our worship in prayer. Whether our prayer is heard and fulfilled or has not yet been fulfilled, we touch God and gain knowledge of Him through prayer. Consequently, we should worship Him. In our prayer we should worship God Himself.

THE CONTINUATION OF PRAYER

If our time for prayer is over and our spirit is exhausted, but our burden related to a particular matter is not yet discharged, we should stop and wait for another time to continue praying for the matter. To pray for a certain matter again and again is the continuation of prayer. Sometimes things are fulfilled as soon as we pray, but other matters require prayer over a long period of time. Some matters require a year or years of prayer in order for them to be fulfilled. God often delights in the continuation of prayer in faith. Continuation of prayer can be compared to placing cards on one side of a scale. Each prayer is like the addition of a card. We should continue to pray until there is enough weight to tip the scale. This is the continuation of prayer.

THE COMPLEMENT TO PRAYER

The complement to prayer is reading the Bible. Reading the Bible and praying complement each other. Good Bible reading needs to be complemented with prayer, and good prayer needs to be complemented with Bible reading. This is what we call reading and praying, praying and reading. These two matters should be mingled so that we cannot distinguish reading from praying. Reading the Bible helps our praying, and praying helps our reading of the Bible. This may be compared to our left and right arms. It is easy for us to lose our balance if either arm is missing. Prayer without reading the Bible makes it difficult for our spirit of prayer to rise up. Therefore, we need to read a portion of the Bible. An appropriate amount of Bible reading can usually uplift, cultivate, and nourish our spirit of prayer. Hence, we need to train ourselves to complement our prayer with the reading of the Bible.

THE TIME TO PRAY

A Set Time

We should all have a set time each day to read the Bible and also a set time to pray. We should pray in the morning, at noon, and in the evening. Instead of praying at irregular times, we should decide on definite times for prayer. If we do not set aside definite times, we will lose the time. Those who are experienced realize that in order to redeem the time, we must set aside the time. Only time that has been set aside can be redeemed. This applies even more to times for prayer. If we do not set a time for prayer, we will not pray regularly. Therefore, to have a proper spiritual exercise, we need to set a time to rise up in the morning, a time to read the Bible, and a time to pray.

In the Morning

Just as with Bible reading, the best time to pray is in the morning. Since our heart and spirit are not yet distracted or troubled by many things in the morning, they are able to be quiet before God. It is also easy for our spirit to open to God and be touched in our fellowship with Him. Moreover, there are fewer distractions in the morning, unlike other times of the day when the telephone or the doorbell rings, the neighbor visits, or troubling and trivial matters arise. The best time for us to pray in a peaceful environment before God is in the morning.

Praying at Other Times

In Psalm 119:164 David said that he praised Jehovah seven times a day. In Psalm 55:17 he said that he prayed to God in the evening, in the morning, and at noon. When Daniel was in captivity in Babylon, he knelt down before God to pray three times a day (Dan. 6:10). Besides praying in the morning, we should also pray at other times.

Not Being Too Long

It is sufficient for the duration of each prayer time to be twenty to thirty minutes. Prayer time that is too long often results in a loss of interest, exhaustion, and hesitancy to pray again. Unless there is a special burden, our prayer times do not need to be very long.

COMPANIONS IN PRAYER

In order to have a good prayer life, we should also find companions to pray with. This will cause our prayer to be strengthened and also help us to maintain a prayer life. For many Christians, it is not easy to pray unless they pray with others. It is especially difficult for those who have a wandering mind to be calm in order to pray alone. If they can pray with two or three others, it is easier for their mind to concentrate and be calm. In this way they can pray for a longer period of time.

If we always pray alone, our learning in prayer will surely be inadequate. If several people pray together, there will be more learning in our prayer. In 2 Timothy 2:22 Paul exhorted Timothy to pursue "with those who call on the Lord out of a pure heart." It is best if every brother and sister would spend some time praying with others, apart from their own individual prayer time.

Christians should also attend prayer meetings. There are many lessons on prayer that can be learned in prayer meetings.

MEETING

We will now consider five aspects of meeting.

GOD'S ORDINATION

God has ordained a way of existence for every living creature in this universe. God's ordination for a creature is the law of existence for that creature. Fulfilling this law enables a creature to survive and be blessed. If a creature does not follow this law, it violates God's ordination and thus suffers unnecessary loss. God has ordained that chickens live on land, not in water; thus, chickens cannot live in water. God has also ordained that ducks live in water, so ducks cannot stay away from water for long. Furthermore, birds must be in the air and fish in the water. This is God's ordination. These ordinations are the law of existence for these creatures.

God has also ordained that Christians must meet in order to live or survive. To Christians, meeting is like water to fish or air to birds. Just as fish need to live in water and birds need to live in the air, Christians need to maintain their life by meeting. Once a Christian stops meeting, he is like a fish out of water or a bird that is not in the air. He has no way to survive. Brothers and sisters, once we are saved, we are a person in the church, and we cannot be individual Christians. To be a Christian, we must be one in the assembly, and this assembly is the church. The meaning of the term *church* is the gathering of the called-out ones. This implies that the nature of the church involves meeting. Without meeting, the church cannot exist, and there will be no church. The life of the church hinges on meeting. Therefore, the church is intimately related to meeting. This is God's ordination.

We must be deeply impressed with this point. Originally, we were descendants of Adam living in the world. When God called and saved us and we answered His call, He immediately set us apart from the world. God does not desire for us to be individual Christians after we have been set apart. Rather, He desires to gather all of the called ones into an assembly, which is the church. Although we cannot say that meeting alone constitutes the church, we can say that the church is in the meetings. If Christians did not meet, it would be difficult to have the church. Deciding not to meet is almost the same as prohibiting Christians to have the church. Whenever we stop meeting, we are separated from the church. If we do not attend the meetings, we are detached from the church.

The need to meet is according to God's ordination. We need to meet just as fish need water, birds need air, and man needs to breathe. This is God's ordination, and it should never be violated.

THE REQUIREMENT OF LIFE

Every kind of life has its own characteristic or characteristics. The spiritual life that we obtained, the life of God in us, has many different characteristics. Staying away from sin and abhorring sin is a characteristic of this life. Desiring to draw near to God and to serve God are also characteristics of the life within us. Flocking together, that is, assembling, is another characteristic of this life. The life within us wants us to flock together with other believers, to assemble with others. This characteristic demands that we be joined to others instead of being individualistic. Our physical life depends upon drinking water. If we do not drink water, we will be thirsty, but we feel comfortable when we drink water. Similarly, the spiritual life within us has the characteristic of wanting to meet with other Christians, of wanting to flock together with other believers.

In the New Testament, the word *flock* is the same as *assembly*. The Lord Jesus said, "I have other sheep...I must lead them also...there shall be one flock" (John 10:16). The flock is the church. A shepherd knows that sheep do not like to be isolated; they like to flock together with other sheep. This is amazing. Sheep do not like to roam about in the mountains and fields on their own. This is a suffering and unpleasant experience. However, sheep feel comfortable and at ease when they are in a flock. Christians are the Lord's sheep. The "sheep's" life in us demands that we flock together and assemble. If a new believer does not come to the meetings, he will not have much joy, peace, or comfort. If he comes to the meetings, however, he will have joy within as he sings, fellowships, prays, praises, and worships with the brothers since this is a characteristic of the divine life. Christian meetings are the issue of this inward requirement of life.

THE IMPORTANCE OF MEETING

There is a personal aspect as well as a corporate aspect of the grace that God gives to man. According to the personal aspect, we can receive grace when we read the Bible, pray, seek after God, and contact God. However, there is a corporate aspect of grace that can never be obtained through just our personal contact with God. It can be received only in the meetings.

We must also realize that the personal aspect of grace is not as weighty even though it is practical and necessary. But the corporate aspect of grace, the grace received in the meetings, is great and weighty. For example, a person can be touched by the gospel and receive salvation when he thinks of God or reads a spiritual book or a portion of the Bible on his own. However, his salvation will not be as strong as it could be if he is in a meeting. Those who are saved in a personal way may not have a salvation experience that is thorough or strong. When a person experiences salvation in a meeting, however, his salvation will be strong and thorough.

The light we receive when we read the Bible by ourselves can be small and limited. But when we read the Bible with others, the light we receive can be great and unlimited. Similarly, although we can touch the Lord's presence in our personal prayer, it is often limited. But there is an aspect of the Lord's presence in the meetings that exceeds an individual experience. Even in our prayer, we are often limited to trivial matters when we pray by ourselves. Our prayer for crucial matters is often ineffective. This is like moving boxes of different weights[We may be able to move a box that weighs twenty pounds, but it is impossible for us to move a box that weighs twenty thousand pounds by ourselves. If we attempt to move such a large box, it will be impossible. If we attempt to move it, it will still be in the same place even after twenty years of effort. In order to move it, we must gather others and move the box together. This is a principle in prayer. There are many things we cannot move by ourselves that must be brought to the meeting.]

There are some spiritual matters for which the personal aspect of grace is insufficient; hence, they must be brought to the meeting. Some people constantly try to overcome a weakness or shortcoming by themselves. They pray repeatedly, but no matter how much they pray, they are unable to overcome. If they would be willing to bring that weakness to the meeting and ask others to pray with them, they will easily overcome it. Likewise, there are matters that cannot be understood through individual seeking, but they can be easily understood if we are willing to seek with other brothers and sisters. This shows the importance of meeting.

There are many examples of this in the Bible. When the Lord Jesus appeared to the disciples on the evening of His resurrection, they rejoiced to see Him. However, since Thomas was not with them, he missed the Lord's appearing (John 20:19, 24-25). Mary Magdalene's experience of the Lord's appearing was fresh on the morning of His resurrection (vv. 1, 14-18). However, the weight and richness of that appearance cannot be compared to the Lord's appearance in the meeting. When the Lord appeared to His disciples, He breathed into them and said, "Receive the Holy Spirit" (v. 22). The Lord also charged them, saying, "Whose sins you forgive, they are forgiven them; and whose sins you retain, they are retained" (v. 23). Such an appearing in which the disciples received the Holy Spirit and were commissioned was not experienced individually. It was experienced in the meeting.

Concerning the two aspects of grace that God gives to man, although the personal aspect is fresh and sweet, it is far less important than the corporate aspect. Thomas missed a great blessing because he was absent from the meeting that evening. However, he was present when the Lord appeared again in the evening of the following Lord's Day, and it was then that he obtained the blessing he had missed (vv. 26-29). If he had been absent from the second evening, he would have suffered a loss that could never have been regained.

On the day of Pentecost, the Holy Spirit was poured out when the disciples were gathered together; He was not poured out while the disciples were having their personal prayer time (Acts 2:1-4). These examples show that if we want the Lord's presence, the Holy Spirit's outpouring, and the Lord's blessing, we must meet together. Understanding the Bible, answers to prayers, understanding God's will, deliverance from sins, and the solving of problems are often matters that cannot be solved individually. But once a person goes to the meeting, there is a way. Therefore, Christians can never be without meetings.

I repeat, there are two aspects to the grace that God gives to man: the personal and the corporate aspect. Grace in the personal aspect can be obtained in private, but grace in the corporate aspect can be obtained only in the meetings. Therefore, a normal Christian should not neglect his personal contact with God, nor should he neglect coming to the meetings to worship God with the saints. To neglect either aspect will cause us to suffer loss. Moreover, the loss suffered by neglecting the corporate aspect is greater than the loss suffered by neglecting the personal aspect. Rarely can Christians who only have a personal aspect and not a corporate aspect continue to stand firm before the Lord. It seems that those who are somewhat loose on the personal side but who continue to meet can still be sustained before the Lord. This shows that the corporate grace is greater, weightier, and more important than the personal grace. Hence, we must meet.

THE MEETING LIFE

Christians should not only meet often but should also meet to the extent that meetings become a habit, and thus, a meeting life is produced. We need to see that meeting is not an occasional act of Christians; rather, it is the Christian life, just as eating and washing daily are part of the human life. Every morning we need to wash ourselves when we rise. Then at noon, we need to wash our hands again. We need to wash our hands several times a day. Furthermore, we need to eat three meals a day and drink water many times. These are not occasional acts; rather, they constitute our living. The meeting of Christians is the same; it is a living, not an occasional act.

If Christians do not meet, it means that they do not live. If man does not eat, he cannot live. He will starve to death. Likewise, if Christians do not meet, it is the same as committing suicide. They are killing the Christian life.

It seems as if the believers at the time of Pentecost did nothing but meet. They met from morning until night. Many people ask us why we meet every day of the week, meeting in the mornings and also in the evenings. Frankly speaking, however, we do not meet as often as the believers at the time of Pentecost. Meeting is the Christian life. As soon as Christians stop meeting, they stop living.

NOT ABANDONING OUR ASSEMBLING TOGETHER

Hebrews 10:25 says, "Not abandoning our own assembling together, as the custom with some is." Abandoning the assembling together will eventually become a habit as well. A Christian who develops a habit of not meeting is in a dangerous state and will certainly be unable to stand firm.

Concerning our meeting together, these five points should be adequate for this lesson. In the following lessons, we will consider how to meet and the different kinds of meetings.

HOW TO MEET

(1)

In the previous lesson we covered the importance of meeting, the benefit of meeting, and the result of not meeting. In this lesson we will consider how to meet.

Although meeting is a spiritual matter, there is still the need of teaching and leading. Many matters related to life require teaching. Teaching, however, is futile if there is no life. But life without teaching and training will be useless. For example, in order for us to speak a human language, we need the human life. However, we will still be unable to speak any language without learning and practice. This principle applies to meeting. A person who is not saved cannot meet because he does not have the life of God. Believers have the life of God; this life requires us to meet and gives us the ability to meet. However, we still need to learn many techniques related to how to meet in order to be skillful in our meeting. Therefore, it is necessary that we be taught.

When we consider the condition of our meetings, we realize that thirty years ago we were like children playing. Although the Lord's mercy was upon us in our childishness and brought us through, we wasted some of our time and energy. After many years we can now say that we have discovered some ways and secrets concerning how to meet. In order to meet we must have a seeking heart and a strong spirit. We also need the presence of the Holy Spirit by the Lord's mercy and blessing. These are crucial matters. In addition, we need to carefully consider the techniques of meeting, which are definitely related to ushering in spiritual blessing. We must pay attention to all these matters.

THE PURPOSE OF MEETING

What is the purpose of meeting? What is its significance? The general concept concerning Christian gatherings is that church members sit in a chapel, listen to the preaching of a pastor, and sing some hymns. After this the pastor will stretch out his hands to give a benediction, and everyone goes home. This is the concept most people have concerning Christian meetings. But we are not speaking of this kind of meeting. Our meeting is by no means a so-called Sunday service. There are four aspects to the purpose of our meetings.

Toward God—Worship

The first aspect of the purpose of meeting is toward God. This can be summarized as worship. Worshipping God involves four points.

Singing

We need to sing hymns in the meeting. Once a person is saved, he needs to learn to sing hymns. Some may have learned music in school and, therefore, have some knowledge concerning singing; this is convenient. But even with this knowledge concerning singing, we still need to adjust our attitude when we sing. Whereas we learned to appreciate music artistically, now we should sing hymns with a heart to praise. The brothers and sisters who have not learned music need to learn a little concerning music. Hence, sometimes it is necessary to teach the brothers and sisters before or after the meetings how to sing hymns.

Singing hymns is closely related to meeting. If the singing is poor, our spirit often cannot be uplifted. If the singing is good, our spirit will be easily uplifted. Sometimes a hymn is begun in a key that is too high for people to follow; at other times the key is so low that it is difficult for people to breathe. Sometimes the singing is so fast that it is difficult for people to keep up; at other times it is so slow that it puts people to sleep. This requires our attention and learning.

Praising

We need to praise God in the meetings. We praise God

with prayers, not with hymns. Good praises are often needed in the meeting. This is not petitioning, asking, begging, or even thanking. This is praising God mainly for His doings and His virtues. We should read the words of praise in the Bible and apply them frequently in the meeting.

Thanking

In the meeting we also need to give thanks to God for His grace and for the works of grace He accomplished for us. Whereas the objects of our praise are God's doings and His virtues, the objects of our thanksgiving are God's grace and His works of grace.

Meditating

We also need quiet moments to meditate during the meetings. In particular this applies to the bread-breaking meeting; the brothers and sisters should exercise to be calm and consider the Lord Himself. Even the prayer meeting needs this.

The brothers and sisters should always consider the Lord quietly before a meeting begins. We should not talk and disturb the spirit of worship. This requires much exercise. We need a kind of contemplation to consider the Lord and His doings.

These four points constitute our worship to God. In the meetings we should sing hymns to God, offer prayers of praise to God for His doing and His virtues, and thank Him for His grace and works of grace. We also need to be calm before God to consider His person and His doings.

Toward Man—Edification

The second aspect of the purpose of meeting is toward man. This is for edification. We attend meetings not only to worship God but also to edify others. We must not think that as a new believer we are unable to edify others. As long as we have spiritual inspiration, the testimony of our salvation experience can edify others, inwardly refreshing them and thereby enlivening them. No matter how young or weak we may be, our attending of the meetings should be to edify others. There are two points related to edifying others.

Releasing and Refreshing the Spirit of Others

Our edification of others is to release and refresh their spirit. For example, we may select a hymn that causes the spirit of the believers to be released and refreshed when they sing. We may offer a prayer of praise that releases and refreshes the spirit of the meeting. Giving thanks to the Lord, reading a few verses from the Scriptures, or speaking a few words may release and refresh others' stale spirit. In principle, our edifying others in a meeting should release and refresh their spirit.

Ministering Life and Light

To release and refresh others' spirit is on the negative side. There is also a positive side in the edification of others, that is, to minister life and light. Whether we speak a few words, offer a prayer, or share a testimony, we should minister Christ and the divine life to others. We also need to minister light. Whether we give a message, read a portion from the Bible with some speaking, or share a testimony, others should be enlightened. This is the second point in the edification of others.

Toward Ourselves—Being Built Up in Life

Third, we also take care of ourselves in the meetings. The meetings are for our spiritual growth. Whenever we attend a meeting, we should have the intention of being built up. This aspect includes three points.

In Life

This point is very broad. A meeting should always result in experiencing a certain amount of being built up. We may not know how to deal with our conscience, but through a testimony we are enlightened and learn how to deal with our conscience. We may not know how to walk by the Spirit, but a brother's testimony of how he was led by the Lord to walk by the Spirit may deeply impress us, and we desire also to live by the Spirit. In this way we are built up and established in the divine life. The enlightenment and supply from the meeting can release us from being entangled by sin, the world, and the flesh, and it can resolve any problem we may have related to prayer or reading the Bible. The more help we receive in the meetings concerning spiritual life, the more we are built up in life.

In Truth

A strong Christian not only needs to grow in life but also needs to know the truth. Truths such as the ground of the church and the way of the church are very important. It is a pity that some brothers and sisters who love the Lord, are zealous, and pursue the Lord are not clear concerning these truths. There is a group of Christians who advocate the universal church because they have not seen the practical aspect of the church being the church in a locality. It is not easy to find the universal church in the Bible, but the local churches can be found in many portions of the Scriptures. There is the church in Jerusalem (Acts 8:1), the church in Antioch (13:1), the church in Ephesus (Rev. 2:1), the church in Smyrna (v. 8), and the churches in Asia Minor (1:4). These are local churches. We acknowledge that the Body of Christ is universal, but the churches we contact on the earth today are local churches. Without the local churches, we have no way to touch the universal church. This is related to the knowledge of the truth.

The Bible also clearly presents matters such as Christian conduct, marriage, family, management of finances, and occupations. We should know these matters. Such knowledge should not be pursued merely on our own. We need to come to the meetings and receive help from others. The more we come to the meetings, the clearer will be our knowledge of the truth. In the meetings we can be built up in our knowledge of the truth.

In Service

A proper Christian should also be active in service, actively coordinating with the brothers and sisters. Christians are priests who serve before God. Thus, the more we meet, the more we should serve. The more we meet, the more we grow in life and know the truth. We can be built up in these three matters in and through the meetings.

Toward the Devil—Shame

In every Christian meeting we worship God, edify others, are built up, and shame God's enemy, the devil. This is the fourth aspect of the purpose of our meetings. If we do not meet, we lose the opportunity to shame the devil. The meetings are the greatest shame to the devil. This is the reason he does not like Christians to meet. Whereas the positive side of Christian meetings is to receive grace, the negative side is to put Satan to shame. Putting Satan to shame involves two points.

Displaying God's Grace

Christian meetings are for the display of God's grace. The displaying of God's grace is a shame to Satan. For example, a brother may stand up in a meeting and testify that he used to live in sin; he was bound by sin because he played mah-jongg and indulged in dancing. But now God has forgiven and saved him, "the foremost of sinners." Another sister may testify of how she was saved from worshipping the devil and how hearing the gospel, she went home and burned all her idols. These testimonies display God's grace. The displaying of God's grace is a shame to the devil.

Exhibiting Christ's Victory

Christian meetings are also an exhibition of Christ's victory. Whenever we gather together, we exhibit Christ's victory. We can exhibit the victory of the Lord Jesus in the meeting by speaking of the Lord in our practical living. This is also a great shame to the devil.

This does not mean that we come to the meeting in order to curse the devil. Some people continually curse Satan in their prayers, saying, "Lord, curse Satan and bind him." This kind of cursing is not very effective. We need to display God's grace to us and exhibit Christ's victorious work upon us. Such a display and exhibition are a shame to the devil.

Christian meetings glorify God and shame the devil. Thus,

we do not meet merely to attend a so-called Sunday service; rather, we meet to worship God, edify others, be built up, and shame the devil. These are great and important matters.

PREPARING BEFORE A MEETING

Having covered the purpose of meeting, let us now consider our preparation before a meeting. We should prepare ourselves before every meeting in order to be ready. There are also four aspects to our preparation—toward God, toward man, toward ourselves, and toward the devil.

Toward God—Dealing with Offenses and Removing Barriers

Before coming to a meeting, we need to come before God to deal with our offenses and mistakes and with any condemnation in our conscience. These need to be dealt with by the Lord's blood one by one. When the sense of condemnation in our conscience is cleared, the barrier between God and us is removed. We should not come to a meeting with a barrier between God and us. If we do, we will bring burden and death to the meeting. Therefore, before every meeting we must come before God and have a thorough dealing. Through prayer and confession, we should ask for forgiveness and cleansing by the Lord's blood. We should comply with whatever God requires of us, and we should remove whatever He wants us to remove. We must remove all the barriers in order to commune with God freely. If we do this, we will be a benefit to the meeting, and we will benefit from the meeting.

Toward Others—Willing to Minister and Help

When we prepare for a meeting, we need to have a desire to minister and help others in the meeting. It is not right for us to have an indifferent and nonchalant attitude. We should care for others and be willing to be used by the Lord to supply and help others.

We must remember that whoever supplies others will be supplied, and whoever helps others will be helped. The more we supply others, the more we are supplied, and the more we help others, the more we are helped. If we stop supplying others and have no desire to help, we will not receive much supply or help.

Even if we were saved yesterday, we should prepare ourselves in this way. We should not think that we cannot offer any help because we do not know anything and cannot do anything. This concept must be changed. No matter who we are, by the Lord's mercy our attitude must be that we are pleased to allow God's grace to flow through us so that others may be supplied and helped. We need to prepare in such a way before the meeting.

Toward Ourselves—
Ready to Receive Grace, Light, Supply, and Help

In preparing for a meeting we need to be ready to receive grace, light, supply, and help. This is toward ourselves. Before coming to a meeting, we should prepare ourselves to receive grace, light, supply, and help in the meeting.

Toward the Devil—Rejecting Distractions,
Hindrances, and a Closed Mouth

Toward the devil, our preparation is to reject. We reject distractions, hindrances, and a closed mouth. The devil has a powerful scheme, which is to keep our mouth closed. He may let us come to a meeting but try to forbid us from opening our mouth. We should reject his attempt to keep our mouth closed. Some brothers and sisters are kept quiet by the devil because they do not see through his scheme. From the beginning to the end of a year, they never open their mouths in a meeting; hence, they cannot supply others or be supplied by others.

We need to prepare ourselves before every meeting, saying, "I want to open my mouth. I will not let Satan keep my mouth closed. Lord, cast out the demon of dumbness from me!" Especially the brothers and sisters who are particularly timid and shy should prepare in this way. In 1 Corinthians 12:1-3 Paul said that the Corinthian believers once served dumb idols, but now they served a God who speaks. When we served dumb idols, we were possessed by a demon of dumbness and were dumb, but now we are serving a speaking God.

His inspiration reaches us, causing us to open our mouth and speak. Therefore, when we come to a meeting, we should reject Satan's scheme to keep our mouth closed.

LEARNING TO TOUCH
THE FEELING OF THE MEETING

The most important thing in a meeting is to touch the feeling and the atmosphere of the meeting. What are the feeling and atmosphere of a meeting? For example, in a wedding meeting everyone is joyful, and we touch a joyful atmosphere as soon as we enter the meeting. In a funeral meeting, on the contrary, we sense an atmosphere and feeling of grief. These two examples clearly show that the atmosphere of a meeting is something concrete. As long as we have feeling, we should be able to sense the atmosphere.

Every meeting has its own feeling and atmosphere, and we need to learn to touch and take care of this atmosphere. It would be insensible for us to begin weeping when we enter a wedding meeting or for us to sit in a funeral meeting looking cheerful. We should never disregard the feeling and the atmosphere of a meeting.

Although most meetings do not have such a distinct feeling and atmosphere, there is always a feeling and atmosphere in a meeting. No meeting is without a feeling or atmosphere. Therefore, if we want to have a good meeting, we need to learn to touch the feeling and atmosphere of the meeting.

In order to touch the atmosphere of a meeting, we need to pay attention to the following points.

Touching the Spiritual Facts of the Meeting

The feeling of a meeting is a spiritual fact. When we touch this spiritual fact, the feeling of the meeting is produced. Thus, in order to touch the feeling of a meeting, we need to learn to touch the spiritual facts. In a wedding meeting, for example, everyone is happy because someone is getting married, and there is the fact of happiness. When we touch this fact in a wedding meeting, we are happy. This is the feeling of the meeting. Another example is a funeral meeting. In a funeral meeting everyone is grieving, and there is the fact of grief. Touching this fact in a funeral meeting causes us to have a feeling of grief. This is the feeling of the meeting. The feeling of a meeting is a spiritual fact, and when the spiritual fact touches man's inward feelings, the feeling of the meeting is produced. We must touch the spiritual fact before we can touch the feeling of a meeting.

Exercising the Sense of the Spirit in Our Daily Living

In order to touch the feeling of a meeting, our spiritual sense must be keen. It is difficult for a person with a dull spiritual sense to touch the feeling of a meeting. For example, a child can run into a wedding meeting crying, even though joy is the fact in the meeting. A child can also scream and yell happily in a funeral meeting when everyone is grieving. This is because his inward feelings have not been exercised and are muddled. In order to touch the fact of a meeting, our inward sense must be keen, not dull. This keenness depends on our daily exercise.

[Our spirit is deeper than our mind, emotion, and will. If we normally do everything by our mind, emotion, and will and disregard the feeling in our spirit, the sense of our spirit will not be developed. Consequently, the sense of our spirit will not be so keen, and it will lose its function when we are in a meeting. However, if we exercise the sense of our spirit for every matter in our daily life, our spirit will be very keen and able to touch the fact of a meeting once we enter the meeting.]

This is similar to learning music. Because a person has been learning music consistently, his ears become very sharp and can distinguish a note that is either sharp or flat. There are also people whose eyes are trained to accurately determine the size of a piece of land without measuring it. This is because they have been trained in their daily living.

Hence, after we are saved, we not only need to love the Lord and follow Him; we also need to exercise the sense in our spirit so that it can be keen. In this way, it will be easy for us to touch the spiritual fact of a meeting and sense the atmosphere in our spirit.

Fellowshipping with the Lord and
Dealing with Everything before the Meeting

Daily exercise of the sense in our spirit is not enough. Before coming to a meeting, we need to fellowship with the Lord in prayer to deal with everything between Him and us. This is dealing with our spirit. Then our spirit will be enlivened and uplifted. Once our spirit is enlivened, uplifted, and refreshed, the feeling in our spirit will be keen, and we can easily touch the feeling of the meeting. Because some people still have many barriers between them and the Lord, they cannot sense the atmosphere of the meeting. Their spirit is dull and numb. Therefore, such dealing is very important before a meeting.

IN THE MEETING

Now we will consider several aspects of how we should conduct ourselves in a meeting.

Putting Aside Our Personal Feelings

When we come to a meeting, we must first put aside our personal feelings. If we have lost our temper before a meeting, we should put aside our anger when we come to the meeting. Otherwise, we will be fully occupied with our feelings throughout the meeting. A brother may be provoked to anger by his wife and then bring his anger to a meeting. Then when he prays in the meeting, his anger can be sensed in his prayer. He does not care for the nature or the atmosphere of the meeting. His only concern is that his wife has provoked him, and his prayer in the meeting is used as an outlet.

Besides this negative example, there are also positive examples. A brother is filled with light and joy through reading the Bible at home and is singing Hallelujahs before a meeting. At the meeting he excitedly speaks of the light he received at home, disregarding the atmosphere of the meeting. This shows that he has not put aside his personal feeling; thus, he cannot touch the atmosphere of the meeting.

This does not only apply to the meetings. Although someone may speak with us for five minutes, and we nod our head in agreement, we may not hear a word of what he said. This is because we did not put aside our personal thoughts. If we are anxiously waiting for an opportunity to speak, we will not hear what others have to say. In order to hear what others are saying and realize what they mean, we must put aside our personal thoughts. In the same way, in order to touch the feeling of a meeting, we must put aside our personal feelings. Whether we are angry or happy, we need to put aside our feeling. Only in this way can we touch the feeling of a meeting.

Opening Our Spirit

A closed person can never touch the feeling of a meeting. Some people come to a meeting with a closed spirit. They come as spectators to watch others perform. They criticize when others perform poorly and applaud when they perform well. Such behavior is from a closed spirit. We must not be like this. When we come to a meeting, we must open our spirit and be prepared to receive the leading of the Holy Spirit.

Exercising the Spirit to Touch the Feeling of the Meeting

When we put aside our personal feelings and open our spirit, we are qualified to exercise our spirit and touch the feeling of a meeting. Once we touch the feeling of a meeting, we should function accordingly.

It is very important that we be able to touch the feeling of a meeting. If we cannot touch the feeling, we cannot enter into the flow of the meeting and be mingled with the meeting. Since our gathering together is the meeting, we cannot have a personal agenda; rather, we should all move together. Hence, we must touch the atmosphere of a meeting and enter into the flow of the meeting.

Knowing the Progression of the Meeting

There is a progression in all meetings: a beginning, a process, and an end. A person who knows how to meet knows the purpose of meeting, prepares himself before a meeting, can sense the feeling of a meeting, and knows the progression of a meeting. There are many points to be considered concerning how a meeting begins, the steps it passes through, and how it ends.

Strictly speaking, a good meeting progresses through eight steps. It may be acceptable for a meeting not to pass through two or three of these steps; however, not passing through more than two or three of these steps will result in a poor meeting. We cannot have a meeting that has a beginning and an end but only a brief progression in between.

Let us briefly explain the eight steps through which a meeting progresses.

Opening—to Begin the Meeting

The opening of a meeting is to begin the meeting. It is not easy to begin a meeting; in fact, the most difficult part of a meeting is the beginning. If the opening is strong, the whole meeting will be strong. If the opening is weak, it will be difficult to strengthen the meeting later. Sometimes a person selects an "inappropriate" hymn at the beginning and kills the entire meeting. If another person adds a deadening prayer, the meeting will be "put in a coffin." Hence, it is not easy to begin a meeting.

In order to have a good opening, we must accurately touch the feeling of the meeting. Once we touch the feeling, it is easier to begin the meeting. We can begin by selecting an appropriate hymn, offering a prayer, or speaking a few words. Some people are very good at opening a meeting, and the meeting is lively from the beginning. Other people, on the contrary, seem to have the "capability" of deadening any meeting they begin. This is like selecting *Hymns,* #183, "Come, let us join our cheerful songs," or *Hymns,* #127, "Hark! ten thousand voices crying," in a funeral meeting. The meeting will be ruined if it is opened in this way. This is the same as singing *Hymns,* #974, "He looked for a city and lived in a tent," at the beginning of a wedding meeting; this is basically a wrong opening. A wrong opening deadens the entire meeting. The opening of a meeting is very important and requires much practice.

Introduction—to Lead the Meeting to the Subject according to the Feeling

No meeting is without a subject or purpose. Once a meeting has begun, we need to lead it to the subject according to the feeling of the meeting. The introduction must be done through prayer, speaking, or singing. For example, at a meeting we may sense that the feeling of the brothers and sisters is that the Lord is in glory; hence, this is the feeling and subject of the meeting. We should rise up to offer a prayer, speak a few words, or select an appropriate hymn in order to lead everyone to the subject. This is the introduction.

Strengthening— to Strengthen the Spirit of the Meeting

After the meeting is led to its subject, the spirit of the meeting may not be strong; thus, it may require some strengthening. Strengthening the spirit of a meeting also requires some skill. Selecting a hymn, offering a prayer, or speaking a few words are the ways to strengthen the spirit of a meeting.

Uplifting—to Uplift the Spirit of the Meeting

If the spirit of a meeting is not high enough after strengthening, it needs to be uplifted. This also requires some skill. The means to uplift the spirit of a meeting is also by singing, prayer, or speaking.

Maintaining—to Maintain the Spirit

When, through strengthening and uplifting, the spirit of a meeting reaches a peak, we should maintain it at this peak for a while. Sometimes after reaching the peak, a meeting goes down too quickly because of a lack in maintaining the spirit of the meeting. As a result, the meeting is not very rich. Thus, maintaining the spirit of a meeting is also very necessary.

The spirit of a meeting is seldom maintained by speaking. This is because speaking does not have much function in this step. Because it is difficult to select a fitting hymn, it is also difficult to maintain the spirit by singing. The most effective way to maintain the spirit of a meeting is for a few brothers and sisters to offer prayers with a strong spirit. I have been in several meetings when some brothers and sisters prayed one after another and thereby maintained the spirit of the meeting. Such meetings edify the spirit of the saints.

Filling the Time—
to Fill Up the Remaining Time of the Meeting

Sometimes although everything is accomplished in a meeting, there is still time left because it is too early to end the meeting. The remaining time should be filled with singing, prayer, or speaking. Filling the time is similar to maintaining the spirit of a meeting, but there is a slight difference. Maintaining the spirit is keeping the spirit of a meeting at the peak after the peak has been reached. However, if a meeting does not have a peak, or if it is somewhat flat, and if it is not time for the meeting to end, there is the need to fill the time. The requirement for filling the time is not that high, but we should avoid routine practices. In filling the time there should be the addition of a spiritual atmosphere and flavor to the meeting.

Ending—to End the Meeting

The ending is to end a meeting. There is much involved in ending a meeting. We have many meetings that have a good opening but a poor ending. Ending can be compared to tying a knot. When we travel, we tie our luggage with a knot at the end of the rope after everything is bundled up. If the knot is not tied securely, the luggage will open up when it is being transported. A meeting that progresses through all the steps but has a weak ending will leave the saints without a solid feeling. In contrast, a meeting that is flat and weak in its progression but nevertheless has a strong ending will leave the saints with a good taste. The ending of a meeting is very important. Those who learn to take the lead in the meeting must learn this matter so that the meeting can end in a strong way.

We can end a meeting with a hymn or with some speaking, but the best way to end a meeting is through prayer. This does not mean that a meeting must always end with prayer. From our experience, however, we know that prayer is the best way to end a meeting. A meeting that does not end with prayer may cause the saints to feel that the meeting has not ended.

Sending Off—to Express
the Lingering Riches of the Meeting

Sending off is derived from Genesis 18 where Abraham sent Jehovah off. Sending off expresses the lingering riches of a meeting. There is the need of sending off when a rich meeting produces a lingering atmosphere. For example, when we sense such a lingering atmosphere, we can stand up and share a few words, even though a brother has already ended the meeting with prayer. This kind of sending off leaves the saints full of a pleasant taste. Instead of speaking a word, we may offer another prayer. Seemingly this is repetitious, but it is not. This is sending off, which strengthens the lingering air of a meeting.

It is also appropriate to send off with a short hymn. For example, after the bread-breaking meeting has ended, we may still sing the last stanza of *Hymns*, #33, "Loving Father, now before Thee / We will ever praise Thy love." This is a sending off.

These are the eight steps in the progression of a meeting. It may not be necessary for a meeting to progress through the steps of maintaining the spirit, filling the time, and sending off. Even the uplifting step may not be necessary. The remaining four steps, however, are necessary in every meeting. Every meeting should have an opening, an introduction, a strengthening, and an ending.

A new believer may not be able to take care of these steps of progression in a meeting, but he needs to know these steps. Gradually, he should learn to take care of these steps in a meeting. We should bring all our meetings through this progression. This is not a law; rather, this is a spontaneous progression. After a meeting begins, there is an introduction, then strengthening, uplifting, and maintaining the spirit. If there is still more time before the meeting should end, there is the need to fill the time before the ending. If there is a lingering air after the ending, there is a need for sending off. A meeting with these steps of progression is rich and supplying.

Correction and Turning

Apart from these eight steps of progression, there are two supplementary steps.

Correcting

Correcting is to correct the selection of a wrong hymn. For example, a hymn on prayer may be selected in a breadbreaking meeting, a hymn to praise the Lord may be selected after we have begun to worship the Father, or a hymn to praise the Lord's glory may be selected while we are remembering the Lord's suffering. These hymns do not match the atmosphere of the meeting; rather, they distract the spirit of the meeting and must therefore be corrected. Sometimes we may wait until the hymn is sung and then select another hymn. Or we may immediately select another hymn, but this must be done carefully. The person being corrected may be offended if this is not handled properly. Any correction should be done gently. We must be skillful in correcting.

Turning

Turning is to turn the subject of the meeting. For example, although the feeling of a meeting may obviously be the Lord's suffering on the cross, a brother calls *Hymns,* #127, which is on the Lord's exaltation. Singing this hymn cannot uplift people's spirit. A brother follows with a prayer, but the spirit is still not uplifted. Another brother may select a hymn on the Lord's love, but this still cannot move the spirit of the saints. However, when the subject is returned to the Lord's suffering, the spirit of the brothers and sisters is released through singing a hymn and prayers. This is because the feeling of the meeting was on the Lord's suffering. There was thus the need for turning.

Although there is the need for correcting and turning, they should not be practiced in a light way. If we do not know how to correct properly, we should not correct. If we do not know how to turn the subject in a suitable way, we should not do it. We need to have some confidence before correcting and turning. We should also be gentle and not harsh in order to avoid hurting others.

HOW TO MEET

(2)

We have covered four points concerning how to meet. We will continue with two more points.

FUNCTIONING IN THE MEETINGS

After touching the feeling of a meeting, we should learn to function in the meeting. We should not come to a meeting merely to listen to a message or to watch others worship; instead, we should come to meet in mutuality. Everyone bears the responsibility for a meeting. For this reason, as we touch the feeling of a meeting, we should learn to fulfill our obligation to function in the meeting.

There are several points we should pay attention to in order to function in a meeting.

Rejecting Improper Things

Before functioning in a meeting, we must first reject every improper thing. If we do not reject these things, they will distract us and hinder our functioning in the meeting. Improper things can be grouped into six categories.

Disturbing Thoughts

If we come to a meeting with disturbing and troubling thoughts, we will be unable to function. Therefore, we must reject all disturbing thoughts in order to function in a meeting. There are three points we should pay attention to related to disturbing thoughts.

Not Receiving Any News

We should not receive any news before a meeting; otherwise, we will have disturbing thoughts during the meeting. When I first learned this lesson approximately twenty years ago, I would not touch any practical affairs half an hour before a meeting. I would put aside any letters or telegrams and read them only after the meeting. Reading letters or telegrams before a meeting can give us disturbing thoughts that we will be unable to drop, even when we are in the meeting. This will damage our functioning in the meeting. Hence, we must learn not to receive any news before a meeting. Regardless of how important a matter may be, it should wait until after a meeting.

Not Exchanging Any News

Not only should we not allow ourselves to be disturbed, but we should also not cause others to be disturbed. Before a meeting we should not receive any news, and we should not share any news with others. We should wait until after a meeting before we speak to others about any news. This is very important. We need to learn not to spread any news when we see one another before a meeting. Even if it is very important, we should wait until the meeting is over.

Not Worrying about Things
That Are Outside of the Meeting

We should not bring any matters that are outside of a meeting into the meeting. Since we desire to meet, we should meet in a proper way. We should not bring any matters related to our family, job, school, health, children, or relatives to a meeting. We should completely forget every matter, even if it is important. We need to have faith and believe that everything is in God's hands. It is useless to worry in a meeting because worrying only distracts and troubles us during the meeting. Therefore, we must learn not to worry about things that are outside of the meeting.

Analysis

In order to function in a meeting, we should reject

disturbing thoughts, and we should not analyze. Once we touch the atmosphere of a meeting and receive spiritual inspiration, we should function immediately. Consideration or analysis merely quenches the inspiration.

Self-consciousness

We should have spiritual awareness, a sense of the spirit, during a meeting. We should not be self-conscious. Self-consciousness is being shy. It is a fear of being laughed at, saying something inaccurate, praying in an improper tone, or other such things. Such a feeling of fear is produced when a person is self-conscious. We must learn to reject self-consciousness in the meeting. Our spiritual sense in a meeting must be very keen, but we must utterly reject self-consciousness.

Accusations

Satan often accuses us in our conscience when we come to a meeting, saying that our condition is improper because we have failed in this or that. We must reject all such accusations. We must also reject his accusations against others. When Satan accuses us, he either reminds us of our own failures so that we are unable to rise, or he reminds us of others' mistakes so that we condemn them during the meeting. We need to believe in the Lord's forgiveness, and we also need to forgive others. All our wrongdoings have been cleansed by the Lord's blood. Since He has forgiven us, we should also forgive others. If we do not reject this twofold accusation of Satan, we cannot receive spiritual inspiration in a meeting.

Burdens

We should reject not only accusations but also burdens. For example, the responsibility of giving a message after a meeting may be a burden on a brother, preventing him from being released in the meeting. We need to give our burdens to God through prayer. No matter what kind of burden we have to bear, whether it is related to our work, our family, or our business, we should put it aside once we come to a meeting. We need to exercise not to bring any burdens to the meeting.

Criticism

Criticism leaves us without spiritual inspiration and affects others. We lose our spiritual inspiration once we begin to criticize others. A criticizing spirit also affects others. Therefore, we need to reject all criticism.

If we desire to function in a meeting, on the negative side, we must learn to reject disturbing thoughts, analysis, self-consciousness, accusations, burdens, and criticism.

Being Aggressive

On the positive side, a person needs to be aggressive if he desires to function in a meeting. A passive person is unable to function in a meeting. In order to function, we must be aggressive. We gather together in order to meet. If our intention is to play basketball, we should not wait for the ball to come to us. Rather, we should actively try to catch the ball. There are five matters that require our attention if we desire to be aggressive in a meeting.

Having a Willing Heart

In order to be aggressive, we must have a willing heart. Our heart must be turned to the Lord, desiring to worship the Lord and to be inspired. Some believers are willing to come to a meeting, but they are not willing to function in the meeting. Because their heart is not willing, they cannot be aggressive. In order to function in a meeting, we must have a willing heart.

Exercising the Will

Since the will is the organ we use to take the initiative, it must be exercised. Even though we have a spirit within us, we are not spirits; we are human beings. Receiving spiritual inspiration is not a matter of being passive. We must exercise our will in order to receive spiritual inspiration. Once we have a sense within, we must exercise our will to function according to that inspiration.

Having Faith

We must believe that we will receive spiritual inspiration

when our heart is turned toward God and we exercise our will to cooperate with Him. We receive inspiration by faith.

Functioning according to Inspiration

Once we take the initiative to exercise our will and have received spiritual inspiration by faith, we should express this inspiration according to our sense. We should not analyze the inspiration with our mind. Once we analyze it, the inspiration will be quenched.

Not Being Afraid

We must not be afraid or timid when we speak according to the inner sense. Being afraid or timid quenches the sense of the spirit.

Functioning

When we reject improper things on the negative side and exercise our will to receive spiritual inspiration by faith on the positive side, we will spontaneously be able to function in the meeting. However, there is much to consider concerning how to function in a proper way so that the meeting can be supplied. Generally speaking, the activities in a meeting do not include more than three items—selecting hymns, praying, and speaking. Let us briefly consider these three items.

Selecting Hymns

Matching the Nature of the Meeting

This point is very obvious. In a prayer meeting we must select hymns that have the nature of prayer; in the bread-breaking meeting we must select hymns related to the Lord's table. The hymns we select in a meeting need to match the nature of that particular meeting.

Matching the Progression of the Meeting

The hymns selected in a meeting should match not only the nature but also the progression of the meeting. A closing hymn should not be selected at the beginning of a meeting, nor should an opening hymn be selected at the end of a meeting. When a meeting reaches its climax, a hymn that is high in content should be selected. Sometimes there is the need to strengthen a meeting, and at other times there is the need to uplift or maintain the spirit of a meeting. The hymns we choose must always match the progression of the meeting.

For example, after singing, "Hark! ten thousand voices crying," a table meeting may reach its climax; at this time, the spirit of the meeting needs to be maintained so that the climax is not diminished. If a brother then selects a hymn that speaks of surveying the wondrous cross, the focus of the meeting will be changed from the Lord on the throne to the Lord on the cross. Such a selection does not match the progression of the meeting, and the spirit of the meeting will be lowered rather than maintained. After singing, "Hark! ten thousand voices crying," it is difficult to find another hymn that can maintain the spirit of a meeting. It is best to repeat a few stanzas from this hymn that are relatively high in content. In this way, we can maintain the spirit that has already been uplifted. The selection of a hymn needs to match the progression of a meeting.

Being according to the Sense in Our Spirit

We must select hymns according to the sense in our spirit. We cannot rely merely on our mind. We should not mechanically consider the nature of a meeting, or even the stage of the meeting, and then flip through our hymnal to find a suitable hymn. Hymns that are selected in such a dead way will not be according to the spirit of the meeting. We must select hymns according to the sense in our spirit. When selecting a hymn, we need to touch our spirit to see if there is an inward confirmation. There must be an inward response so that when we sing the hymn, we will be inspired.

Calling the Number of a Hymn Clearly and Slowly

After selecting a hymn, we need to consider how to call out the hymn number. We should not call a hymn too loudly, too softly, or so fast that others are unable to hear the hymn that has been called. Rather, we should call a hymn number slowly and clearly. When some brothers call a hymn, it is like a gust of wind that passes by so quickly that other people do not know which hymn number was called. Other brothers call hymns in a manner that can be compared to a loud clap of thunder; it frightens people and causes them to lose their spiritual inspiration. Still others call hymns with a voice that is so quiet that even those sitting next to them have difficulty hearing the number. This also disturbs the spirit of the meeting. Because the spirit of the meeting is quite tender and can easily be disturbed, all the activities in the meeting must be refined. We must call a hymn clearly and slowly. Our voice should neither be too loud nor too soft. People must be able to hear us clearly and not be disturbed. We should not think that these are trivial matters. These matters have much impact on a meeting.

Praying

Matching the Nature of the Meeting

Our prayers, just as our selection of hymns, should match the nature of a meeting. If a sister begins to pray for her son, crying bitterly with tears, this will greatly affect the feeling of the meeting. This is because her prayer does not match the nature of the meeting.

Matching the Progression of the Meeting

The bread-breaking meeting has two sections. The first section is for remembering the Lord, and the second section is for worshipping the Father. After the bread and the cup have been passed around, someone may pray long-windedly concerning the Lord's humbling Himself to be born in a manger and His dying on the cross. Because such prayer does not follow the progression of the meeting, even though it may match the nature of the meeting, it disturbs the entire meeting. For this reason, our prayers must follow the progression of the meeting.

Being according to the Sense in Our Spirit

It is normal for our prayers to be according to the sense in our spirit.

Using a Clear Voice

Our voice should not be too soft when we pray. It is difficult to hear some people when they pray, even if we strain to listen. For this reason, we should not spare our throat and hurt the ears of the brothers and sisters when we pray. At the same time, we should not yell and shout like thunder when we pray. Such ear-quivering prayers make people feel uncomfortable. The tone of our voice in prayer must be moderate, neither too high nor too low, and the pronunciation should be clear.

Using Brief Sentences

We should use simple words in our prayer, and our sentences should be short, not long.

Exercising Our Spirit

We should pray with the exercise of our spirit so that our spirit comes out and releases the spirit of others.

Being Brief

When we pray, our sentences should be brief and our prayer should be brief. Long prayers often kill a meeting. C. H. Mackintosh said that long prayers torture the children of God. He would ask others not to punish the brothers and sisters by long prayers. D. L. Moody was in a meeting where a sister was praying nonstop, exhausting the endurance of the brothers and sisters. He stood up and wisely recommended that while the sister was still praying, they should sing a hymn. We all need to avoid long prayers in the meeting.

Considering the Response of Others

When praying in a meeting, we must consider the response of others. If there is not a response of Amen, we should stop our prayer. A lack of Amens means that others are not responding. Why should we continue praying if they are not responding? We should always consider the response of others to our prayer. We should stop praying when the spirit of others does not follow.

Speaking

Concerning the activities in the meeting, there is also speaking in addition to selecting hymns and praying. Speaking includes testifying, exhorting, and releasing the light we have received from the Bible. In principle, the points that apply to selecting hymns and praying also apply to speaking.

Matching the Nature of the Meeting

When we speak in a meeting, we should follow the nature of the meeting; otherwise, our speaking can interrupt the atmosphere and even kill the spirit of the meeting.

Matching the Progression of the Meeting

Our speaking in a meeting must match the progression. In our speaking we must take care of this point.

Being according to the Sense in Our Spirit

Although our speaking must also follow the nature and take care of the progression of a meeting, we must speak according to the sense in our spirit, not merely according to dead knowledge.

Bible Reading Being Brief and Fitting

If there is a need to read a portion from the Bible, only the verses that are appropriate should be read. Reading an entire chapter or a few chapters can be as unbearable as long prayers. By reading only succinct portions, we can save time and not consume people's energy. Our Bible reading needs to be brief.

Being Brief, Succinct, and Focused

When speaking in a meeting, we need to be brief, succinct, and focused. When some brothers stand up to speak, they speak about everything from atomic bombs to missiles, changing subjects without any inward restraint. Speaking in an unfocused way disturbs the meeting and must be avoided.

Not Being Afraid

We should not be too bold and arrogant, nor should we be afraid when we speak. We need to be calm, not nervous, anxious, timid, or frightened. Being frightened and nervous can weaken the spirit.

Using a Clear Voice

We should also pay attention to our voice when we speak. Our voice must be clear and audible so that it can easily be heard and understood by everyone. A soft and muffled voice is not only difficult to understand, but it can also cause the atmosphere of the meeting to sink.

Using an Exercised and Released Spirit

The most important point related to speaking is to exercise our spirit so that it can be released. We should not be like a robot, speaking only from our throat and mind but not from our spirit. Our spirit is released when our whole being is exercised. Once the spirit comes out, we will have a feeling when we open our mouth to speak, and when people hear us, they will be moved. This requires much practice.

Considering the Feeling and Response of Others

We must also consider the feeling and response of others when we speak. If we continue speaking, even though some saints have fallen asleep during our speaking, we disregard the response of the saints. If the saints fall asleep when we are speaking, we can either stop speaking and immediately sit down, or we can change our manner of speaking. This requires our attention and practice.

Taking Care of the Time

We must also take care of the time when we speak in a meeting. We should not speak for half an hour or an hour as it pleases us. We must take care of the time.

Avoiding Two Things

Pretense

There should not be pretense in the activities in a meeting.

For example, it is pretentious to cry when we have no feeling to cry. To pretend in a meeting is very ugly. All the activities in a meeting must be genuine.

Imitation

We should not imitate the behavior of other people in a meeting. More than a decade ago, a group of young sisters in Tsingtao tried to imitate an elderly sister who often coughed when speaking the truth. These young sisters imitated her coughing. This imitation made people very uncomfortable. Imitation, however, may not be intentional. It is unavoidable to be influenced by other people after being with them for a long period of time. For example, the brothers and sisters who meet with us pray in a tone that is completely different from believers in the denominations. This is an understandable influence, not an imitation. We need to be careful not to imitate others intentionally. All our activity in a meeting must be genuine.

Being Submissive

When functioning in a meeting, we also need to learn the lesson of submission.

To the Advice of the Responsible Brothers

In a meeting the responsible brothers may give advice in any of three points.

Concerning the Voice

The responsible brothers bear the responsibility to remind the brothers and sisters to raise their voice when they speak too softly.

Concerning the Time

The responsible brothers should tell the saints who speak too long to be brief or to finish their speaking soon.

Concerning the Content

The responsible brothers should also remind the saints to

adjust their speaking when their speaking is not appropriate or is cumbersome and repetitive.

We should submit ourselves to the advice of the responsible brothers in all the activities in a meeting, especially when we speak. Their feeling often represents the feeling of the brothers and sisters.

To the Spiritual Inspiration of Other People

According to 1 Corinthians 14:30, if something is revealed to another sitting by, the first should be silent. This is being submissive to the spiritual inspiration of others. In this way, the order in a meeting is maintained without confusion.

KNOWING THE HYMNS

In order to function properly in the meeting, we must also know the hymns. If we do not know the hymns, we will be unable to select them in a meeting. In order to know the hymns and to select appropriate hymns in a meeting, we must pay attention to five points.

The Category

We need to know the categories of the hymns. For example, some hymns are for the gospel, some are for edification, and others are for worship.

The Subject

Although there are many hymns in the same category, they may not all have the same subject. For example, the subject of some gospel hymns is vanity, and the subject of other gospel hymns is the cross of the Lord Jesus. Some of the hymns on remembering the Lord have the Lord's glory as their subject, and others in the same category focus on the Lord's suffering. For this reason we need to know the subject of the hymns as well as their categories.

The Feeling of the Hymns

Some hymns may be in the same category and of the same subject but have a different feeling. Every hymn has its feeling. For example, "It passeth knowledge, that dear love of

Thine" (*Hymns,* #154) is a hymn for remembering the Lord and has the Lord's love as its subject. The feeling of this hymn is fine, sweet, and tender. The feeling of other hymns may not be as fine as this one, even though their subject is the Lord's love. Some hymns have a fine feeling and are also poetic. Other hymns, however, may not be poetic. In learning the hymns, we need to know their categories and subject so that we can further distinguish them according to their feeling.

Matching the Progression of the Meeting

To know the hymns by their nature, subject, and feeling is one thing, but to select hymns in the meeting is another. When we select hymns in a meeting, we must match the progression of the meeting. For example, because it is not easy to have an uplifted spirit at the beginning of a meeting, we should not begin the meeting with "Hark! ten thousand voices crying." Hence, our selecting of hymns must match the progression of a meeting.

Memorizing the Number
and the First Line of the Hymns

Memorizing the number and the first line of the hymns enables us to select hymns in a meeting according to spiritual inspiration. We may have spiritual inspiration and know which hymn to select but forget the hymn number. As a result, the atmosphere of the meeting may change by the time we find the hymn, or someone may grasp the opportunity and call another hymn. This is often a loss to the meeting. For this reason, we need to be familiar with and memorize the number and the first line of the hymns so that we can select the proper hymns when there is a need.

We need to spend time to practice these points. Otherwise, our meetings will not be strong. Let me repeat: our meetings are not a Sunday service. In Christianity and in the Catholic Church, the Sunday service is altogether for the pastors and the priests, who undertake all the activities. Our meetings, on the contrary, are for the brothers and sisters to coordinate with one another and to function together. This applies to prayer meetings, bread-breaking meetings, Bible-study meetings, and fellowship meetings in which we exercise our gifts. The meeting for the ministry of the word is the only exception. Hence, we all need to practice the skills for meeting. If we are not strong in these skills, the meetings will be poor, weak, dead, and depressed. In order to have meetings that are lively and rich, every brother and sister must know how to meet and must possess the skills for meeting. May the Lord bless us in this matter.

LESSON ELEVEN

VARIOUS KINDS OF MEETINGS

(1)

In this lesson we come to the various kinds of meetings and their natures. It is evident that a person must know the focus and activities of each meeting if he desires to serve and function in the meetings. We will first consider the bread-breaking meeting.

THE BREAD-BREAKING MEETING

Acts 20:7 and 1 Corinthians 10:21 and 11:20 show that the bread-breaking meeting is the gathering of the saints to partake of the Lord's table and to eat the Lord's supper. We must know that this meeting is divided into two sections. The first section is for the remembrance of the Lord, and the second section is for the worship of the Father. Since this meeting is divided into two sections, the activities in this meeting are also of two natures. The activities in the first section are to remember the Lord. The activities in the second section are to worship the Father.

The First Section— for the Remembrance of the Lord, Taking the Lord as the Center

The purpose of the first section is to remember the Lord; therefore, we should never bring in any activity related to the worship of the Father into this section. The focus in this section is on breaking the bread. Our coming together to break bread is for the remembrance of the Lord. This section of the meeting has two aspects.

Eating the Lord's Supper
Being to Remember the Lord

As clearly presented in 1 Corinthians 11:20-25, eating the Lord's supper is the first significance of this aspect of the bread-breaking meeting. Eating the Lord's supper is for the proper remembrance of the Lord. There are three points for us to understand related to the Lord's supper.

First, the bread signifies the Lord's body that hung on the cross for us. This was His physical body that was given for us. The Lord's body was given and broken for us on the cross so that we may obtain His life. Every time we come to the bread-breaking meeting and see the bread on the table, we should have a strong feeling in our spirit. We should have the realization that the bread signifies that the body which the Lord clothed Himself with in His incarnation was broken for us on the cross so that we may have His life. At His supper we partake of the bread that signifies His body that was given for us that we may obtain His life. Our receiving and enjoying the Lord is our remembrance of Him. This is what the Lord meant on the night of His betrayal when He took the bread, gave thanks, broke it, and gave it to His disciples, saying, "This is My body which is being given for you; do this in remembrance of Me" (Luke 22:19).

Second, the produce of the vine in the cup signifies the Lord's blood, shed for us so that our sins may be forgiven. On the positive side, the bread signifies the Lord's body given for us so that we may have His life. On the negative side, the cup signifies the Lord's blood shed for us so that we may be delivered from sin and everything we have that is outside of God.

It is very strange that while the bread on the table is identified as the bread, the blood on the table is not identified as the blood, but as the cup. If the cup was referred to as the blood, it would denote only redemption. However, the significance of the cup encompasses much more than merely redemption. In the Bible the cup signifies a portion, a blessing. Psalm 16:5 says, "Jehovah is the portion...of my cup." Therefore, the cup denotes the portion we obtain from God.

The portion God measures out to us according to our condition is the cup God has given to us. Therefore, Revelation 14:9-10 says that the fallen sinners who worship the beast and his image receive the cup of God's wrath as their portion.

According to our true condition, we also deserve the cup of God's wrath. But we thank God that the Lord drank the cup of wrath for us on the cross. Before His crucifixion, the Lord prayed in Gethsemane, saying, "My Father, if it is possible, let this cup pass from Me; yet not as I will, but as You will" (Matt. 26:39). When He was arrested, He said to Peter, who drew the sword to protect Him, "Put the sword into its sheath. The cup which the Father has given Me, shall I not drink it?" (John 18:11). These verses show that on the cross the Lord drank the cup of God's wrath for us who have sinned, fallen, and should perish. On the cross He was judged by God and shed His blood. Therefore, the Lord's blood is proof that He bore our sins and was judged by God. His blood declares to the universe that He drank the cup of God's wrath that we, the fallen sinners, should drink, and He suffered the punishment that we should suffer. He fulfilled the righteous requirement of God. Hence, the Lord's shed blood indicates that He has washed away our sins before God.

The Lord has also established a covenant by His blood. This covenant enables us to receive God Himself and all of His blessings. This covenant established by the Lord's blood is included in the cup. This cup speaks forth that God Himself and all of His blessings have become our portion. The cup that we have received from the Lord is the cup of salvation in Psalm 116:13 and the cup that runs over in Psalm 23:5. On the negative side, this cup speaks of the Lord's blood that has washed away our sins before God. On the positive side, it speaks of the blood of the Lord that has paid the price for us so that God and all that belongs to Him are now our portion for our enjoyment. This is our blessed portion.

Hence, the bread denotes life, and the cup signifies blessing. The bread always refers to life; it is the bread of life. The cup always refers to blessing; it is the portion that man receives from God. By receiving the bread, we testify that we receive the Lord as life in our spirit. Our receiving and enjoyment of Him in this way is our remembrance of Him. At the same time, by receiving this cup, we testify that we receive all that He has accomplished for us by the shedding of His blood on the cross. Hence, every time we receive the bread and the cup, we have a fresh receiving of the Lord Himself and what He accomplished for us by the shedding of His blood on the cross. This receiving is in spirit for our inward enjoyment. Our receiving Him, enjoying Him, and eating and drinking of Him are our true remembrance of Him.

Here we see that our remembrance of the Lord is completely different from the worldly commemoration of famous people and memorials of relatives. In the world people exercise their mind to contemplate the ways, conduct, works, and love of the one whom they are remembering, but there is no element of receiving. When we remember the Lord, however, we do not merely meditate on Him; this is but a small part. The focus of our remembrance of the Lord is our eating and drinking of Him. The Lord said, "This is My body, which is given for you; this do unto the remembrance of Me...This cup is the new covenant established in My blood; this do, as often as you drink it, unto the remembrance of Me" (1 Cor. 11:24-25). The Lord's words clearly state that to remember Him is to receive Him as the One who was given for us and to receive all that He has accomplished. Our eating, drinking, and enjoying Him in such a way is to remember Him.

Hence, every time we come to remember the Lord, we should not remember Him merely by meditating in our mind. We need to receive Him and all that He has accomplished in our spirit as our inward enjoyment and allow Him to mingle more with us. This is the true remembrance of the Lord.

The significance of bread-breaking is also the meaning of our Christian living. The Christian living is a life of eating, drinking, and enjoying the Lord day by day in order to allow Him to mingle with us. We should not do this merely on the first day of the week when we come to the bread-breaking meeting. This should be our daily living. As saved ones, we live by eating and drinking the Lord.

If our understanding of bread-breaking to remember the Lord is not up to this standard, our bread-breaking may be merely something superstitious. This would be like the mass in the Catholic Church. Catholics believe that they come to God by keeping the mass and that they are thereby forgiven and able to receive His blessings. This is altogether superstitious. The significance of our coming to eat the Lord's supper by remembering the Lord is absolutely different. We declare to the universe, testifying that we live by eating, drinking, and receiving Him so that He can enter into us to be our life and be mingled with us. This is not merely an outward ritual; it is the reality of our daily living. Only those living in this way are truly remembering the Lord; otherwise, bread-breaking is but a superstitious religious ritual.

Third, when we come to break the bread and drink the cup in remembrance of the Lord, our focus is on eating, drinking, receiving, and enjoying the Lord, not on thinking about the Lord. Hence, when we come to the bread-breaking meeting, we should not consider the Lord too much with our mind; rather, we should exercise our spirit to contact the Lord and have fellowship with Him. We must have a deep realization regarding this point. According to our human concept, we may think that as we break the bread, we should tremble at the sight of the bread. We may also think that when we touch the cup, we should consider each drop the Lord shed of His blood. We may remember how the Lord left His throne, was born in a manger, went to Nazareth, went up to Jerusalem, was crucified, was buried in a tomb, and then ascended to the throne after His resurrection. We often hear people pray in this way at the bread-breaking meeting. This is man's natural concept.

We need to know that when the Lord established the supper, He passed the bread to His disciples and told them to take and eat it. He also passed the cup to them and told them to drink of it. He told them to do this in remembrance of Him. The main focus in the bread-breaking meeting is not to remember the Lord in our mind but to fellowship with the Lord in our spirit, receiving the Lord whose body was broken for us and whose blood was shed in order to redeem us. When we have such fellowship with the Lord in our spirit by eating, drinking, and enjoying Him, we are fed in our spirit. This can be compared to being invited to a feast in which the host does not want us to think about the dishes that he has prepared; rather, he wants us to eat to the full what he has prepared. This is the Lord's revelation regarding the bread-breaking meeting. This is completely different from man's natural concept.

The Lord desires that we eat the bread and drink the cup in our remembrance of Him. He said, "This do unto the remembrance of Me" (v. 24). When we contact the Lord in this way, we will spontaneously think of His acts and of what He has done for us. However, this is not the focus of our remembrance of the Lord. The focus is our eating, drinking, receiving, and enjoying Him.

Partaking of the Lord's Table
Being to Fellowship with All the Saints

Eating the Lord's supper, as presented in 1 Corinthians 11, is mainly for our remembrance of the Lord. Partaking of the Lord's table, as presented in 1 Corinthians 10:16-17 and 21, is mainly for our fellowship with the saints. First Corinthians refers to the matter of bread-breaking two times. In chapter 11 it speaks of the Lord's supper with the focus of remembering the Lord. In chapter 10 it speaks of partaking of the Lord's table with the focus of fellowshipping with the saints.

The apostle says, "The cup of blessing which we bless, is it not the fellowship of the blood of Christ? The bread which we break, is it not the fellowship of the body of Christ? Seeing that there is one bread, we who are many are one Body" (10:16-17). He then explains that to have fellowship in the Lord's blood and the Lord's body is to "partake of the Lord's table" (v. 21). Since partaking of the Lord's table is for us to share in His table, the focus in this aspect is not on remembering, receiving, and enjoying the Lord but on having fellowship with all the saints in the Lord. There are many things a Christian can do individually; he can pray, read the Bible, and even preach the gospel. But he cannot break the bread and drink the cup by himself at home. The reason for this is that the bread-breaking meeting has an aspect of eating the Lord's supper to remember the Lord and an aspect of partaking of the Lord's table with all the saints. The Lord's table is for all the saints to partake of together. Having mutual fellowship with all the saints in the Body of Christ is not an individual matter. There are three points for us to consider related to the Lord's table.

First, in the aspect of eating the Lord's supper, the bread on the table signifies the Lord's body that was given for us on the cross. However, in the aspect of partaking of the Lord's table, the bread on the table signifies the Body that is comprised of all the saints who have been regenerated through the Lord's death and resurrection. Hence, the apostle says, "Seeing that there is one bread, we who are many are one Body" (v. 17). This Body is different from the Lord's physical body that hung on the cross. The Lord's physical body died on the cross for us. The Body in verse 17 is His mystical Body produced by the Lord's death and resurrection, and it is composed of all the saints. Therefore, each time we break the bread, we come to enjoy the Lord, remember Him, and receive the body that He gave for us on the cross. In addition, we also enjoy His mystical Body that was brought forth through the Lord's death and resurrection. This indicates that we have fellowship with all the saints in the Body.

Therefore, from the aspect of partaking of the Lord's table, the breaking of the bread is our fellowship in the Body of Christ, testifying of the oneness of the Body of Christ. This concerns our relationship with all the saints and our relationship with the Lord Himself. Today Christians pay attention mainly to remembering the Lord but neglect the fellowship of the Body of Christ.

Second, in the aspect of partaking of the Lord's table, the bread and the cup are the common portion that we enjoy in fellowship with all the saints. The apostle says, "The cup of blessing which we bless, is it not the fellowship of the blood of Christ? The bread which we break, is it not the fellowship of the body of Christ?" (v. 16). Therefore, the bread and the cup are the common portion that we enjoy in fellowship with all the saints.

Third, in the aspect of eating the Lord's supper, the focus is on eating, drinking, and enjoying the Lord. In the aspect of partaking of the Lord's table and having fellowship with all the saints, the focus is on having <u>mutual fellowship</u> in the <u>blood</u> and in the <u>Body of Christ.</u>

The Practical Aspect

Having a Focus

The Lord must be the goal of our singing, praying, speaking, meditating, and fellowshipping in the first section of the bread-breaking meeting. We must also have a focus. Every bread-breaking meeting should be focused. If we touch the Lord's love in the atmosphere of the meeting, our focus should be the Lord's love. The focus may also be the Lord's name, His death, His humbling of Himself, His living on the earth, His sufferings, His ascension and glorification, His splendor, or His sweetness. Regardless of the focus, the selecting of hymns, praying, giving of thanks, praising, and sharing should point toward this focus. After singing a hymn on the Lord's love, we should not follow with a prayer on the Lord's suffering and then with a word on the Lord's ascension. Such inconsistency confuses people. Therefore, each meeting should have a focus.

Everyone Coordinating and Cooperating

In order to be focused in a meeting, everyone must coordinate and cooperate. For example, after singing a hymn on the Lord's love, I may offer a prayer on the Lord's love in order to digest the hymn. A brother may follow by reading some verses from the Bible to strengthen this feeling. Another brother may then select a hymn to strengthen the singing on the Lord's love. <u>This is our coordination and cooperation.</u> There should never be a situation in which one brother selects a hymn without considering the general feeling in the meeting, then another brother prays without considering the feeling of the hymn, and still another brother stands up to speak, not caring for the feeling of the prayer. Such a situation would indicate that everyone is acting individually. This will cause the meeting to be chaotic. Therefore, in the bread-breaking meeting we must learn to coordinate and cooperate with one another. When we coordinate, cooperate, and have a focus, the spirit of the meeting will be sweet.

Having a Climax

In addition to having a focus and coordinating and cooperating together, we need to move toward a climax in every meeting. This enables the meeting to climb higher and higher. Once a meeting reaches the climax, the bread and the cup should be blessed and passed. We should not make the meeting a ritual, thinking that at a particular time the bread and the cup should be blessed and passed, regardless of whether a climax has been reached. Such a meeting does not have much spiritual inspiration and cannot give its participants a feeling of satisfaction. Every bread-breaking meeting should reach a climax when everyone truly touches the Lord with their spirit. This gives the participants a deep sense of satisfaction.

Thanksgiving and Praise

There should be prayers only of thanksgiving and of praise, not prayers of supplication, in the bread-breaking meeting. Prayers of supplication should be left for the prayer meeting. In the bread-breaking meeting we should remember only the Lord, giving thanks and praise to Him. Prayers of supplication drag the meeting down and ruin the atmosphere of the meeting.

The Second Section— for the Worship of the Father, Taking the Father as the Center

The second section of the bread-breaking meeting is entirely for the worship of the Father, taking the Father as the center. There are five points for us to consider in this section.

First, let us consider the basis in the truth for the worship of the Father. The salvation we have received consists of two sections. In the first section we met the Lord, received Him as our Savior, and received all that He accomplished for us. After receiving the Lord in this way, we immediately came to the Father's house, and the Father accepted us. This is the second section. Hence, in the process of our salvation first we received the Lord, and then the Father accepted us. First we are forgiven by the Lord, and then we are accepted by the Father.

This is clearly portrayed in the three parables in Luke 15. The first parable presents the Lord as the good Shepherd, who left the Father's house to seek us, the lost sheep. He found us, carried us on His shoulder, and brought us back to the Father's house. In the third parable we see that the lost sheep was the lost son, the prodigal son. The Lord brought us back to the Father's house, and God the Father accepted us. From our experience of salvation we see that the One who came to seek us is the Son, and the One who accepted us into the house is the Father. When we were in the position of sinners, we met the Son. After we received Him as our Savior, He brought us to the Father's house, and there we met the Father who accepted us.

Therefore, it is very clear from our salvation that there are two kinds of receiving. One is our receiving the Lord, and the other is the Father's receiving us. Having only one kind of receiving is not a full salvation. If we merely receive the Lord without the Father receiving us, we would not have a full salvation. One side of our salvation is our receiving the Lord, and the other side is the Father receiving us. Therefore, we are not only saved, but we have also returned home. We not only have the Lord, but we have the Father also. The Lord is the Son. First John 2:23 says, "He who confesses the Son has the Father also"; we first have the Son, and then we have the Father. Since our receiving the Son makes us sons, the Father accepted us into His house.

Since there are two sections in our salvation, there should also be two sections in a meeting where proper worship is rendered. In the first section we remember the Lord. This is related to our receiving the Lord. In the second section we worship the Father. This is related to the Father's receiving us. In the first section we remember our Lord, who saved us. In the second section we worship the Father, who accepted us as His sons.

Second, we know that the Lord Jesus was the only Begotten from the Father (John 1:14). However, when the Lord Jesus died on the cross, the life within Him was released and imparted into all those who believe in Him. When the life of the Son enters into us, we are made sons of God as well. This is the one grain of wheat falling into the ground to die and bearing much fruit (12:24). Now the only begotten Son becomes the Firstborn of many brothers (Rom. 8:29). Formerly, God had only one Son, but now He has many sons. Before His death, the Lord Jesus was the only begotten Son, but after His resurrection from the dead, He became the Firstborn among many brothers.

Therefore, in the morning of the Lord's resurrection, He appeared to Mary and said to her, "Go to My brothers and say to them, I ascend to My Father and your Father" (John 20:17). Before the Lord's death and resurrection, He never called His disciples brothers; at the most He called them friends. But once the Lord was resurrected from the dead, His life was released into the disciples to make them the many sons of God; thus, the disciples became His brothers. Therefore, Hebrews 2:11 says, "He is not ashamed to call them brothers," because they have His life, and they "are all of One." Just as He is the Son of God, having the life of God, all those who believe into Him and receive Him as life also become sons of God. He now is the Firstborn among many brothers.

Third, Hebrews 2:10 speaks of the Firstborn "leading many sons." Quoting Psalm 22:22, Hebrews 2:12 says, "I will declare Your name to My brothers; in the midst of the church I will sing hymns of praise to You." This is the Lord leading us to praise the Father in the church. The One for whom are all things and through whom are all things is leading many sons into glory. To accomplish this the firstborn Son leads the many sons to praise and worship the Father in the church of the firstborn, which is also the church of the many sons (12:23). This is what we do in the second section of the bread-breaking meeting. Our worship of the Father is based upon the history of our salvation. No other meeting is more suitable than the bread-breaking meeting to render this kind of worship.

Among Christians today, the fellowship of the Body of Christ is a much neglected aspect, and the Son's leading many sons to worship the Father is almost a non-existent aspect. We should not neglect these two points. Instead, we must care for them solemnly so that the Father can gain worship from His many sons with His Son.

Fourth, in this section our singing, prayer, and fellowship should be directed toward the Father, taking the Father as the center. There is no need for contemplation in this section.

Fifth, in this section the spirit of the meeting should climb to the highest peak, higher than in any other meeting. Therefore, there are two peaks in the bread-breaking meeting: one in the section of our remembrance of the Lord and the other in the section of our worship to the Father. If the bread-breaking meeting has these two peaks, the Lord's presence will be prevailing, the moving of the Spirit will be apparent, and the spirit of the saints will be greatly satisfied.

VARIOUS KINDS OF MEETINGS

(2)

We will continue considering various kinds of meetings.

THE PRAYER MEETING

The second kind of meeting is the prayer meeting. Acts 4:24 to 31 and 12:5 and 12 are two portions in the Bible that speak of the church gathering and praying together corporately. When an important matter was encountered, they had prayer meetings. There are not as many details about the prayer meeting as there are about the bread-breaking meeting. Among the various kinds of meetings, the bread-breaking meeting has the most details. Since the prayer meeting is relatively simple, there are only a few matters for us to consider. Nevertheless, these few matters are quite important; if we neglect them, the prayer meeting will be killed and nullified.

There are four important points that we need to pay attention to in the prayer meeting.

Being in One Accord

The first point is to be in one accord. The Chinese Union Version of the Bible translates *one accord* as "the same heart and the same will." This word in Greek refers to the harmony in a musical composition. The better a musical composition, the more harmonious it is. When a musical composition is performed, the pitch should be neither too high nor too low, and the tempo should be neither too fast nor too slow. If both pitch and tempo are appropriate and regulated, the musical sounds will be very harmonious. This same kind of harmony in human society can only be the result of people having the same mind and the same will, that is, of their being in one accord. Without a oneness of heart and agreement in will, it is impossible for people to be in harmony. In order to be in harmony, the heart of a people must be one and their will must be in agreement. Hence, it is acceptable for the Chinese Union Version to translate *one accord* as "the same heart and the same will." However, this is a translation based upon the meaning; it is not a literal translation.

Meeting together to pray always exceeds personal prayer in weight, value, authority, and power. There is a principle in the Bible that one chases a thousand, and two put ten thousand to flight (Deut. 32:30). According to mathematics, if one person chases a thousand, two should chase two thousand. But the Bible says that one person chases a thousand and two put ten thousand to flight; this exceeds the mathematical calculation by eight thousand, which is a fourfold increase. This is the principle of a meeting. The strength in Christian meetings is increased by multiplication, not merely by addition. This also applies to prayer. Individual prayer is powerful, but corporate prayer is much more powerful.

This is the reason the Bible, especially in Acts, shows the church meeting together to pray whenever important matters were encountered. This can be compared to moving an object. Although one person may be able to move a fifty-pound object by himself, no one can move an object that weighs one thousand pounds. Even if one thousand people were to take turns pushing the object, no one would be able to move it. But if a concerted effort was made to move it together, we would not need even fifty people. We would need only ten or more people to move the object. We need to see this. Even if ten thousand people tried to move the object individually, they would not be able to do it. But if we combine our efforts, there would not be a need for ten thousand people to move the object. It could be moved by a few people working together. This is the power of corporate prayer. The Lord Jesus said that if there were two or three gathered into His name, He would be in their midst, and what they ask for in harmony will be done for them (Matt. 18:19-20). Two or three praying together is the principle of corporate prayer.

Regardless of how many of us pray together, we must be one person, not just *like* one person. When we pray together, we must pray as one person. A prayer meeting in which we are not in harmony, in one accord, is not effective. If we pray as many people, instead of as one person, there is no harmony, one accord, in the prayer meeting. If there is no harmony, it would almost be better not to pray corporately because prayer in discord, without harmony, divides and kills. Such prayers are even inferior to personal prayers, because they annul prayer. Therefore, the first crucial point for the prayer meeting is to be in one accord.

Matthew 18 presents the Lord's teaching concerning one accord in a prayer meeting. Acts 1:14 gives an example of meeting together to pray in one accord. In Acts there were about a hundred and twenty persons praying in one accord for a period of ten days. Even though one hundred and twenty were praying, in the eyes of God only one person was praying. Therefore, as a result of their prayer the Holy Spirit descended on the day of Pentecost. This proves that one accord is the most important point concerning the prayer meeting.

Being Genuine

The second point is to be genuine. This means that our prayers should not be feigned. We should neither feign nor make up a prayer, both of which are false and not genuine. Although we should consider others when we pray, we should not pray for others to hear; rather, we pray for the Lord to hear. If we pray for others to hear, there will definitely be the element of pretense and embellishment in our prayer. Embellishment brings in falsehood. In the prayer meeting we need to consider others' response and feeling, and we need to learn to pray before God, as if no one else were with us. Only such prayers are without pretense and embellishment.

This is not easy, but we must practice. Although some do not weep in their personal prayer, they weep when they pray in a meeting. Their weeping is for others. There are others who weep when they pray alone, yet they are reluctant to weep when they pray in a meeting. Both their weeping and not weeping are under the influence of others; thus, they are feigned and not genuine.

Of course, sometimes when we are by ourselves before God we may cry and laugh aloud, but we should have some restraint when we pray with others. This is according to 2 Corinthians 5:13, which says, "Whether we were beside ourselves, it was to God; or whether we are sober-minded, it is for you." However, being sober-minded is different from being pretentious. Being sober-minded is genuine, and being pretentious is false. The more genuine our prayers in the prayer meeting are, the better.

Being Short

The third point is to be short. We should not be a person with a mouth that does not open or a mouth that does not shut once we begin to pray. Some people seem to have problems with their mouth in the prayer meeting. Either they cannot open their mouth to pray, or when they do open their mouth, they cannot conclude their prayer and close their mouth. Long prayers kill the spirit of the meeting, causing the spirit of the meeting to sink. Therefore, prayers must be short in the prayer meeting.

Not Having Too Many Subjects

The fourth point is not to have too many subjects for prayer. In order to have a good prayer meeting, there should not be too many prayer items. The prayer meetings in our localities often commit the mistake of having a long list of prayer items. Many items on this list never change and are unnecessary. Hence, before each prayer meeting the responsible brothers should seriously consider what matters are in need of prayer. It is best to pray for only one item in every prayer meeting. Of course, this is not a rigid principle. However, we should not bring trivial matters to the prayer meeting; instead, we should pray for important matters.

In the prayer meeting we usually pray for the various meetings, the personal problems of the brothers and sisters, gospel preaching, training meetings, and so forth; we cover many items. The brothers and sisters in the prayer meeting have the ability to pray for many items. If each one prays through their list of items, the whole prayer meeting will consist of giving reports. We may pray for every item on the list, yet none of the items will be covered thoroughly.

The Bible does not record examples of prayer meetings with many subjects. In Acts 4:24-31, when the believers gathered together, they specifically prayed for the church in Jerusalem under persecution. Even though all the participants must have prayed, the focus of their prayer was to ask the Lord to strengthen the church and to stretch out His hands. After they prayed, the place in which they were gathered was shaken, proving that God had answered their specific prayer.

In chapter 12, verses 5 and 12, the church gathered together to pray fervently concerning Peter, who had been arrested by Herod, put into prison, and was about to be harmed. Their specific prayer was effective. Peter was rescued by an angel, his chains fell off, and the prison gates were opened.

Our prayer should also be specific. In a prayer meeting the responsible brothers may ask the brothers and sisters to pray specifically regarding the sickness of a certain brother so that the Lord's will would be made known. Does the Lord want to heal this brother? What does the Lord want to do? If it is the Lord's will to heal him, we then ask the Lord to stretch out His holy hand. When the whole church beseeches the Lord specifically concerning the sick brother praying for this matter, it is proper and right.

The Chinese have a saying that speaks of biting off more than one can chew, which means to take on more than one can handle. If there are too many items in a prayer meeting, nothing will be accomplished. If there are too many items to pray for in every meeting, eventually everyone will be worn out, feeling as if every item is of equal importance and, consequently, does not have much meaning. As a result, they will not come to the meeting as often, and even if they come, they will seldom pray. In the end, some responsible ones, like those staging a show, will offer a few prayers to quickly conclude the meeting. There will be no burden, not to mention impact. This kind of prayer meeting is merely a meeting, without genuine prayer, and it completely misses the significance of the prayer meeting. I am afraid that this is the condition of the prayer meeting in many places. Even though this is not due to one single matter, having many common subjects for prayer is certainly a factor.

This is the reason it is best to pray for only one item in each meeting. Even if more than one item needs to be prayed for, they should be brought up one by one. We should not bring up a second item before everyone has finished praying for the first. Once the first item is thoroughly covered with prayer, the second item can be presented. This can be compared to accomplishing different tasks. It is important to finish the first task before beginning the second task. There should not be more than three items to pray for in a prayer meeting.

There must be a specific burden for prayer. The purpose of the prayer meeting is for us to come together to pray corporately for items that are too great to be borne by one person. Hence, there must be a specific burden. May the prayer meetings in every locality be adjusted according to these points. The saints must be in one accord, the feelings must be genuine, the utterances must be brief, and the subjects must be specific. We must exercise according to these four points.

THE MEETING FOR THE EXERCISE OF GIFTS

The third kind of meeting is for the exercise of gifts as presented in 1 Corinthians 14:26-40. The bread-breaking meeting is a meeting of the church where all the saints function in mutuality. The prayer meeting is a meeting of the church for all the saints to function in mutuality. The meeting for exercising our gifts is also a meeting of the church for all the saints to function in mutuality. In the past we held a weekly fellowship meeting that was similar in nature to a meeting for the exercise of gifts spoken of in 1 Corinthians 14. Initially, we separated the brothers and the sisters. The brothers had their meeting, and the sisters had theirs, but later these two meetings were combined. Regardless of whether the brothers and the sisters met separately or whether their meetings were combined, the meeting was not successful. It did not have the practice of everyone exercising his gift according to 1 Corinthians 14.

Even though the church in Taipei has a bread-breaking meeting, prayer meeting, and also a ministry meeting, we do not have the kind of meeting spoken of in 1 Corinthians 14, which is for the exercise of the gifts. According to the principle of the Bible and the teaching of the New Testament, there should be many such meetings in the church because this kind of meeting affords the saints an opportunity to supply others and receive the supply from others.

For example, the church in Taipei is always concerned about how to lead the newly baptized brothers and sisters. Many are baptized, but few remain. I feel that one of the reasons for this is that the church has no specific meeting for them to give their testimonies. They have received the Lord's grace but are not given the opportunity to express it. Thus, they continue to hold back the grace within them. After holding back this grace for a long time, they become depressed, deadened, and cold, and they lose their freshness and vitality. Eventually, it is difficult to take them forward. Therefore, even if it is only for the sake of newly baptized brothers and sisters, there is a need for this kind of meeting for the exercise of the gifts, testimonies, and fellowshipping.

Concerning the meeting for the exercise of gifts, there are a few points that require our attention.

Being for the Building Up of the Church

First, this is not a meeting for the display of gifts but for the edifying, the building up, of the church. It is not for someone to sing a spiritual song so that others will know how well he sings. No, but when a spiritual song is sung, it should be for the edification of those who are listening. We should not bring anything that cannot edify others to this meeting. This is not an exhibition or a performance but a meeting for the exercise of the gifts for mutual edification.

A more accurate translation of the word *edify* in the Bible is "build up." However, being built up is slightly different than being edified. Building up includes edification, but edification may not involve building up. Edification only perfects an individual, and it does not necessarily build many individuals up together. The exercise of gifts that we are speaking of should be for mutual edification, not individual edification. Thus, the building up includes edification, but the ultimate goal is the building up of all the saints as God's dwelling place. We must have this kind of realization concerning edification.

Everyone Being
Able to Exercise His Gift

Second, everyone can exercise his gift. In this meeting every person has an equal opportunity to exercise his gift. The meeting should not be taken over by a few. We must bear in mind that this is not for an exhibition or a performance. On the contrary, it is for the building up of the saints. Hence, even though everyone can exercise his gift in the meeting, the principle of building should not be violated. Some brothers may be timid even though they have a gift; hence, they need some encouragement. It may be easy for other brothers to stand up and speak because they are too bold. Their boldness may issue in the exercise of a debate, not a gift. Two brothers may even debate openly until their faces are red. This is not building up. It is tearing down. We must avoid this. The principle in this meeting is that all the saints have an opportunity to exercise this gift, neither burying nor frustrating it and neither misusing nor abusing it.

Exercising Every Kind of Gift

Third, every gift should be exercised. Everyone can exercise his gift, and every kind of gift should be exercised. Someone may stand up to speak from the Scriptures. This is the gift of a teacher. If his expounding of the Scriptures is proper, logical, and full of light and supply, this gift should be exercised. If someone can speak in a tongue, he should speak a few sentences in the tongue by spiritual inspiration. Then another who can interpret the tongue should interpret it so that everyone can benefit spiritually. In this way, the meeting will be very rich because the various gifts in the church are given the opportunity to be exercised.

Prophesying

Fourth, as for prophesying, the principle is that there should be only two or three, and they must speak in order. This is explicitly instructed in the Bible. There should not be too many who speak, and there should not be any confusion in the order.

Sisters Not Being Permitted to Teach

Fifth, in a meeting for the exercise of gifts, sisters are not permitted to teach, that is, to preach the word. This is God's governmental arrangement. First Corinthians 14:34 says, "The women should be silent in the churches." This means that the sisters are not permitted to teach or preach the word as teachers. This is because the sisters, typifying the church, should stand in a position of being subject to authority and not stand in the position of teaching and instructing others as the head.

Everything Being Orderly

Finally, a basic principle of this meeting is that all things must be done properly and in order, without any confusion. Such a meeting should not be like a secular meeting where everyone competes to be the first to speak. If someone wants to sing, there is no need to preempt him by preaching the word, or if someone wants to preach the word, there is no need to preempt him by offering a prayer. Every person in this meeting should learn to be restrained. According to the principle in 1 Corinthians 14:29-30, we should be willing to stop as soon as another is led to speak. Even if we are speaking, we should be willing to stop if another wants to speak. All our activities should be in the principle of being led by the Spirit. If everyone keeps this principle, there will not be any striving to speak while another is speaking. Since a person is being led, we should go according to order and not cause confusion.

BIBLE-STUDY MEETING

The fourth kind of meeting is the Bible-study meeting. In

this meeting the saints gather to read the Lord's Word. Acts 15:30-31 and Colossians 4:16 both refer to this kind of meeting. There are five points for us to consider related to the Bible-study meeting.

Reading Together

First, we should read together. One person should not read to the others, and neither should merely a few read to the rest. All the saints should read together. It is even better to read the portions at home before coming to the meeting.

Fellowshipping Our Gain

Second, everyone should release and fellowship with others what they have gained, that is, the spiritual inspiration they have received from their reading. However, verbose and worthless words that waste people's time should be avoided.

Having a Focus

Third, although everyone reads together and has the opportunity to fellowship what they have gained, the meeting should still have a focus. Every kind of meeting should have a definite and clear focus. This will leave everyone with a deep impression after the meeting.

Avoiding Debates

Fourth, we should avoid debates. We can study and discuss with one another in the Bible-study meeting, but we should never debate. Debating kills the spirit of the meeting and does not benefit anyone; therefore, we must try our best to avoid debating.

The greatest temptation in the Bible-study meeting is to debate. No meeting provides as much opportunity for people to debate as a Bible-study meeting. This is because there can be different views regarding the same portion of the Scriptures, and since everyone thinks that his view is better, he tries to strike down other views. This gives rise to debates. Therefore, we must be careful to restrain our views and never initiate a debate. Debates annul the purpose of the Bible-study meeting.

Needing Someone
to Steer and Close the Meeting

Fifth, there is a need for someone to "steer the helm" and to "draw the rein," and to close the meeting. We all know what it means to steer the helm and draw the rein. Those who sail a boat need to steer the helm so that the boat does not drift randomly. Those who ride a horse must draw the rein so that the horse does not run wildly. Similarly, even though we read together in a Bible-study meeting, there is still a need for one or two experienced brothers to steer the helm and draw the rein so that the meeting does not turn or drift randomly without a goal or direction. There is also a need for someone to close the meeting and give the meeting a satisfactory conclusion.

THE MINISTRY MEETING

The fifth kind of meeting is the ministry meeting. The scriptural basis for this relatively simple meeting is found in Acts 20:7. However, in this verse there was first a bread-breaking meeting and then the ministry of the word.

Having a Seeking Heart and an Open Spirit,
and Not Attending a "Sunday Service"

First, one must have a seeking heart and an open spirit in a ministry meeting. A seeking heart and an open spirit prepare a person to listen to the ministry of the Word, rather than merely attending a "Sunday service."

There are "services" every Sunday in Christianity. The participants attend mainly for the Sunday service, not so much to listen to the ministry of the Word. Listening to the ministry of the Word is completely different from attending a Sunday service. We do not have Sunday services. The closest meeting we have to a Sunday service would be our bread-breaking meeting. However, because the words *Sunday service* do not appear in the Bible, we do not use the term *Sunday service*. We have prayer meetings, meetings for the exercise of gifts, and meetings for the ministry of the Word, but we do not have Sunday services.

The Lord's Day morning message meeting that we have at present is nearly the same as a Sunday service. When the brothers and sisters come to the meeting, they neither open their heart nor open their spirit. They come to the meeting hall to attend a "Sunday service." After the meeting they do not have an impression of the message they heard that day. They even say that they came to worship God, not to listen to man, sounding quite spiritual. The practice of attending a "Sunday service" is not pleasing to the Lord. If this is our condition, it may be better not to have this meeting; rather, we should change it to a gospel meeting. In any case, we must correct this practice.

There must be the feeling that we are coming to a ministry meeting to listen to the Lord's word. The Lord's revelation and light are in His Word; therefore, we must have a seeking heart and an open spirit in order to hear and receive the Lord's revelation and light. This is entirely different from attending a religious Sunday service.

Willing to Be Taught in Humility

Second, when we come to the ministry meeting, we should always be humble and willing to be taught. If we are even a little proud, we will not receive any benefit. It will be difficult to receive any benefit if we have a critical heart concerning the speaking of others. We should not come to criticize; rather, we should come to be taught. If this is our motive, every sentence we hear will be received into our spirit and become our enlightenment and supply.

We must resolve the question of whether God is speaking among us. If God is not speaking among us, the meeting for the ministry of the Word will be completely empty and false. If, however, the ministry of the Word releases God's speaking to the church, then all the children of God should have a respectful heart to be taught in humility. We should never criticize, discuss, or judge others casually. Rather, since God is speaking, we should have an attitude and desire to show respect and receive His word in humility. Only this type of heart can be blessed and not offend God.

THE GOSPEL MEETING

The sixth kind of meeting is for the preaching of the gospel. This meeting is also very important. In particular, new believers should exercise to participate in this meeting.

Bringing People

All the brothers and sisters should bring people to hear the gospel. We should not merely come by ourselves, but we should try our best to bring people to hear the gospel. How do we bring people? We need to make a list of our relatives, friends, classmates, colleagues, and those who are close to us. From this list we should invite those who have never heard the gospel. Sometimes we may be unable to bring them directly; rather, we may need to use various means, such as inviting them for a meal or preparing a ride for them. We should not be discouraged if we need to invite them repeatedly. We know from experience that once a person has been invited, that invitation will influence him even if he does not come. The more he is invited, the greater the responding power within him will be. Then when he does come, he will be saved dynamically. Thus, we should never give up on those who decline our first invitation.

Sitting beside People

After bringing a person, we need to accompany him by sitting beside him. When we sit with him, we should do five things.

First, we should help him locate the Bible verses. When the speaker mentions a certain book, a certain chapter, or a certain verse, we should help him find it.

Second, we should help him find the hymn. If the hymn is written out, we should point it out to him; if the hymn is in the hymnal, we should look it up for him.

Third, we should explain the hymn. There may be some special terms in a gospel hymn; if the speaker does not explain them clearly, we should explain them to him.

Fourth, we should pray for him. While we sit with him and help him, we need to observe his condition and silently pray for him.

Fifth, we should help him receive the Lord. When the speaker asks everyone to indicate a willingness to receive the Lord, we should not leave him to his own discretion and let nature take its course. Rather, we should encourage him a little without being rude or forcing him to stand up. All these should be done appropriately and properly.

Contacting and Speaking with People

After the meeting, we should contact and speak with the one we brought. If it is inconvenient to speak with him, we can ask other brothers and sisters to speak with him. In speaking with him, we need to pay attention to three things.

First, we should strengthen the message that he heard. We should not discuss another subject with him. Based on the message spoken, strengthen the meaning of the message and his response to the message.

Second, we should lead him to pray. After speaking with him for a short time, we should lead him to pray. Speaking too little does not save people, and neither does speaking too much. Sometimes we miss the opportune time for prayer because of our excessive speaking. Consequently, it is difficult for people to be saved. Therefore, after speaking with our guest, we need to lead him to pray. This prayer will often result in his salvation.

Third, we should help him to leave his name and address to facilitate further contact with him.

Visiting People

After the gospel meeting, we should bear the responsibility to visit people.

First, we should visit according to a schedule.

Second, we should take some brothers and sisters with us. The brothers and sisters can help us to solve any problems we would be unable to solve on our own.

Third, we should continue to visit until the person we are visiting is saved, baptized, and enters into the church life. Then the church can help bear the responsibility for him. However, we often still need to be responsible to visit him for a period of time after his baptism. May we all enter into a proper practice of the bread-breaking meeting, the prayer meeting, the meeting for the exercise of gifts, the Bible-study meeting, the ministry meeting, and the gospel meeting so that the church and all the saints can be greatly blessed.

WHAT THE CHURCH IS

Knowing the church is a very practical matter. Today everyone would admit that the situation in Christianity is chaotic. After believing in the Lord, we must know the church and the proper way of the church. We cannot know the church merely by studying the truth but rather by taking the proper way to follow the Lord after we are saved. We will cover this matter in a clear and concise way in six messages. First, we will cover what the church is.

THE CHURCH NOT BEING A PHYSICAL BUILDING

Christians often have the incorrect concept that a chapel is the church and that going to a chapel is going to church. In the Western world, the word *church* is often understood to be a chapel. This is an erroneous concept. Chapels, gospel halls, evangelistic halls, and assembly halls are not the church. According to the Bible, the church can fear and pray (Acts 5:11; 12:5); therefore, the church is a *living* entity, not a *dead* structure. Considering a dead structure to be the church is not only wrong but also very nearly heretical. Hence, we should not think that this is simply a matter of speech and that it is a small thing.

THE CHURCH NOT BEING AN ORGANIZATION

The church is not a physical building; neither is it an organization or a group in Christianity. It is not a mission, evangelistic society, or a denomination. In any large city there are many denominations, such as Presbyterian, Baptist, Lutheran, Wesleyan, etc., and numerous missions and evangelistic societies. These Christian groups and organizations are not the church. The Bible says that the church is the Body of Christ (Eph. 1:22-23; Col. 1:18). A body is an organism with life, a living organism, not a dead organization. The numerous groups in Christianity are religious organizations that emphasize formalities and neglect life. Considering these organizations and religious groups as the church is also wrong.

THE CHURCH BEING THE CALLED-OUT CONGREGATION

The Greek word for *church* in Matthew 16:18 and 18:17 is *ekklesia,* which is composed of two words. The first is *ek,* meaning "out of," and the second is *klesia,* meaning "calling." When these two words are combined to form one word, the meaning is the called-out congregation or the assembly of the called-out ones. Thus, according to the literal meaning, the church is the congregating, the gathering together, of a group of people whom God has called out of the world.

Although the Old Testament does not speak of the church explicitly, using the Israelites, it presents a picture of the condition of the church. The children of Israel left Egypt, arrived at Mount Sinai, and were arranged and grouped by God. Thus, they were coordinated together and gathered before God. They formed a corporate body with the Tent of Meeting at the center and the twelve tribes encamped around the Tent of Meeting (Num. 2). That was the *ekklesia,* the gathering of the called-out ones. Therefore, the New Testament also calls the children of Israel an *ekklesia* in Acts 7:38. The word *assembly* in this verse is *ekklesia* in the original text. On the one hand, God called them out of Egypt, which typifies the world; on the other hand, they were a congregation gathered before God. Of course, the children of Israel did not have the nature of the church. They were only a type, a picture, showing that the church is an assembly of people whom God calls out of the world to gather before Him through His redemption and the power of His salvation. This is one aspect of the meaning of the church.

THE CHURCH BEING THE BODY OF CHRIST

The book of Ephesians is the one book in the Bible that

speaks specifically concerning the church. Ephesians 1:22-23 says that the church is the Body of Christ. This is a divine revelation showing what the church is in a thorough and distinct way. We will cover this in six points.

Being the Fullness of Christ

Ephesians 1:22-23 says that the church is the Body of Christ and that the church is "the fullness of the One who fills all in all." This shows that the church as the Body is the fullness of Christ. We all understand that the human body is the fullness of a human being. We identify a person mainly by his face. Without seeing the head of a person, it is not easy for us to identify him. Hence, the distinction of a person is in the head and the face. However, the fullness of a person is his body. If a person has only a head without a body, he will have no fullness. A person's fullness is manifested in his body.

Fullness and body are not two items but one item. The fullness equals the body, and the body equals the fullness. When people speak of the church being the Body of Christ, they usually emphasize ability and function. Rarely do they realize that the Body is the fullness. But when Ephesians, which is a book on the church, speaks of the church as the Body of Christ, it emphasizes fullness and building, not ability and function. Fullness is the expression of the Body, and building produces the fullness. If there is no building, there will be no expression of the fullness.

May the Lord intensify our feeling so that whenever we speak concerning the church as the Body of Christ, our first feeling would be that of the fullness. The Body of Christ signifies not only that the church is spiritual, living, heavenly, and functioning, but it also signifies that the church is the fullness of Christ. The church as the Body of Christ is the fullness of Christ. Christ is full, and the overflowing of Christ from His fullness is the church. If Christ does not have the church, there would be no way for His fullness to be expressed in the universe. When the fullness of Christ is expressed, it becomes His Body, which is the church.

When the Bible says that the church is the Body of Christ, the primary significance of the church is its fullness, not its functions. Whereas our emphasis on function is often according to a natural human understanding, the emphasis on fullness is according to God's revelation. Without the revelation of God, man has no way to realize that the Body is a matter of fullness.

The first thing people see when they look at a person is not his ability and function; rather, they see his proper appearance. This is a matter of fullness. If we take a photograph of only a person's head, there is no fullness. If it were possible for four people to place just their heads side by side on a bench, would it look nice? It would scare people away! However, it would be a pleasant sight to have the four of them sitting on the bench as complete persons. Therefore, a man without a body lacks something. He does not look like a man. The church is the same to Christ. The church is the fullness of Christ, just as a man's body is his fullness.

Ephesians 1:23 says that Christ fills all in all. Sometimes people translate this word *all* as "pan." For example, *pan* in "Pan American Airlines" is Greek for the word *all*. Christ is the One who is "pan" in "pan"; He is all in all. This shows how rich Christ is.

The verses prior to Ephesians 1:23 also show how great and high Christ is. Verses 20 and 21 say that God raised Christ from the dead and seated Him at His right hand, far above all rule, authority, power, lordship, and every name that is named, not only in this age but also in that which is to come. This is His greatness, His height, and His transcendence. Not only so, God subjected all things under His feet and gave Him to be Head over all things to the church. He is above all, and all things are under His feet. He is the Head over all things. We cannot fully realize His greatness and His transcendence.

Brothers and sisters, we need to know our great and surpassing Lord. Only when we realize His surpassing greatness will we know His fullness. His fullness requires a large vessel in order to be expressed. This vessel is the church. However, because the church has not been built up, it does not completely express His fullness. When the fullness of the times comes and God's chosen ones have been filled, the church will truly be the fullness. Today the church is still being filled. The church needs more saved ones and more local churches. Christ is so full that He needs an immeasurably large vessel to express Him. This vessel is the church. Therefore, the church as the fullness of Christ is a tremendous matter.

Even though Satan has damaged the church and done a divisive work, we can still see the great matter of the fullness of the church. In spite of Satan's dividing and damaging work, we cannot deny the greatness of the church in its nature and condition. This is the fullness of Christ.

Coming out of Christ

The church as the Body comes out of Christ. In the Bible God uses the type of the building of Eve in Genesis 2:21-24 as a clear and definite illustration of how the church as the Body of Christ, the fullness of Christ, in Ephesians 1:22-23 is brought forth in 5:30-32. These verses show that Adam and Eve are a type of the relationship between Christ and the church. Just as Eve came out of Adam, the church also comes out of Christ. Just as Adam and Eve are one flesh, Christ and the church are also one. Although Eve came out of Adam, she was not separate from Adam. She belonged to Adam, because she was a part of Adam. This also applies to Christ and the church.

Today people have a poor view of the church. They think that the church is merely an organization or an association for a multitude of people. This concept is absolutely wrong. We need to see that the church is something that came out of Christ. When God wanted to build a counterpart for Adam, He opened Adam's side, took out a rib, and formed Eve. Hence, Eve came out of Adam. Likewise, when the Lord was nailed to the cross, His side was also opened and out came blood and water (John 19:34). Blood is for redemption; water is for life-impartation. The life that the Lord released and imparted into us produces the church.

As believers, we all have Christ within us. If we do not have Christ within us, then we do not belong to Christ, and we are not saved. Since we are saved, we all have Christ within us. The church is the Christ within you and me. When the Christ within you, the Christ within me, and the Christ within others is added together, that is, when the Christ within all who belong to Him is added together, this equals the church. The church is the new man, and in this new man there cannot be Greek, Jew, or any other kind of people (Col. 3:10-11). In the church as the new man, there is only Christ. The church is not you plus me plus others; the church is the Christ within you plus the Christ within me plus the Christ within others. This is the church.

We cannot bring our natural man into the church because there is neither you nor I in the church. In the church there is neither Chinese nor Japanese. In the church there is only Christ. In the Chinese Union Version of the Bible, Colossians 3:11 says, "There is no distinction between Greek and Jew, circumcision and uncircumcision, barbarian, Scythian, slave, free man." However, the original text does not say "no distinction"; rather, it says, "there cannot be." In the church there cannot be this or that; there can be only Christ.

If the new believers have such a realization of the church, the following subjects on the ground of the church and the way of the church will be easily understood. People are not clear about the ground and the way of the church because the things of man have been mixed with the church. Through the cross of Christ, we must eliminate the things of man. A brother rightly said that though the cross looks like the mathematical sign of addition, the work done by the cross for the church on the believers is always one of subtraction. The cross eliminates man's old creation so that it has no place in the church. If the element of Adam was put off from the saints and only the element of Christ within them was present, the result we would see would be the church. Hence, the church is only that which comes out of Christ.

Being Joined to Christ as One

Although the church comes out of Christ, the church and Christ are not separate. Just as Eve came out of Adam, returned back to him, and became one flesh with him, so is the church in relation to Christ (Eph. 5:31-32). We should never consider that after coming out of Christ, the church is separate from Christ. No, we are still one. Christ and the church are one. Even though this is incomprehensible to man, if we have God's revelation, we will realize that this is true.

The church comes out of Christ and returns to Christ; hence, Christ and the church are one. Any condition, action, or work in the church that is apart from Christ is not the church. Whenever we touch the church, we need to test it by asking whether Christ is in it. Is it something out of Christ? Is it something in Christ? Is it something joined to Christ? This is a serious test. If a church cannot pass this test, it is not the church, not the Body of Christ, but it is merely an organization in Christianity. As the Body of Christ, the church comes absolutely out of Christ and also returns to Christ, being joined to Him as one and becoming one entity with Him.

Being Christ Himself

First Corinthians 12:12 clearly speaks of the church as the Body of Christ; however, it does not say that this Body is the church but that this Body is Christ. Actually, the church is the enlargement of Christ. Christ enlarged is the church. Therefore, the church is Christ. A proper determination of the ground of the church and the way of the church must be based on this understanding.

The church on the earth today is Christ Himself. This is a sobering matter. If a person has this light and this vision, do you think that he will still bring elements other than Christ into the church? Absolutely not! A person who has this vision touches the cross whenever he touches the matter of the church and the things concerning the church. The cross separates the things belonging to Adam from the things belonging to Christ and the things that are of Adam from the things that are of Christ. The cross keeps the things that are of Adam and all things that belong to Adam apart from the church, allowing only the things that are of Christ and the things that belong to Christ into the church. As a result, everything of the church is just Christ Himself.

If we have this light, we cannot acknowledge that the Catholic Church is the church, and neither can we acknowledge that the Protestant denominations are the church. No denomination is the church; rather, they are Christian organizations or religious groups. Although there may be some who belong to Christ in these denominations, these denominations, groups, or organizations do not belong to Christ. These are of man and of the world.

We did not leave the Roman Catholic Church, the Protestant Church, or any of the other denominations in Christianity simply because they were unscriptural, but because they were not of Christ. I can testify that when I left the denominations thirty years ago, my feeling was simply that there were errors among them. However, after seven or eight years I saw that even if there were no errors in the denominations, I would still leave because their ground was wrong. Their sectarian ground was the ground of division. Slowly, after a few more years, I saw that the Protestant denominations were not only wrong related to their ground, but their organizations were not of Christ and did not have Christ. Yes, there were some among them who were saved, and these saved ones had Christ in them. However, there was no Christ within these denominations. Christ had no ground in these denominations. The organization of these denominations was full of man's arrangements and worldly things. Hence, around 1935 we frequently said that we left the denominations, the sects, of organized Christianity not only because they were not according to the truth but also because there was no Christ in them. They were not the Body of Christ, not the organism of Christ, but mere organizations.

We need to see that the church is Christ Himself and that it is also the Body of Christ, an organism of Christ. In the church we can neither depend on organization, arrangement, nor on methods and regulations. Rather, we depend only on the living Christ. If a condition in the church prevents us from being spiritual and manifesting our spiritual function, that church is wrong and is degraded. In the church there should be opportunities for us to manifest our spiritual measure and function. Even though there should be coordination, there should not be any restriction. The Holy Spirit must have absolute freedom, and the saints must be able to manifest their spiritual condition and function. Such a situation proves that the church is an organism, not an organization. This organism is the Body of Christ and also Christ Himself.

Being Formed through Baptism in the Holy Spirit

The church is composed not only of one person or several persons but of millions of people. These millions have become one Body not only because they are of Christ but also because they have all been baptized in one Spirit into one Body (1 Cor. 12:13). The life of Christ within you causes you to be of Christ, and the life of Christ within me also causes me to be of Christ. The life of Christ in every believer causes them to be of Christ. Furthermore, we who are of Christ have been baptized in one Spirit into one Body. The divine life causes us to be of Christ, and the Holy Spirit causes us to be mutually joined together. Having the divine life, we are of Christ, and being in the Holy Spirit, we are mutually joined together. Thus, we become one Body.

The church as the one Body is formed by coming out of Christ and by being baptized in the Holy Spirit. By coming out of Christ and being baptized in the Holy Spirit, the church becomes one Body. Both are indispensable. Without the life that comes out of Christ, there would be no church, and without the Holy Spirit who baptizes the saints into the Body of Christ, there would also be no church.

We often say that we need to be in life. This is not enough. Being in life mainly emphasizes our relationship with Christ. We also need to learn to live in the Holy Spirit. It is only by being in the Holy Spirit that we can be joined mutually with all the saints. On the one hand, we need to have the life that comes out of Christ; on the other hand, we also need the Holy Spirit who baptizes us into the Body of Christ. This coming out and baptizing into cause the Body of Christ to be formed. Therefore, to live in the church in reality, we need to live by Christ as life, and we also need to live in the Holy Spirit. Our walk and work need to be in the Holy Spirit. We should now have a general understanding concerning the church. The church is something high, mysterious, heavenly, living, and spiritual.

Expressing Christ

The church as the Body expresses Christ. Christ expresses Himself in the Body. For us to express ourselves, we must use our body. If we do not have a body but have only a spirit and soul, we cannot express ourselves. Likewise, Christ expresses Himself in the universe, on the earth, among men, and in this age entirely by the church as the Body. Where the church is, there is Christ. Where the church is, there is the expression of Christ. The expression of Christ cannot be separated from the church. Since the church is the fullness of Christ, the Body of Christ, it is the expression of Christ.

However, Roman Catholicism is not the expression of Christ, and every denomination in Protestantism is not the expression of Christ. They are but human organizations and religious groups, not the Body of Christ. Because there is little element of Christ and little ground for Christ within them, they are not the expression of Christ. The Body of Christ is full of Christ within and is entirely Christ. Only such a Body and such a church is the expression of Christ.

THE CHURCH BEING THE HOUSE OF GOD

First Timothy 3:15 speaks of the church as the house of the living God. The Bible mentions the house of God in many places. The Chinese Union Version translates each instance as the temple of God. The tabernacle and the holy temple in the Old Testament were the house of God (Judg. 18:31; 1 Kings 6:1); thus, they typified the church. This shows that in relation to God, the church is the house of God, just as the tabernacle and the holy temple in the Old Testament were the house of God. There are at least two important significances here.

Being God's Dwelling Place

A house is a person's dwelling place, his place of living. It is the place where a person prefers to live. The church is the house of God, the dwelling place of God on earth where He can dwell in peace and where He can entrust Himself. Hence, Ephesians 2:22 says that the church is the "dwelling place of

God in spirit." In order to identify, distinguish, and discern whether a gathering is the church, we need only to see whether God can make His home, dwell in peace, entrust Himself, and be at rest there. If He is able to do this, such a gathering is the church and has not lost the nature of the church. If He is not able to do so, such a gathering is not the church. Very likely, it is only a religious organization.

Being the Place Where God Is Expressed

A house is also the best place for a person to express himself. A person cannot be fully expressed in any place other than in his own house. There are certain things a person cannot say, will not say, and dare not say in a place other than his home. He cannot express certain intentions in other places, but he can once he is in his home. It is inconvenient to do certain things if he is not at home. Hence, a home is the place where man can best express himself.

A house occupied by a person from China expresses the ways of the Chinese; if it is occupied by a person from Japan, it expresses the ways of the Japanese; and if it is occupied by a person from America, it expresses the ways of the Americans. Simply by looking at the condition of a house, we can determine what kind of person lives there. We can look at the house and tell whether a clean person lives there or a messy person lives there. We do not need to see a person in order to know whether a person of high class or low class lives there; we only need to look at his house. In order to fully know a person, we often need to look at his house. For example, someone may dress neatly, but his house may be a mess. Someone may be dignified in appearance, as if he is a rich man, but his house may be in utter poverty. Therefore, we must look at a man's house in order to know a person. His house is an expression of himself.

The church is the house of God, and it is also the place where God expresses Himself on the earth. First Timothy 3:16 speaks of the church as the great mystery of godliness, that is, God manifested in the flesh. God not only desires to make His home, settle down, and gain a place of rest, but He also desires to express Himself in the church. God desires to carry out His plan, express His desire, and manifest His glory in the church. All He is, all He has done, and all He desires to obtain must be expressed in the church as His house.

On the one hand, the church is the Body, the fullness, and the expression to Christ. On the other hand, the church is a house, a dwelling place, for God to express Himself. Both God and Christ are expressed in the church. This is the church.

THE EXPRESSION OF THE CHURCH

In the previous lesson we saw a general sketch of the church and briefly touched the concept of the church. These, however, are primarily abstract theories regarding the church and are not so definite. In order to know the church in a definite way, it is necessary to make the church concrete and tangible, bringing the church out of the air to the earth. Hence, we need to speak about the expression of the church.

The church has an expression. The church is not something mysterious, abstract, or suspended in the air but is practical. We can touch the church, contact the church, and be in the church. Therefore, the church must have an expression. Without this expression, our speaking concerning the church is but empty talk, and people cannot touch it. We may see that the church is not a structure such as a chapel or gospel hall nor an organization such as a denomination or mission. We may also realize that the church is the assembly of the called-out ones, the Body of Christ, and the house of God. Nevertheless, if the church is not practical and concrete, we cannot touch the church, contact the church, and much less be in the church. Because we are still on the earth, the church must have an expression. Without an expression, the church means absolutely nothing.

Many people in Christianity have an unscriptural view and understanding of the church. In particular, the seeking ones, who see the desolation and confusion of the church, believe that it is impossible for the church to be on the earth today. They say that the church is spiritual and invisible and that the oneness of the church can be achieved only in heaven in the future. Hence, it is difficult to discuss the matter of the

practical church today. They also say that it is sufficient
for Christians to preach the gospel to save people and help
them to be spiritual. This kind of talk is not only extreme but
also erroneous. We must bear in mind that the church is not
something in the future, something in heaven, or something
hidden and invisible. The church is expressed in time and
space. It can be touched and contacted on the earth today, and
the believers can be in it today. Thus, the church must have
an expression today. This matter is important.

The expression of the church is the practicality, reality,
concreteness, and substantiality of the church. The church
must have an expression in order to be practical, real, concrete, and substantial. Otherwise, the church is nothing
but an empty theory, something of the imagination, something abstract, and something suspended in the air. To us, the
church must be practical not theoretical, real not imagined,
concrete not abstract, and substantial not suspended in the
air. For this reason the church must have an expression.

We will briefly cover twelve points regarding the expression of the church.

THE EXPRESSION OF THE CHURCH
BEING IN LOCALITIES

The Bible clearly shows that the expression of the church
is local. Some say in a general and vague way that there is
only a universal expression of the church. This is inaccurate.
The church was first expressed in the city of Jerusalem (Acts
8:1); it was surely and definitely expressed in a place called
Jerusalem. Obviously, to be expressed in Jerusalem is to be
expressed in the universe, because Jerusalem is a place in the
universe. However, to say that the church is expressed only
universally is too general. The universe is vast; if we say that
there is only a universal expression of the church, we will
not know where to find it. Therefore, if a person does not consider the local expression and says that the expression of
the church is only universal, he will cause people to think
that the church is remote and elusive. Although this kind of
speaking concerning the universal church was popular and

prevailing in past decades, by the Lord's mercy we are seeing that the church is local, having an expression in localities.

We cannot find the expression *universal church* in the Bible. On the contrary, everywhere in the New Testament we can find local churches, that is, churches appearing in different localities, in locality after locality. For example, there is the church in Jerusalem (v. 1), the church in Antioch (13:1), the church in Corinth (1 Cor. 1:2), the church in Ephesus (Rev. 2:1), and the church in Smyrna (v. 8). These examples show that the church has a local aspect; the church is expressed locally. Thus, to emphasize only the universal church is inaccurate.

Taking the Jurisdiction of a Community as the Boundary

The boundary of the local expression of the church is the jurisdiction of a community. This jurisdiction can be as large as a city or as small as a town or a village. A city can be the jurisdiction of a community, or a village can be the jurisdiction of a community. The jurisdiction of a community can be a city as large as New York, London, or Tokyo with a population of almost ten million, or it can be a small village with only a few hundred people. At the time of Pentecost the church had an expression in the large city of Jerusalem (Acts 8:1). Jerusalem was the jurisdiction of the community. Later, the church also had an expression in many small cities in Asia (Rev. 1:11). These cities were the jurisdiction of a community. If a person reads carefully through Acts, the Epistles, and Revelation, he will conclude that the church is expressed in the jurisdiction of a community.

Taking the Principle of One Church in One Locality

On the one hand, the expression of the church takes the jurisdiction of a community as the boundary, and on the other hand, it takes the principle of one church in one locality. There can be only one expression of the church in a local jurisdiction; there definitely cannot be two or more. There can be only one church in one locality. This means that there can be only one church in one locality. In a small locality there can be only one church; likewise, in a large locality there can be only one church. Although Jerusalem was a city with a large population, there could be only one church in Jerusalem, not two or more. Although the cities in Asia were small and the population was sparse, there was only one church in a locality, and two localities were not combined to form one church. In the Bible there was the church in Jerusalem and the church in Antioch, not the churches in Jerusalem or the churches in Antioch (in Acts 8:1 and 13:1, *church* is singular in Greek). Hence, the Bible clearly shows that there should be one church in one locality.

However, since a region or a province can include many jurisdictions, the Bible does speak of *churches* in a region or province. For example, Acts 15:41 refers to the churches in Syria and Cilicia; Galatians 1:2 and 1 Corinthians 16:1 speak of the churches of the province of Galatia; 1 Corinthians 16:19 speaks of the churches of the province of Asia; and 2 Corinthians 8:1 speaks of the churches of the province of Macedonia. All these places were either a region or a province, including many community jurisdictions; therefore, there was more than one church in these regions and provinces. This shows that the expression of the church is local and is according to the principle of one church in one locality.

**BEING IN A LOCALITY MEANING
BEING ON THE EARTH AND EXISTING TODAY**

Since the church is expressed in a locality, it is on the earth and exists today. Hence, as far as space is concerned, the church's expression is on the earth; as far as time is concerned, this expression exists today. Some say that the church will be expressed in the future and in heaven. This kind of speaking is too far off. We do not need to wait until the future for the church to be expressed, because the church is expressed today. Neither do we need to wait for the church to be expressed in heaven, because the church is expressed on earth today. Yes, the nature of the church is heavenly, but the expression of the church is on the earth. Moreover, this expression is on the earth today. Yes, the nature of the church is eternal, but the expression of the church is in time.

As we have seen earlier, the Bible clearly says that the church in Jerusalem was in Jerusalem and that the church in Antioch was in Antioch. These churches were in localities and in time. Moreover, the Lord Jesus Himself confirmed that the church is something on the earth. Acts 9 records that on the road to Damascus the Lord appeared to Saul, who was persecuting the church, saying, "Saul, Saul, why are you persecuting Me?" (v. 4). In this verse *Me* is a very great "Me." Saul could have said to the Lord, "I am on the earth. How can I go up to heaven to persecute You? I have only persecuted Peter, James, Stephen, and others who were with them, but I have never persecuted You." Yet the Lord said, "Saul, Saul, why are you persecuting Me?" The Lord said this because the church is the Lord's Body, that is, the Lord Himself. Persecuting the people of the Lord, His church, is persecuting the Lord. The Lord and His church are one. Therefore, the *Me* in verse 4 does not simply refer to the Lord in heaven but also to His church on the earth. It refers not only to the Lord in eternity but also to His church in time.

The Lord's word here strongly refutes the general assertion that the expression of the church will be in heaven in the future. These people say that the church on the earth today is a mere formality, and since the genuine church is heavenly, it must be in heaven, eternal, and in the future. The Lord's word, however, completely refutes this kind of speaking. The Lord fully acknowledged the church in Jerusalem as His Body, Himself. This is the reason the Lord said to Saul, "Why are you persecuting Me?" This clearly shows that although the church is heavenly, the church is expressed on the earth, and although the church is eternal, the church is expressed today.

THE EXPRESSION OF THE CHURCH IN THE UNIVERSE
BEING ITS EXPRESSION IN LOCALITIES

The local expression of the church is for the universal expression. The church must be expressed locally in order to be expressed universally. It is through the expression in localities that the church is expressed in the universe. Therefore, it is not possible for the church to abandon the boundary of locality. Once the local expression is abandoned, there cannot be a universal expression of the church. Once the local expression of the church is abandoned, the church is but an empty theory. If there were no churches in localities, there would be no church in the universe. We fully agree that the nature of the church is universal and that the church is expressed universally, yet this universal expression is realized through local expressions. Hence, without localities, it is simply impossible to have the church.

THE CHURCH IN THE UNIVERSE
BEING CALLED THE UNIVERSAL CHURCH

Although the expression *universal church* cannot be found in the Bible, it is not unreasonable to refer to the church as being universal. The church referred to in Ephesians 1:22-23 can be called the universal church. However, we must remember that the expression of the universal church is local. Since this expression is local, the church is a local church. Thus, to say that the church is only universal is merely theoretical, and to say that the church is local is practical.

Let me repeat, it is not wrong to call the church in the universe the universal church, but over the past two thousand years no one has ever seen the universal church. If we asked Paul, he would say that the churches were in definite places, such as Ephesus and Antioch. Therefore, to speak of the church as being only universal is to engage in vain talk. In reality, the expression of the church is in localities. The churches spoken of in Acts 15:41; 1 Corinthians 11:16; 16:19; 2 Corinthians 8:1; and Galatians 1:2 and 22 point to the fact that in reality the expression of the church is in localities. Although the church is universal, the church is expressed locally. Since the church is expressed in many localities, the local expressions are called churches.

EVERY LOCAL CHURCH BEING THE EXPRESSION
OF THE UNIVERSAL CHURCH IN THAT LOCALITY

The church in a locality is the expression of the universal church in that locality. Hence, every local expression of the church is a local church. We must remember, however, that a local church is the expression of the universal church in a locality. The local church represents the universal church and is part of the universal church. Hence, not acknowledging the local churches is the same as not acknowledging the universal church, and not contacting the local churches is the same as not contacting the universal church. This is because a local church is the expression of the universal church in that locality.

THE SUM TOTAL OF THE LOCAL CHURCHES BEING THE UNIVERSAL CHURCH

Since every local church is the expression of the universal church in that locality, the sum total of the local churches throughout time is the universal church. Individually, there are churches in different localities. In totality, all the local churches in time constitute the universal church.

THE LOCAL CHURCHES BEING MINIATURES OF THE UNIVERSAL CHURCH

The local churches are miniatures of the universal church. Every local church is a miniature of the universal church. This is similar to calling young chickens chicks, because they are miniature chickens. Likewise, the expression of the church in a locality is a miniature of the universal church. Even though there is a difference in size between the expression in a local church and the expression in the universal church, in nature and in principle the expression is exactly the same. Therefore, when we contact a local church, we contact the universal church.

THE LOCAL CHURCHES BEING THE PRACTICALITY OF THE UNIVERSAL CHURCH

The practicality and reality of the universal church are absolutely dependent on the local churches. Without the local churches, the universal church is abstract and in the air, an empty theory, something of the imagination, and impossible to practice. For the universal church to be practical and concrete, the local churches are needed. Hence, the local churches are the practicality of the universal church.

The Building of the Universal Church
Being through the Local Churches

In Matthew 16:18 the Lord said, "Upon this rock I will build My church." The building that the Lord referred to is the building of the universal church. Nevertheless, the carrying out of this building must be through the building of the local churches. In other words, the Lord's building of the local churches is His building of the universal church. Without building the local churches, it is altogether impossible to build the universal church. Therefore, the building of the universal church is through the local churches. Sadly, some say that it is too narrow and rigid to focus on building the local churches. They do not want to build the local churches because they want to build the church of Christ, the universal church. How can they build the church of Christ without building the local churches? How can they build the universal church apart from the local churches? By building the local church in Jerusalem, were Peter and John not building the church of Christ? By building the various local churches among the Gentiles, was the apostle Paul not building the universal church? To speak of building only the universal church is impractical, empty talk.

The Local Churches Being Necessary
for the Administration of the Universal Church

The first reference to the church in the New Testament is in Matthew 16:18, where the Lord spoke of building the church. In Matthew 18:15-20 the Lord spoke of the church the second time, speaking concerning the administration of the church. It is obvious that the administration of the church in these verses refers to the administration of the local church. Verses 15 through 17 say, "If your brother sins against you, go, reprove him between you and him alone...But if he does not hear you, take with you one or two more...And if he refuses to hear them, tell it to the church." It is clear that the church here is the local church. If this were the universal church, where would we go to tell the church? Where is the universal church? God wants us to live in the local church and not wander in the universe. Therefore, if there is no local church, there cannot be any administration of the church. In order to carry out the administration of the church, there must be local churches.

Some advocate rejecting the local churches but keeping the universal church. They say, "Why should there be local churches? Did the Lord not say in Matthew 18:20 that He is in the midst of two or three who are gathered in His name? Does this not indicate that as long as two or three are gathered into the Lord's name, they are the church?" Although this understanding seems logical, if we examine it, we will find it to be in error. First they say that the local church is not the church because the church is universal. But then they turn around and say that the church can be as small as two or three people because the gathering of two or three people is the church. Let us read Matthew 18 carefully. "If your brother sins against you, go, reprove him...But if he does not hear you, take with you one or two more" (vv. 15-16). These two or three cannot be the church because verse 17 clearly says that if he refuses to hear these two or three, they should "tell it to the church." If these two or three were the church, why do they still need to tell it to the church? If there is a church in a locality, two or three believers gathered together cannot be considered as the church by themselves; they are merely two or three members of that local church. If they have a problem that they cannot solve by themselves, they need to bring it to the church. Thus, the two or three who are gathered into the Lord's name in Matthew 18 are not the church. If they were the church, there would be no need of the local church. This would result in "street churches" and "alley churches." This is an erroneous understanding. Brothers and sisters, God is truly wise in setting the boundary of locality for the expression of the church. This is because the boundary of locality is the only means of keeping the church from confusion. Today all the confusion in the church is the result of people not stressing and keeping the boundary of locality.

The Lord's charge that we should tell the church of a problem that we have with a brother and then let the church take care of the problem shows that the administration of the church is in the local church and carried out through the local church. This is the first time the Lord spoke of the administration of the church in the Bible. The Lord spoke not only of the building of the church but also of the administration of the church. The administration of the church is for the building of the church, and the administration of the church is in the local churches and carried out by the local churches. If there were no local church, there would be no administration of the church.

In Titus 1:5 the apostle charged Titus to appoint elders in every city. Acts 14:23 says that the apostles appointed elders in every church. Appointing elders in every city or in every church shows that the administration of the church is in the local church. Where would the elders be appointed if there were no local churches but only the universal church? Where would the elders serve as elders? Where would the administration of the church be carried out? Therefore, for the carrying out of the administration of the universal church, there must be the local churches.

The Universal Church Being Intangible and the Local Churches Being Real to the Workers and Believers

The Work of the Workers Being in the Local Churches

Whether in Acts or the Epistles, all the work of the apostles was carried out in the local churches and for the local churches. The Epistles written by the apostles were addressed to local churches. The Epistles to the Corinthians were written to the church in Corinth (1 Cor. 1:2), the Epistles to the Thessalonians were written to the church in Thessalonica (1 Thes. 1:1), and the Epistle to the Ephesians was written to the church in Ephesus. None of the Epistles were written to the universal church. Apparently, the Epistle to the Ephesians addresses the matters of the universal church, but it was sent to saints in Ephesus (Eph. 1:1). This proves that the apostles' work was altogether in the local churches. Unless their work was in the local churches, there would be no way for them to work in the universal church. To the workers, the universal church is intangible; only the local churches are real.

The Believers' Corporate Living and Coordinated Service Being in the Local Churches

If there were no local church, the saints would be unable to have a corporate living and a coordinated service. If we live in Taipei but do not live and serve with the brothers and sisters in the church in Taipei, where would we have our church life and service? Could we live and serve in the universal church, which is intangible? Hence, to the believers, the universal church is abstract; only the local churches are real.

Touching the Universal Church Only by Touching the Local Churches

Since the local church is the practice and the expression of the universal church, only when a person touches the local church can he touch the universal church. The more we speak concerning the universal church, the more vague and intangible the church will be to us, but once we speak concerning the local church, the church becomes concrete and real to us.

THE ADMINISTRATION OF THE LOCAL CHURCHES BEING LOCAL AND INDEPENDENT— THE LOCAL ADMINISTRATION

The administration of the local churches is by locality. If the administration of the church is not local and independent, the local nature of the church will be lost. Thus, to preserve and maintain the local nature of the church, the administration must be independent in each locality. Church A should not intervene in the practical affairs of church B; likewise, church B should not intervene in the practical affairs of church A. Although churches in villages and towns may be small, they are still the church in that locality, and other churches can neither intervene nor interfere with their practical affairs. If a local church loses its independence in its administration, it immediately loses its local nature.

Acts 14:23 and Titus 1:5 reveal that the church in each locality has its own elders. This proves that the administration in a church is independent. Elders oversee and administrate a particular church. If the administration of a local church is not independent, there is no need to appoint elders in every city. It would be sufficient to appoint elders in a central location. However, there is no central location because the expression of the church is in localities. All the local expressions, that is all the local churches, are equal and have their own elders. Hence, the administration of the local churches is independent in each locality.

THE FELLOWSHIP AMONG ALL
THE LOCAL CHURCHES BEING UNIVERSAL AND ONE—
THE FELLOWSHIP OF THE BODY

Although the administration of the local churches is independent in each locality, the fellowship of the local churches is of the Body and is universal. First Corinthians 10:16 says, "The bread which we break, is it not the fellowship of the body of Christ?" This indicates that the fellowship of the church is of the Body. It is universal, not local; it is in oneness, not independent. With respect to administration, the local churches are independent, but with respect to fellowship, they are one. If the church in a locality is not one in fellowship with the other local churches, that local church becomes a local sect. Once a local church loses its independence in administration, it loses its local aspect, and once a local church loses the oneness in fellowship, it becomes a local sect. These two aspects are serious. On the one hand, a local church loses its local aspect when its independence in administration is lost; on the other hand, a local church becomes a local sect when it loses the oneness in the universal fellowship. There should be a local aspect, but there should never be local sects. Retaining the local aspect is a great protection to the church, enabling the church to avoid many errors, heresies, and divisions. There have been many problems throughout history because the church lost and abandoned its local nature. At the same time, a church should never become a local sect; fellowship with all the local churches must be maintained. Hence, while the church's administration is local, the church's fellowship is universal and of the Body.

God's arrangement is truly wise and wonderful. Because all the local churches are independent in administration, the local nature of the constitution of the churches is not lost. Moreover, because all the local churches are in one fellowship, the oneness of the Body of Christ is kept, and the churches do not become local sects.

ALL THE LOCAL CHURCHES
LIVING DIRECTLY BEFORE THE LORD

All the local churches live directly before the Lord and are responsible directly to Christ the Head; hence, they should not form a federation or have a head church. Revelation 1:11-20 shows that the seven lampstands, that is, the seven churches, have the Lord Jesus in their midst. They live independently before Christ the Head and are directly responsible to Him. Among these churches, there are no so-called federations, head churches, or subsidiary churches.

Some people depict the seven lampstands in Revelation as being seven lamps on one lampstand. This conveys the wrong impression that churches can be united together to form a central church, a central lampstand. However, this is not what Revelation shows. Revelation 1:11 through 13 and 20 speak of seven different lampstands. The lampstand with seven lamps was the golden lampstand in the tabernacle in the Old Testament; this is not the case in the New Testament. The seven lampstands in Revelation 1 are independent and equal, each standing before Christ the Head. Therefore, among the churches, there is no higher-level church or lower-level church, no head church or subsidiary churches. The highest church is a local church, and the lowest church is also a local church. Both the highest and lowest church are a local church. No local church is higher than another church, and no local church is lower than another church. In this way, the authority of Christ the Head is not usurped or damaged among the local churches. If there were higher-level and lower-level local churches, the lower-level churches would have to obey the commands of the higher-level churches, and the result would usurp the authority of Christ the Head in the local churches.

The administrative independence of the local churches allows the Holy Spirit to move freely among the churches without any hindrance. Sadly, the organization in Christianity today is multi-level, with one level controlling another level, so that there is absolutely no room for the authority of the Head and the moving of the Holy Spirit. This is offensive to the Lord and to the Holy Spirit. Therefore, there should never be distinctions such as federated churches, head churches, higher-level churches, or lower-level churches. The church in Jerusalem was the largest church, but it was not so large that it became the head church among the local churches. Before the Lord the smallest local church is by no means lower than the largest local church. Whether it is the largest local church or the smallest local church, all the local churches are equal before the Lord, being absolutely under the authority of the Head and the control of the Holy Spirit. This gives the Head and the Holy Spirit the absolute ground and authority among the churches.

<h3 style="text-align:center">ALL THE CHURCHES
BEING THE SAME IN THEIR ACTIONS</h3>

Although the local churches are independent in administration and are not unified as an organization, they should be the same in their spiritual move and testimony. The action and testimony of the one universal church should be the same in all localities. For the convenience of management, leading, and edification, there is no better way than to have the local churches administrated by locality. However, as far as spiritual living and testimony are concerned, the local churches should all be the same.

First Corinthians was written by the apostle Paul to the church in Corinth, but 1:2 says that it was also written to "all those who call upon the name of our Lord Jesus Christ in every place." This is because the commands concerning spiritual living and service contained in this Epistle are to be kept unanimously in all the local churches. All the local churches should be and do what the church in Corinth is and does.

What the church in Corinth does, the other local churches should do. This is not a matter of organization; rather, this indicates that all the local churches should be the same in principle, nature, and testimony. Thus, the apostle's charge to the church in Corinth was also his charge to all the other churches (7:17; 16:1). When a custom is not found in one church, it should not be found in the other churches (11:16; 14:34).

In 1 Thessalonians 2:14 the apostle said, "For you, brothers, became imitators of the churches of God which are in Judea in Christ Jesus." This refers to the persecutions and sufferings they encountered because of their testimony for the Lord. Hence, in the matter of being persecuted for the testimony of the Lord, all the churches should follow the same footsteps and be one; a local church should imitate the pattern of the other churches.

Although each epistle written by the Lord to the seven churches in Revelation was written to a particular local church, at the end of each epistle it says, "He who has an ear, let him hear what the Spirit says to the *churches*" (2:7, 11, 17, 29; 3:6, 13, 22). Just as there should not be idols in the church in Thyatira, there should not be idols in the other local churches; just as the church in Pergamos should not follow the teaching of Balaam, the other local churches should not follow the teaching of Balaam. These examples show that the churches should be one in their actions. While the local churches should be separate and independent in administration, they should be one in their fellowship and in their living and actions for the Lord's testimony. In this way, the expression of all the local churches will be balanced, stable, and proper.

THE ONENESS OF THE CHURCH

We have seen that the church is the Body of Christ and the house of God, the vessel through which God can be expressed in the universe. The expression of the Body of Christ, the house of God, is local, and there is only one expression in each locality. On the one hand, the administration of each church is local; on the other hand, all the churches are one with regard to their move, having the common goal of upholding God's testimony on the earth.

It is not sufficient for us to realize only this; we need to know the oneness of the church. The oneness of the church is also the unity of the church. However, we do not like to use the term *unity* because the church is one from the beginning; there is no need for the church to be united. If we use the word *unity,* we are implying that there was a time when the church was not one. Hence, we prefer to use the term *oneness* to describe the church. The word *oneness* can be applied to something that is produced out of one source, one origin, and according to one principle. Therefore, it is not only permissible, but it is appropriate to say that the church is one because the source, origin, nature, and principle of the church are all one. The church is truly something that is one. The church cannot be two and cannot be divided; once the church is divided, it is through. We must preserve the nature of the oneness of the church.

We will consider the oneness of the church in the following six points.

THE SOURCE, PRODUCING, NATURE, PRINCIPLE, EXISTENCE, ADMINISTRATION, FELLOWSHIP, TESTIMONY, AND EVERY ASPECT OF THE CHURCH BEING ONE

Everything that is related to the church is one. Whenever

the church loses the oneness, it immediately is divided and falls apart. The church comes out of the Triune God; hence, the source of the church is one. The church is produced by the Triune God entering into man to be his life; hence, the producing of the church is one. The nature of the church is the Triune God coming into man as life; hence, the nature of the church is one. The principle that is produced out of this nature must also be one. The administration of the church is one regardless of where the church is expressed. In the universe the church has only one fellowship. The testimony of the church is also one. Every aspect of the church is one. Therefore, the church is altogether a matter of oneness.

THE CHURCH RECEIVING ONE SPIRIT, ONE LORD, AND ONE GOD THROUGH ONE FAITH AND ONE BAPTISM TO BECOME ONE BODY AND HAVE ONE HOPE

Ephesians 4:3-6 speaks of seven ones: one Body, one Spirit, one hope, one Lord, one faith, one baptism, and one God. These seven ones are all concerning the oneness of the church. The Body is the focus of the seven ones. The Body is produced from people who have one faith. Through this faith, the content of what we believe, we receive the Lord and eternal life, and we are saved. In the Gospel of John this is the faith through which we believe into the Son and receive eternal life (3:15). In the book of Romans it is the faith by which we are justified (5:1). This faith does not refer to whether we believe in pre-tribulation rapture or post-tribulation rapture or whether we should keep the Sabbath. These things are not the faith; they are merely views and opinions. One person may believe in the pre-tribulation rapture, and another person believes in the post-tribulation rapture. One person may believe in keeping the Sabbath, but another person may not believe in keeping the Sabbath. These are merely views and opinions. There is only one faith that causes man to be justified and saved and to receive God as life. Hence, the Bible calls it "one faith." As long as a person is saved, this faith is in him regardless of whether he believes in a pre-tribulation or post-tribulation rapture or whether he believes in keeping the Lord's Day or the Sabbath.

The Body is also the result of one baptism. This baptism is not a matter of being immersed or sprinkled but of being baptized into the name of the Lord and being buried together with Him. Through baptism, those who have believed into the Lord have died, been buried, and resurrected with the Lord. Hence, they have been delivered from everything that is of the old creation. Through one faith we enter into the new creation, and through one baptism we are delivered out of the old creation. Through one faith we become the new creation in Christ, and through one baptism the old creation in Adam is terminated. Through one faith and one baptism we are transferred out of Adam into Christ.

When we receive the Lord and are put into Him through one faith and one baptism, we receive the Spirit. The Lord, the Spirit, and God are one. Thus, we receive the Triune God—the Father, the Son, and the Spirit. The Father is in the Son, the Son is in the Spirit, and the Spirit enters into us (John 14:17). When we receive the Spirit, we receive the Son who is in the Spirit, and we also receive the Father who is in the Son. With regard to order, the Father comes first, the Spirit comes last, and the Son is in the middle. With regard to the Triune God's reaching us, the Spirit comes first. When we receive the Spirit, we receive the Son, and when we receive the Son, we have the Father.

Through one faith and one baptism, we have received one Spirit, one Lord, and one God, and this produces the one Body. The one Body is the church. The church is produced in this way. The one faith and one baptism are the history of the one Body; they are accomplished facts. However, the Body is not something merely from the past. The Body also has a glorious future, that is, a hope. This one hope is to enter into glory, to be the same as the Triune God. Therefore, our hope is also one.

Each of the seven ones is indispensable to every believer. Believing in a pre-tribulation rapture or post-tribulation rapture or keeping the Sabbath or the Lord's Day does not matter because they do not affect our salvation. However, if we lack any of the seven ones, we are not saved. We must have the faith that causes us to be saved and the baptism that delivers us from the old creation. We must receive the Spirit, the Lord, and God who make us part of the Body. We must also recognize this Body and admit that the future of the Body is the hope of glory. If we are short in any one of these seven points, there is a problem with our salvation.

These seven ones are the very elements that constitute the church: one faith, one baptism, one Spirit, one Lord, one God, one Body, and one hope, to enter into glory. The elements that constitute the church are all one. Its history is one, and its future is one. Its inner life is one, and its outer form is one. Since everything concerning the church is one, the church is one. When we see this, we will understand why we should never do anything that would cause the church to be divided. Whenever the church is divided, the church is destroyed.

THE CHURCH EXISTING AS ONE IN THE UNIVERSE

There is only one church in the universe. There are not many churches in the universe; there is only one church. Since the source and production of the church are one, the existence of the church must also be one. According to the nature of the oneness of the church, the existence of the church in the universe must be one. According to the principle of the oneness of the church, the existence of the church in the universe should also be one. Therefore, the church is uniquely one in the universe; there is only one church. This is the aspect of the church emphasized in Ephesians 1:22-23.

THE CHURCH IN EACH LOCALITY BEING ONE

There is only one church in the universe, and there is only one church in each locality. Regardless of whether the city was Jerusalem (Acts 8:1), Antioch (13:1), Ephesus (Rev. 2:1), or Corinth (1 Cor. 1:2), there was only one church in it. There can be only one church, not two or more, in each locality. If there are two or more in one locality, the oneness of the church is immediately damaged. All the saints in the universe belong to the universal church. In the same principle, all the saints in one locality belong to the church in that locality. If the believers in one locality become divided and form two churches, the oneness of the church is damaged.

Regardless of the locality, there can be only one church. In Taipei there is one church, and in Tainan there is also one church. In Tokyo there is one church, and in New York City there is also one church. In a large locality there is one church, and in a small locality there is also one church. The church is one. However, in today's situation there are so many "churches" that there is almost one on every corner. There can be an East Gate Church on one corner, and a Baptist Church on another corner, or there can be a Lutheran Church on this street and a Wesleyan Church on the next street. This can be compared to a "church" market. If we see the light concerning the oneness of the church, we will abhor this situation. Such a condition completely contradicts the oneness of the church by establishing more than one "church."

This can be compared to God's creation of man and woman. God ordained that a man should marry one woman and that a woman should be married to one man. There should not be polygamy. People in both the East and the West abide by this ordination. A person who is married to more than one person is looked down upon because in the human concept, marriage is meant to be between one man and one woman. A man can have only one wife, and a woman can have only one husband. This also applies to the church. There should be only one church in each locality. If there are many "churches" in one locality, it is a big problem. This is not a small mistake. It is a serious sin (3:3-4). It is a sin greatly abhorred by God.

Some people may say, "Surely there are believers in these 'churches.' Surely some love the Lord zealously." Yes, I agree that there are believers there. However, I would like to ask, "Are there not believers and pious ones also in the Roman Catholic Church?" However, Revelation 17 says that the Roman Catholic Church is a great harlot. Brothers and sisters, this age is dark, and the condition of the church is confused. We truly need God's mercy. To those who have blurry eyesight, the Roman Catholic Church is a religion of piety, teaching man to believe in God, attend mass, and worship the crucified Savior. Little do they know that in God's eyes, Roman Catholicism is a great harlot. Hence, we should not ask whether they are a Christian organization, or whether they preach the same gospel, or whether they speak the truths in the Bible. We should not assume that there is no problem as long as these conditions exist. We cannot merely look at these things. They may have all these things, but in the Lord's eyes there is abominable confusion within. As another example, even though some are of the church of Jesus Christ, why should they hang a sign of Wesley? Why should they hang a sign of Luther? This is not a small thing. If this is not spiritual fornication, what is it? A church that has several names is no different from one woman who has several husbands!

In 1954 some believers went to Baguio in the Philippines. When a renowned preacher from China heard that we were coming, he left. Before leaving Baguio, he asked a brother whom he knew very well to ask me why we considered only ourselves to be the local church. I responded, as if jesting, and asked the brother to convey the following analogy to the preacher: "One day, Mrs. Chao saw Mrs. Lee, Mrs. Liu, Mrs. Wang, and Mrs. Chang. Being jealous, they asked Mrs. Chao, 'Why do you consider only yourself to be Mrs. Chao?' Mrs. Chao replied, 'Why do you even ask me such a question? Do you not call yourselves Mrs. Lee, Mrs. Liu, Mrs. Wang, and Mrs. Chang?'"

The one church has been divided. This is something very offensive to the Lord. It offends the Lord even more than immoral sins. The church that should be of Christ openly and shamelessly puts up a sign of Lutheran or of others. Oh, what a shame! This is the same as Mrs. Chao calling herself Mrs. Chang. Today the Protestant churches condemn the Roman Catholic Church, calling her a great harlot, but what about the Protestant churches? Are they a pure and chaste woman in the eyes of the Lord? Those who have light will painfully admit that the Protestant churches have also become harlots!

MANY LOCAL CHURCHES NOT BEING MANY KINDS OF CHURCHES

Although there are many local churches, there cannot be many kinds of churches. There is only one kind of church. "Many" is a matter of quantity, but "kind" is a matter of nature. For example, there are many churches in Taiwan. There is a church in Tainan, a church in Taipei, a church in Taichung, and a church in Kaohsiung. Since there are many localities, there are many churches. However, these churches cannot be many kinds of churches. Since the nature of the church is one, there can be many churches in many localities, but there cannot be many kinds of churches. The church in Taipei and the church in Tainan are of the same nature. However, today in many places there are not only many "churches" but many kinds of churches. This shows that the oneness of the church has been lost and that the nature of the oneness has been changed.

We must see that the church is one; just as the church is one universally, the church is also one locally. Although there are many churches in different localities, the nature of these churches is one; they are of the same kind.

THE CHURCH BEING INDIVISIBLE

The church is one universally and also one locally. The nature of the church is one, and there is only one kind of church. Therefore, the church is indivisible.

The Church as the Body of Christ Not Being Divided

If a physical body is divided, dismembered, it will fall apart. Since the church is the Body of Christ, the church cannot be divided.

The Church as God's Dwelling Place Not Being Divided

The church is the dwelling place of God. A dwelling place is a house. If a house is divided, it will not be able to stand (Mark 3:24). Therefore, as God's dwelling place, the church cannot be divided.

REASONS FOR DIVISION

Deformed Christianity, however, uses many invalid reasons for division, resulting in the current state of confusion. We must realize that the church cannot be divided, and we must also beware of the following reasons for confusion.

Being Divided on the Basis of Spiritual Giants

The Lutheran Church took Martin Luther as their basis and divided. The Methodist Church took John Wesley as their basis and divided. Martin Luther and John Wesley were both greatly used by the Lord, but they should not have become the basis for division.

First Corinthians 1:12-13 and 4:6 explicitly condemn division on the basis of persons. Some believers in the church in Corinth said, "I am of Paul," others said, "I am of Apollos," and yet others said, "I am of Cephas." This indicates that they took spiritual giants as the basis for dividing themselves from others. However, even though they were divisive, they had not yet established a "church of Paul," a "church of Apollos," or a "church of Cephas" in the way that people today openly put up Lutheran and Methodist signs. Since the Holy Spirit condemned the divisiveness in the church in Corinth, will He not even more condemn the denominations today?

Being Divided on the Basis of the Person Who Is Instrumental to Our Salvation or Edification

In the church in Corinth some probably said they were of Paul because they were saved through Paul. There were others who probably said they were of Apollos because they had received edification from Apollos. This is the same as someone saying, "I was baptized by Pastor So-and-so; therefore, I belong to his church." However, the apostle Paul said that we should never consider ourselves as belonging to those who are used by God in order to separate ourselves from others (3:3-8, 21-23). We belong to only One—our Lord Jesus Christ. Belonging to those through whom we were saved, by whom we were baptized, or from whom we received edification is condemned by the Holy Spirit.

Being Divided Because of Spiritual Facts

Those in the Pentecostal Church have received the gift of the Holy Spirit; hence, they call themselves the Pentecostal Church. Those in the Holiness Church stress holiness; hence, they call themselves the Holiness Church. These denominations use a certain spiritual fact to promote themselves and make this a reason to separate themselves from others. Division on this basis is also not right.

In 1 Corinthians 1:12-13, the Holy Spirit not only condemned those who claimed to be of Paul, of Apollos, and of Cephas, but He also condemned those who claimed to be of Christ. This is because they separated themselves from others based on the fact that they belonged to Christ. Although it is right to belong to Christ, it is not right to make this the basis of division. Therefore, there is no reason that allows us to be divided from other believers. There is, however, nothing we can do if believers decide to divide themselves from us. In such a case, even though there is division, it is not our responsibility.

Being Divided Because of Differences in Doctrinal Views

There was a group of believers in northern China who insisted that believers would all be raptured after the great tribulation. Therefore, they became a post-tribulation rapture sect. There were others who believed in rapture before the tribulation and became a pre-tribulation rapture sect. These two groups of believers were divided. Some groups insist on keeping the Sabbath, but other believers say that since the Sabbath is of the Old Testament, they should keep the Lord's Day in the New Testament. Still other groups are divided because of different views concerning immersion and sprinkling. Then there are some who divide because of different opinions concerning head covering. Even items related to the breaking of bread, such as using a large or small cup, eating wafers or bread, or drinking grape juice or grape wine, are the basis for divisions among believers. Forgive me for saying this—there are too many divisions among Christians. In the sixty-six books of the Bible there are so many points that can cause contentions. May the Lord preserve us that these points would not be reasons for division.

Not Considering Doctrinal Views as the Faith

The basic Christian faith consists only of the seven ones spoken of in Ephesians 4:4-6. Apart from these seven ones, nothing should be considered as basic to the faith. Our funda-mental faith can have only this "one faith." If we consider the many possible different doctrinal views as being part of the "one faith," the fundamental faith, there will surely be many divisions among God's children. This should not be so.

Practicing Differently and Being Divided from Others Based on Doctrine Being Fleshly

Galatians 5:19-21 speaks concerning the works of the flesh. One of the items is sects or heresies. The Greek word for "heresies" in the Chinese Union Version means "divisions due to different doctrines." Therefore, any act of causing divi-sion because of different doctrines is the work of the flesh.

Receiving Those Who Are Weak in Faith

Romans 14 speaks of not passing judgment on others' con-siderations but rather of receiving one another: "One believes that he may eat all things, but he who is weak eats vegeta-bles. He who eats, let him not despise him who does not eat; and he who does not eat, let him not judge him who eats, for God has received him...One judges one day above another; another judges every day alike" (vv. 2-3, 5). This portion of the Word makes it clear that none of us should pass judgment on others. Even if a person is a vegetarian and keeps the Sab-bath, the Bible says that we should still receive him. Being a vegetarian and keeping the Sabbath are not according to New Testament truths. Nevertheless, the Bible tells us to receive one who is a vegetarian and keeps the Sabbath. We should receive one who has different views and opinions. Hence, God does not allow any division based on differences in doctrinal views.

The Scriptures Acknowledging Doctrinal Differences but Not Permitting Division Based on These Differences

Although the Bible acknowledges that man has different views with respect to doctrines, it absolutely forbids man from being sectarian and divisive based on different doctrinal views. First Corinthians 1:10-13 and Titus 3:10 show that the

Bible forbids people from being factious. Even more, the Bible condemns those who form parties and cause divisions. As long as there is the oneness on the seven points of the fundamental faith spoken of in Ephesians 4, the Bible does not forbid different doctrinal views if they do not hinder the oneness of the church. However, the Bible absolutely prohibits people from forming parties and causing divisions based on these doctrinal views. The Bible condemns any kind of sectarianism and denominationalism.

Being Divided Because of Racial Differences

First Corinthians 12:13 and Colossians 3:11 say there cannot be Jew or Greek in the Body of Christ. Jews are a certain race, and Greeks are another race. Division because of racial differences is not permitted in the Bible. Therefore, a "church" based on an ethnic group should not be established.

Being Divided Because of Differences in Nationality

The fact that 1 Corinthians 12 and Colossians 3 say there cannot be Greeks or Jews means that there cannot be divisions based on race or nationality. Divisions according to nationality, such as the Anglican Church in England, which is either the Church of England or the Episcopalian Church, and the Church of Christ in China, are neither right nor permitted in the Bible.

Being Divided Because of Differences in Social Rank

First Corinthians 12:13 and Colossians 3:11 also say that there cannot be slave or free in the church. Therefore, it is not permissible to have divisions based on social rank. There cannot be a church of university professors, just as there cannot be a church of rickshaw pullers. In the past there was a "church of the rickshaw pullers" in Shanghai. We should bear in mind that although there are different social classes in society, there cannot be such a thing in the church. A university professor must be able to sit beside a brother who is a rickshaw puller in the meetings. This is a lovely matter.

Being Divided Because of
Spiritual Weakness or Mistakes

In five of the seven epistles written to the seven local churches in Asia, the Lord rebuked the churches because of their weaknesses and mistakes (Rev. 2—3). However, because those five were local churches, the Lord did not ask anyone to leave. Although the spiritual condition of those churches was weak, and there were even serious mistakes among them, the Lord still wanted the believers to be overcomers in these churches.

All of the above points show that the church is one; therefore, it should never be divided. There is absolutely no reason for the church to be divided. Any reason for division that goes against the seven points of the fundamental faith spoken of in Ephesians 4 is wrong. Once the church is divided, it is no longer one, and the result is confusion. This confusion is spiritual fornication. May the Lord preserve us to continually live in the oneness of the church.

THE GROUND OF THE CHURCH

With respect to knowing the church, we have covered three lessons concerning what the church is, the expression of the church, and the oneness of the church. Now we come to the fourth lesson on the ground of the church. This matter can be said to be the key to knowing the church in today's chaotic situation. If someone desires to know the church, he must know the ground of the church.

Every matter, whether according to fact or according to principle, depends first on its ground and then on its condition. For example, if we want to determine whether a family is the Chang family, we should not look at its condition but rather at its ground. If the members of this family are descendants of the Changs, having the Changs' lineage and calling themselves Changs, this family has the ground to be Changs. On the one hand, the condition of this family may be desolate and improper, but as far as the ground is concerned, they are still the Chang family. On the other hand, the Wang family may be very proper, but they do not have the ground of the Chang family. Hence, we should not acknowledge them as the Chang family. This shows that condition and ground are two separate matters.

From the seventeenth century until now, pursuers of spiritual life acknowledge that Madame Guyon was a spiritual person, and many people received some amount of help from her. Madame Guyon and those who were with her at that time, such as Father Fenelon and Francois LaCombe, were quite spiritual. When they gathered together to fellowship and pray, they truly touched the presence of the Lord. As far as their condition is concerned, it was truly spiritual. But we must ask, where were they? They were in the Roman Catholic Church. We should never assume that as long as people are spiritual, there is no problem with their ground. It is quite possible for people to be spiritual yet their ground be wrong. If we want to know the church, we must separate condition from ground and never confuse the two.

In fact, in determining the correctness of a church, the matter of condition is secondary; the primary matter is the ground. Sadly, people's knowledge of the church is mainly based on the condition of the church, and they neglect the ground of the church. When speaking concerning a certain Christian group, they feel that there is no problem if the people are zealous, holy, and spiritual. This is to know the church based on condition, not on the ground. This is dangerous.

Our sight will be blurred if our discernment of the church is based merely on condition. If we do not want the church to be divided, we must pay attention to the matter of the ground. Using the example of the Chang family, can we say that a family is the Chang family simply because its condition is good? Absolutely not. If we want to determine whether a family is the Chang family, we must take a look at their genealogy, lineage, and name. This is a matter of the ground. If this family actually has the Changs' genealogy, lineage, and name, every member of the Chang family must admit that they are the Changs, even if their condition is very poor. They can do their best to improve and build up their family, but they will always be Changs. Likewise, in order to know the church, we must recognize the ground of the church. Condition is relative, but the ground is absolute. Some may say that a Christian group has no problem because its condition is good. However, condition is a relative matter because there is no standard for measuring a good or bad condition. If the condition is good, it is good, and if it is very good, it is still good. There is no standard for determining what degree of good is truly good. Moreover, different people have differing judgments on what is good and what is bad. We may think that something is good, but someone else may not agree; we may think that something else is very good, but others may think that it is not good enough. Different standards cause disagreements. Similarly, there are no definite standards for what is spiritual. A slight degree of spirituality is spiritual, a higher degree of spirituality is spiritual, and an even higher degree of spirituality is spiritual. This also applies to loving the Lord and living for the Lord. We cannot say that a person absolutely does not love the Lord or live for the Lord. Neither can we say that a person fully loves the Lord and lives for the Lord. There is no standard for these things; they are all relative.

In the church in Corinth, some thought that Paul was spiritual and wanted to be of Paul, others thought that Apollos was more spiritual than Paul and wanted to be of Apollos, and yet others thought that Cephas was the most spiritual, so they wanted to be of Cephas. This is a relative matter. One person thinks that Paul is spiritual, another thinks that Apollos is spiritual, and yet another thinks that Cephas is more spiritual. But is it possible to determine who is the most spiritual? This is troublesome.

Moreover, conditions may change. Someone may not love the Lord today, but perhaps tomorrow he will love the Lord very much. A particular group may not be spiritual today, but next year they will become very spiritual. Therefore, the assessment of a church can never be based on its spiritual condition but on its ground. Its ground is absolute and can never change. If a family has the ground of the Chang family, whether they are highly educated or illiterate, they have the ground of the Chang family. Being a millionaire or being penniless does not change the fact that they have the ground of the Chang family. Likewise, the local ground of the church is absolute and cannot be altered.

If the children of God can abandon all conditions and keep the local ground, the church would not be divided. Whenever we deviate from ground to condition, the church will be divided. This is a dangerous matter. Let me repeat, whenever we leave the ground and pay attention to spiritual condition, the church will be divided.

This does not mean that we should not be spiritual and good. We need to ask the Lord for His mercy that our condition would progress and improve day by day. Whether a church is proper does not depend on its condition but on the ground of the church. Whenever we leave the ground, our assessment of the church will immediately become unstable.

Let me say a few solemn words. If the Lord delays His coming, we will one day go to the Lord, and this testimony will spontaneously fall on the shoulders of the young ones. If we do not stand firm on the ground of the church with absolutely no deviation, these young ones will be confused regarding the church. Not only so, there will be divisions among us. If this word is tragically fulfilled one day, please remember that the reason for such a division is that we have paid attention to spirituality and put the ground aside.

In regard to knowing the church, if we depart from the ground and focus our attention on anything else, regardless of how good it is, danger awaits us in the future. Sooner or later, there will be division. No doubt we should pay attention to spirituality and the pursuit of life, but we should set our pursuing feet firmly on the ground of the church. This is our safeguard against any division. Whenever our hearts pursue spirituality and our feet are set on spirituality, division will follow. Once we leave the ground, our pursuing and our spirituality will turn into something dangerous.

I do not know if these words are clear enough. Whether a church is proper does not depend on its condition but on the ground. If the ground is correct, the church is proper even if the condition is poor. If the ground is not correct, the church is improper no matter how good and spiritual its condition is. This is a crucial point.

This matter is not for ourselves; it is for God's recovery at the end of this age. A strong recovery involves fierce warfare. We must see that the ground is much more important to the church than its condition. If we desire to know the church, we must know the ground of the church.

THE CHURCH NEEDING A GROUND

The church must have a ground. What do we mean by the ground? The ground is where something is placed. This podium needs to be placed somewhere. That place is the ground of the podium. Similarly, the church, being something so great in the universe, needs a definite place, a site where it can be placed. The church is real, concrete, great, and weighty. In order for the church to be expressed in the universe, it must be on a site; this site is its ground. Without a ground, speaking of the church is vanity because there is no way for the church to be displayed. In order for the church to be displayed, there must be a ground. This is a principle, a law.

The Bible says that the church is a house built by God as His dwelling place. In order to build a house, there must be a base. This base is the ground. We must differentiate the base of a building from its foundation. The foundation is the lowest part of a building, but the base is the piece of land that is underneath the foundation. Therefore, as the house built by God, the church needs a ground.

When discussing the ground of the church with people, some quote 1 Corinthians 3:11, which says, "Another foundation no one is able to lay besides that which is laid, which is Jesus Christ." From this verse they concluded that the Lord Jesus is the ground of the church. Their speaking has confused the ground with the foundation. The ground and the foundation are two absolutely different things. The foundation is the lowest part of a building, and the ground is the base upon which the building is placed. Since the church is the dwelling place of God, the building of God, it not only needs a foundation but also needs a ground.

Even from the point of view of individual believers, it is not good to be a wandering Christian. Nevertheless, some people are "wandering" Christians; they do not belong anywhere but come and go from place to place. They are like the wandering stars spoken of in Jude 13. This is not acceptable. As a Christian, we need to be stable and settled. In order for us to be settled, we need a place, a ground. Because conditions change, we cannot be settled merely based on a condition. We can be settled only in a place. Therefore, both the church and even individual believers need a ground.

THE GROUND OF THE CHURCH BEING LOCAL

The ground of the church must be local because the expression of the church is in a locality. In lesson 14 we saw that the expression of the church is in a locality. Since the expression of the church is in a locality, the ground must also be local. For example, as I am standing at the podium, I am being expressed at the podium; consequently, the podium is spontaneously my ground. Since the church is expressed in a locality, the locality is the ground of the church. The universe is not the ground of the church. If the church is not expressed in a locality, it cannot exist in the universe because the universe is something in the air, without a solid ground.

This is a point of dispute that others have had with us in the past few years. They always speak concerning the universal church, but we insist that there must be local churches. Sometimes I have said to them, "You speak concerning the universal church, but can you show me where it is? When I speak concerning local churches, I can immediately point out definite places, including Jerusalem, Antioch, Ephesus, Corinth, Rome, London, New York City, and Taipei. However, you cannot show me the universal church. You may speak concerning the universe, but really, you are in a locality, and if you were not in a locality, you would not be in the universe." Do we see this? Speaking of the universe is too vague; only a locality is practical. Thank the Lord that the ground of the church is local, not universal.

Where does the Lord place the church? We need to see clearly that the Lord places the church in localities. Therefore, in the New Testament there are many churches in different localities, such as the church in Jerusalem (Acts 8:1), the church in Antioch (13:1), the church in Corinth (1 Cor. 1:2), the church in Ephesus (Rev. 2:1), the church in Smyrna (v. 8), the church in Pergamos (v. 12), the church in Thyatira (v. 18), the church in Sardis (3:1), the church in Philadelphia (v. 7), and the church in Laodicea (v. 14). All of these churches were in different localities. It is a pity that people do not see the word *in* when they read these verses in the New Testament.

The word *in,* which many people often miss when they read the Bible, is used in two important ways in the New Testament. The first *in* relates to being *in* Christ: "There is now then no condemnation to those who are *in* Christ Jesus"

(Rom. 8:1); "so then if anyone is *in* Christ, he is a new creation" (2 Cor. 5:17); "obey your parents *in* the Lord" (Eph. 6:1); "rejoice *in* the Lord always" (Phil. 4:4). Many people read *obey your parents* but do not read *in the Lord;* they read *rejoice always* but do not read *in the Lord.* The second *in* relates to the churches *in* a locality: "the church *in* Jerusalem," "the church *in* Antioch," etc. We need to see the significance of the second *in.* Being *in* Christ is a matter of our redemption and enjoyment of God, and being *in* a certain locality is a matter of our knowing the church.

Over the past twenty years it has become very clear that if we do not resolve this matter of locality, the problem of the church will never be solved. When we studied church history in the beginning, we received significant help on the matter of the church from the light the Brethren received over one hundred years ago. But the help they gave us did not solve all the problems, because their light regarding locality was not very clear. In 1933 after spending much time and effort in the Word, Watchman Nee saw the second *in.* The believers are *in* Christ, and the church is *in* a locality. Once we are detached from Christ, we lose our position of salvation; once we are detached from a locality, we lose the ground of the church. It is true that in the spiritual aspect, the church is also in Christ, but in the aspect of practicality, the church is altogether in a locality. Without being in a locality, the church cannot be contacted and touched. Since the church is expressed in a locality, the locality is the ground where the church is placed. Let me repeat, the ground of the church is local. Concerning this matter, we need to pay attention to several points.

The Local Ground
Being the Ground of the Body

The local ground of the church is the ground of the Body. Since a local church is the expression of the Body of Christ in that locality, the ground of the local church is also the ground of the Body of Christ. We should never think that the local ground is detached from the Body of Christ. No, even though it is the local ground, it is the ground of the Body, not the ground of a sect. The ground of locality never results in a sect.

The Local Ground Being the Unique Ground

There is only one Body of Christ. Since the local ground of the church is the ground of the Body of Christ, it is the unique ground. Moreover, since a locality should have only one expression of the church, there can be only one ground of the church in a locality. This one ground of the church is the local ground. There should not be two churches or two grounds in one place. Therefore, the local ground is the unique ground. Besides this local ground, there should not be any other ground in a place. Once there are other grounds, there will be divisions into different sects and denominations.

Regardless of the place, if there are two "churches" in a certain locality, either one of them or both of them are wrong. Once there are two congregations, there are two grounds. Once there are two grounds, there is at least one sect or denomination. The local ground is of the Body and cannot be divided; therefore, it is also the unique ground.

The Local Ground Being the Ground of Oneness

Since the local ground is the unique ground, it is also the ground of oneness. Wherever there is the local ground, there is oneness. Nothing apart from the local ground can cause Christians to be one. The local ground is the only place where Christians can practice oneness.

For example, some who practice the Sabbath take the Sabbath as their basis of oneness. This kind of "oneness" divides them from others. Others come together because they have the same opinion concerning head covering. This kind of "oneness" also divides them from others. Still others come together because they have the same opinion concerning baptism, whether it is by immersion or by sprinkling. Once they come together in this way, they divide themselves from others.

We must see that apart from the local ground, any kind of "oneness" that is based on the same opinion is actually a division. When we are united with a group of people based on a certain opinion, we are automatically divided from other believers. Only on the local ground can there be oneness without division. For example, in the locality of Taipei there are brothers who agree on baptism by immersion, brothers who agree on baptism by sprinkling, and brothers who keep the Sabbath, pursue holiness, and focus on the Pentecostal experience of the Holy Spirit. Even though these believers have different opinions, they are all in Taipei. If they stand on the local ground, however, they will spontaneously be one. But this is not the actual situation. When some who agree on baptism by immersion come to Taipei, they form the Baptist Church. This shows that they have a ground other than the local ground, which divides them from other Christians. Those who agree on baptism by sprinkling, keeping the Sabbath, pursuing holiness, or focusing on the Pentecostal experience of the Holy Spirit also gather together with others of the same opinion. Each group has its own ground apart from the local ground. They take their opinion as the ground. As a result, the local church in Taipei is divided.

I believe that the brothers and sisters can see clearly that when we stand on a certain opinion, rather than on the local ground, there is division. When we stand only on the local ground rather than our opinions, there is oneness. Therefore, the local ground is the ground of oneness. It would be a great blessing if the brothers who agree on baptism by immersion would not take this as their ground, even though baptism by immersion is scriptural. It would also be a great blessing if the brothers who agree on baptism by sprinkling would not take this as their ground. Similarly, it would be a great blessing if those who keep the Sabbath, pursue holiness, and focus on the Pentecostal experience of the Holy Spirit would also abandon their ground. If they would all give up their ground as a result of seeing that their different opinions cannot be the common ground of oneness among Christians, all the brothers with different opinions would be on the local ground, and everyone would spontaneously be one. Therefore, the ground of oneness can be preserved only on the local ground.

Today many Christians say, "We are all one in Christ." Although this sounds nice and spiritual, we cannot be one if we are only in the Lord but not in a locality. There is an annual convention in England called the Keswick Convention that is attended by many people from different denominations and sects. At this convention they often like to sing a hymn, which basically says, "We are one in Christ." However, once the convention is over, each believer returns to his respective sect or denomination, and once again they are divided. Their oneness is temporary. Once they leave the Keswick Convention, they are divided again. This confirms that oneness cannot be practiced only "in the Lord," without the local ground.

Over the past thirty years I have met many such believers. They shake hands joyfully with me and say, "Brother Lee, we are one in the Lord." I often replied, "Brother, when we are in the Lord, we are one, but if we are in the denominations, we are not one." To merely speak of oneness in the Lord is not practical; it is an empty theory. If we are still in denominations, the oneness in the Lord is damaged. We may hold other people's hands and say that we are one in the Lord, but this is a oneness only in word, not in reality. In order to have the oneness in reality, we must leave every division and come to the local ground. Is merely holding hands and declaring that we are one in the Lord sufficient for the oneness if we remain Baptists, Lutherans, and Wesleyans? This is not possible. Let me repeat: to be one merely in the Lord is not practical; in order to be one in reality, we must come to the local ground. When we abandon all grounds other than locality, we will be one.

The Local Ground
Being Local yet Universal

All the matters related to the church are real only on the ground of locality. Even the universality of the church is real only on the ground of locality. Those who speak only concerning the universal church have not touched the universal church in actuality. They are touching sects and divided groups. The genuine universal church must be expressed in localities. Therefore, the local ground is universal. Although this ground is local, the universality of the church is real only on this local ground.

THE BENEFITS OF THE LOCAL GROUND

The local ground is the unique ground, the ground of oneness. It is also the ground of the Body and of the universal church. Consequently, all of the benefits of the church come from this ground. Once this ground is lost, the church suffers severely. We greatly benefit by standing on the ground, because several problems can be avoided.

Guarding against Organizational Unification

In lesson 14 we saw that the churches in each locality should be independent, each living directly before the Lord and not forming organizations such as federations or headquarters (Rev. 1:11-20). The local ground is the best safeguard against forming organizations and federations. The local ground always restricts the local churches in every locality from forming federations beyond the boundary of a locality, thus losing the nature of locality. The church in every locality should be administered locally; there should be one church in one locality. The church in Jerusalem did not interfere with the church in Antioch; neither did the church in Antioch interfere with the church in Jerusalem. These local churches did not form a federation. Hence, Revelation 1 shows that the seven churches, signified by the seven lampstands, are independent, each on its local ground. Once the local ground is abandoned, the churches in different localities can immediately be united to form a large, "unified" church. This is how the Roman Catholic Church was produced. The Roman Catholic Church became so influential because the restriction of the local ground was not kept. They do not have the local ground; they only have the ground of the Roman Catholic Church. Since they have abolished the local ground, all the localities are unified into a large religious sect. Furthermore, the Roman Catholic Church is like a religious kingdom, with the pope as the head. This kingdom has its own judicial body, its own police force, and also its own administrative authority. In 1929 Mussolini signed a treaty with the Holy See to formally acknowledge the Roman Catholic Church as an independent nation. Such a large kingdom developed when the local ground of the church was abandoned. The Catholic Church is not standing on the ground of locality but rather on the ground of the Roman Catholic Church. They establish the Roman Catholic Church in many places. They do not establish a local church in a locality. Rather, all the problems in every place are brought to Rome to be settled. The Holy See is their imperial court.

We should not damage the local ground, because it guards against this kind of unification. If the church in every locality stands firm on the local ground, it will be impossible to have large organizational unification. If the churches in each locality are administered locally and are not ruled by other localities or ruling over other localities, the local nature of the church will be preserved.

Guarding Against Division within a Locality

The church in a locality should not be divided into many groups. For example, here in Taipei, there is a Ho Ping East Road Church and a Chungshan North Road Church. There are many "churches" on different streets and alleys; these are small divisions. In lesson 15 we saw that according to the Bible, there should be only one church in a locality, not many "churches." There should be only one local church in a locality; there should not be many "churches" on different streets and alleys in the same locality. If there are many "churches" on different streets and alleys in a locality, these are small divisions.

The open Brethren had many such divisions in a locality. If there were different opinions in a gathering, they would say, "We should not argue or quarrel. We should love one another in the Lord, but since we now have different opinions among us, let us meet separately. You meet on that road, and we will meet on another road. Then we can love one another and not strive with one another." Because of this way, they had many meetings in one locality.

Because of this practice among the open Brethren we encountered the problem of determining what the boundary of the church in a locality should be. In 1933 after much studying of the Word, Watchman Nee found that the boundary of the local church should be neither larger nor smaller than the locality itself. Anything larger than a locality is an unscriptural federation, and anything smaller than a locality is an unscriptural division. By keeping the local ground, we guard against organizational unification or small divisions.

We need to see that this is not a simple matter. If the light concerning the local ground is not sufficiently strong among us, sooner or later we will be divided. The Taiwanese brothers may say, "Since we cannot communicate with those from other provinces, and our temperament is not compatible, why should we suffer? Others can form a Mandarin 'church,' and we will form a Taiwanese 'church.'" If this happens, we will be divided immediately.

Only the local ground can guard against such a danger. There can be only one church in one locality. There is no basis for any division. There were Jewish and Gentile believers in the church in Antioch (Acts 13:1). Niger was a Gentile, and so was Manaen, the foster brother of Herod. Out of the five prophets and teachers there, at least two were Gentiles. However, neither a Hebrew-speaking church nor a Greek-speaking church were formed in Antioch. In the church in Corinth as well, there were Greeks and Jews. But they did not form a Greek-speaking church and a Hebrew-speaking church. There was only one church in Corinth. Therefore, 1 Corinthians 12:13 says, "Whether Jews or Greeks." In one locality there can be only one church. Languages cannot be the ground, and neither can ethnicity be the ground; only the locality can be the ground. If we are not clear concerning this matter and do not hold fast to this matter, sooner or later we will be divided.

For thirty years the Lord has preserved us from division. This is not because we are in absolute agreement in all of our opinions; rather, it is because we have all seen that no opinion is good or sufficient enough to be our ground for establishing the church. The church has no other ground but the local ground. There can be only one church in a locality, and there should not be any division regardless of the reason.

Therefore, the local ground has a great advantage of guarding against small divisions. If we are not satisfied with the church in a locality, we cannot form another church in that locality. The only thing we can do is to move to another locality. If we are not satisfied in Taipei, we can go to Tainan. If we are not satisfied again with Tainan, we can go to Chiayi. Regardless of the situation, we can only leave, not divide.

This is a serious matter. If there is no local ground, the church will have no protection and can be divided at any time. The reason for the formation of different sects and denominations in Protestantism is the lack of emphasis on the boundary of the local ground. At the time of the church in Corinth, there were four parties: those belonging to Paul, those belonging to Apollos, those belonging to Cephas, and those belonging to Christ, but they were not yet divided into four churches. Nevertheless, the apostle Paul still reprimanded them severely. Today, however, people openly put up signs of the "Lutheran Church" and the "Methodist Church." This is because of a lack of light. Therefore, we must see that the local ground is a serious matter; it guards against large federations and also avoids small divisions. The Roman Catholic Church has forsaken the local ground and has thus become a large federation; the Protestants have neglected the local ground and have thus become many small divisions.

Guarding against Confusion

The local ground can also guard against confusion. The situation of the church today is chaotic. Some people open their homes and gather a few people to pray together and thus form a house "church." Some professors gather a few students to meet together and thus form another type of "church." For this reason I sometimes say that today it is more convenient for people to establish a church than to open a tea house. In order to open a tea house, one needs to register with the government, but anyone can establish a "church." In order to avoid this kind of confusion, there must be the local ground. Once the local ground is confirmed, there cannot be unification, division, or confusion. However large a locality may be is the size of the church in that locality, and however small a locality may be is the size of the church in that locality as well. Thus, there will not be a federation that is larger than a locality, nor will there be a division that is smaller than a locality. At the same time, there will not be confusion related to the ground. If there were only one ground and one church in each locality, there would not be such confusion today. These are the benefits of the local ground.

FORSAKING ALL OTHER GROUNDS
AND RETURNING TO THE LOCAL GROUND

Since the local ground is the unique ground, all other grounds must be forsaken. Therefore, we need to forsake all other grounds and return to the local ground. This is what we mean by leaving the sects and denominations. Today it is not sufficient for us to merely love the Lord, be fervent, preach the gospel, perfect others, and be holy and spiritual while ignoring the matter of the ground. Speaking in lofty tones, many people today say that it is sufficient to love the Lord, be fervent, preach the gospel, perfect others, and be holy and spiritual. If there were no church, it might be acceptable merely to be such individual Christians. However, Christians are not alone; they must live a corporate life. The church is a reality. Hence, we must take care of the matter of the ground. In order to take care of the ground of the church, we must forsake all other grounds and return to the local ground.

As Christians, we need a ground for everything. We need a ground to fellowship with others, to meet, to serve God, to coordinate, to pursue holiness and spirituality, to work, and even more, to build up the church. The ground that is required for all of these is the local ground. The local ground is needed for fellowship, meeting, serving God, coordination, pursuing holiness and spirituality, working, and all the more, for building up the church. Only by being on the local ground can we be in the church. Therefore, we must forsake all other grounds and return to the local ground.

THE DIVISION OF THE CHURCH

We have already seen what the church is, the expression of the church, the oneness of the church, and the ground of the church. It is clear that there is only one church in the universe, and there is only one church in each locality. However, in today's deformed Christianity there are "churches" everywhere, clearly indicating that the church is divided. Therefore, we must now look at the division of the church.

THE CAUSES OF DIVISION

In brief, there are two causes for division: Satan's damage and man's fleshly preferences.

God's intention is to build up His church locality by locality so that there would be a local church in every place as the expression of the Body of Christ in order to express Christ. God is wise in His intention. If there were only one church in each locality with no confusion or divisions, and if all the local churches were one in expressing Christ, preaching Christ, and leading people to know God on the earth, this would be glorious. The church in each locality as an expression of the Body of Christ is a foretaste of the coming New Jerusalem, the expression of God.

Satan does not want such an expression; thus, he tries his best to damage it. Satan damages the church through man's preferences. When people appreciate a certain person, they establish a "church" based on that person; when they appreciate a certain truth, they establish a "church" according to that particular truth. All the different sects and denominations in Christianity today simply express man's preferences. The Corinthian believers were an example of this. Some of them chose to be of Paul, others to be of Apollos, and still others to be of Cephas (1 Cor. 1:12). Paul said that they had preferences because they were of the flesh (3:4). These preferences were of the flesh. The situation of division in Christianity today also comes from the preferences of man's flesh. Satan utilizes the preferences in man's flesh to damage the work of the church. This is the true situation.

THE EFFECTS OF DIVISION

With any matter, there is a cause and there is an effect. With the division of the church, there is a cause and there is also an effect. The effect has two aspects.

Damaging the Body of Christ

The church as the Body of Christ is one both universally and locally. However, once the church is divided, the oneness of the Body of Christ is lost. The situation of division that is prevalent today causes the Body of Christ to be "cut into pieces." Hence, instead of being one, the Body has been dismembered.

Producing Sects and Denominations

According to rough statistics, there are approximately two thousand sects in Christianity. In other words, there are approximately two thousand different kinds of "churches" on the earth today. This is truly a terrible result of the division of the church.

When I speak with people concerning the gospel, I am often asked, "If the Jesus whom you preach is the same as the One preached by Such-and-such Church, why are there so many different churches in your Christian religion?" This is a difficult question for new ones to answer. The division of the church is truly a shame to the Lord.

We must know the source of division. Divisions in China were brought in mainly by brothers from the West. We thank the Western brothers for bringing the gospel to China, and we are grateful to them for bringing us the Bible. Sadly, however, they brought their sects and denominations as well. We must acknowledge that bringing so many different denominations was a huge mistake. They should not have been divided into denominations, and they should have brought us only one church. How pleasant it would be if no one divided themselves into denominations, but everyone stood on one ground and took the same way. Regrettably, today's Christianity is full of sects and denominations, whether in the West or in the East. They have been divided and set in their divisions for many years. These many sects and denominations are the result of the division of the church.

THE RESPONSIBILITY OF DIVISION

With every matter, there must be someone who bears the responsibility. Related to the division of the church, there must also be someone who bears the responsibility. We must be clear concerning this. A careful and logical examination will show that the responsibility of division should be borne completely by those who stand on the ground of the denominations, not by those standing on the local ground.

After my return to Chefoo from Tientsin in 1937, a brother invited me to dinner. I can never forget that evening. Other older, well-known people from Christianity had also been invited. At dinner an elderly brother questioned me, saying, "Mr. Lee, you always say that the church is one and that it should not be divided, yet you have taken a group of people with you and separated yourself from us. In doing so, is not your group another division? We have a rare opportunity today to sit together, and we would like to hear from you." I said, "Wonderful! I have also been looking for such an opportunity to clarify this matter, and this account should be settled clearly." The older brother agreed and said, "Very good. Let's settle this matter today." I then said, "First, Paul condemned the Corinthian believers because they said that they were of Paul, of Apollos, or of Cephas. It was obvious that they should not have had such divisions. I would like to ask you all, is it correct for one to say, 'I am of the Chinese Church of Christ, I am of the Baptist Church, or I am of the Presbyterian Church'?" He said, "Of course, this is not correct, there is no question about this." I said, "Wonderful, we have settled the first point. Second, do you want me to belong to the Presbyterian Church, the Baptist Church, the Chinese Church of Christ, or some other denomination?" He said, "We do not want you to belong to the Presbyterian Church, the Baptist Church, the Chinese Church of Christ, or any other denomination." I said, "Very good, this point is also settled. Third, may I ask, having received mercy and grace from the Lord, can I preach the gospel and bring people to the Lord?" He said, "Of course, you can preach the gospel." Then I asked, "After I preach the gospel and some are saved, where should I bring these ones? If I myself do not go to a denomination, can I bring these ones to a denomination?" He said, "Of course not. If you yourself do not go there, you should not ask others to go there." I then continued, "Then what should I do with these ones who are saved? Should they not meet?" He said, "Of course, they should meet." I said, "Good. Since they should meet, where should they meet? If I bring them to the Baptist Church, we will be divided from the Presbyterian Church. If we go to the Chinese Church of Christ, we will be divided from the Presbyterian Church. Where should we meet?" At that point everyone became silent. I then continued, "As elderly ones, please consider this. Today we are meeting on Fourth Street (at the time the meeting place of the church in Chefoo was on Fourth Street). We desire that all of God's children would be one. However, your stand in the denominations, which divides you from other Christians, has forced us to humbly rent a house on Fourth Street to meet there. We have not formed a division, but you are maintaining a division. The responsibility of division is not on us, but on you. Because you are maintaining a division, we have been forced to find another place to meet. However, since you are all representatives of various denominations, let me ask, would you be willing to remove your denominational names—the Baptist Church, the Presbyterian Church, the Chinese Church of Christ, the Inland Mission, and so on? If you would do this, I would immediately go back and ask the brothers to close the meeting on Fourth Street, because there would no longer be any divisions." When they heard this request, they were shocked and replied, "We cannot do this!" I responded, "If this cannot be done, what else is there for us to say? Since you are set in your division, what else can we do? We have no choice but to meet in a place that does not belong to any denomination. Even though you say that we are divided from you, who bears the responsibility of this division?"

I believe this is clear; the responsibility for division is not with us but with those in the sects. It is impossible for us to go to the sects today, and it seems that by doing this, we are divided. However, the responsibility for this is not on us but on those in the sects.

All the Christians in Taipei today should meet as the church in Taipei. If we all take the locality of Taipei as the boundary and the ground, there would not be other "churches." However, some say they are the Baptist Church, others say they are the Presbyterian Church, and still others say they are the Methodist Church or another "church." They have all drawn a small circle around themselves, leaving only a small number who are not within a circle. Who should bear the responsibility of this division? Obviously, those who are in the small circles should bear this responsibility. Those who have not drawn a circle around themselves should not bear the responsibility of division. Although we seem to be divided from others, this is not because we have drawn a circle around ourselves. If others were willing to remove their circles, there would be no divisions. If everyone met in the church in Taipei, there would be no division. Regrettably, within the boundary of Taipei, small circles have been added—the Baptist denomination, the Lutheran denomination, the Presbyterian denomination, and others. This has resulted in many small circles within the large circle of a locality. What should have been a simple, single circle has been filled with many circles; this has resulted in division. It is obvious that the responsibility of division rests on those who are in the many circles.

Therefore, we should not allow our conscience to be weakened by the wrong and unreasonable condemnation of others. I was young when I heard these accusations in 1933, and I felt that I could not lift up my head. Many condemned us, saying, "You want the church to be one, but you divide yourself from others." At the time I also felt that what they said sounded right. However, as I went to the Lord and sought His shining, I was unveiled within to see that their word of accusation was a lie. It was not we who had formed a division, but they. They had left us in a position of division. They had drawn a circle around themselves and left us out of their circle. Hence, the responsibility of division was entirely on them.

Standing for the ground of the oneness of the church is a battle. For over thirty years, many brothers and sisters have struggled. Even though there will be many hardships ahead of us as we stand on the ground of the church, we must be faithful in order for the Lord's will to be accomplished and for our future generations to have a way to advance.

THE NEED FOR DISCERNMENT

In today's divided situation where sects and denominations are rampant, Christians must have the discernment to know what is proper and what should rightly remain. We must have this discernment because Christians must have a church; we cannot be without a church. A person in the world needs to be saved and become a Christian; after becoming a Christian, he needs the church. However, there are too many "churches" today; not only is there the Roman Catholic Church, but there are also numerous sects and denominations in Protestantism that call themselves "churches." Which one should he choose? Which one should he be in? This truly is a problem. Therefore, we must have the discernment; we cannot say that it is sufficient as long as there is a "church." We should not say this! We should not be in the Roman Catholic Church, and neither should we be in the numerous sects and denominations in Protestantism. We must exercise discernment regarding all these so-called churches. There are three principles that should be applied in our discernment.

Not Taking Spirituality as a Basis

When we discern a "church," we should not take spirituality as a basis. We should not say that a church is proper simply because its spiritual condition is good. Brother Andrew Murray was considered to be a spiritual person in the nineteenth century. The spiritual books he wrote have rendered us much help. However, the church that he was in was not proper because he was still in organized Christianity. He was a pastor and kept the title of a pastor. According to spiritual condition, the church that he was in might have been acceptable, but it was a part of organized Christianity. Madame Guyon, whom everyone agrees was very spiritual, was in the Roman Catholic Church. Furthermore, Dr. F. B. Meyer from England was very spiritual, and the books he wrote have benefited many, but he was also in organized Christianity. This proves that spiritual condition cannot be taken as the basis in discerning whether or not a church is proper.

Not Taking Personal Taste as a Basis

Since every person has his own preference, he also has his own taste. If our discernment is according to our preference and taste, it will be difficult to make a proper judgment. Those who prefer quietness will find a group that is quiet. Those who prefer solemnity will find a place with high cathedral ceilings, stained glass, and subdued lighting in order to have a feeling of solemnity when they enter. Those who prefer stories will find a place with superficial sermons. Those who prefer attention will find a place where they can preach and be a leader. If one "church" will not allow them to preach or be a leader, they will go somewhere else. These are all matters of man's taste. It is terrible to discern a church according to personal taste. There are as many different tastes in Christianity as there are different kinds of restaurants and menus. Tastes that are according to our personal preference are not necessarily proper. They may be contrary to God's will and the truth in the Bible. Therefore, under no circumstance should we discern a church according to our personal taste.

Taking the Ground as the Only Basis

When discerning a "church" in the confused and divided condition of the church today, we should not consider whether it is good; rather, we must consider whether it is proper. Being proper is different from being good. Being good is a matter of condition, but being proper is a matter of the ground. Knowing how to differentiate between being proper and being good will give us a solid understanding of the church. Of course, the condition of a church should be good, but having a good condition does not mean that it is a proper church. We need to see its ground.

For example, the Lee family may be quite good. The husband and wife love each other, the children are obedient, and no one ever quarrels. This family, however, is not the Chang family. Even though this is a good family, it is not the Chang family. In the Chang family the condition may not be good. Everyone always quarrels, and the condition is not good, but the family has the name Chang. What should be our basis in determining which family is the Chang family? Obviously, our basis should be only the ground, not the condition. It would be foolishness for us to determine who is the Chang family according to a good or bad condition.

There is a difference between the ground of the church and the condition of the church. Some people come and meet with us either because our condition is good or because our speaking helps and supplies them, not because our ground is proper. They care only for the condition of the church, not the ground. But we must focus on the ground of the church, because whether a "church" is proper or not depends on its ground.

The church has a definite ground. We must discern according to the ground of the church. This is the only basis. We should not carelessly discern on the basis of human opinions and views. In the previous lessons we covered what the church is, the expression of the church, the oneness of the church, and the ground of the church. These are all equivalent to the constitution of the church. Our determination of whether a church is proper must be according to the truths covered in these lessons. A city can have only one city government. It should never have more than one city government. The only city government that can be considered legal and proper is established according to the law of that country. The authenticity of such a city government cannot be denied even if its administration is poor. Despite its poor administration, its ground is still proper. This is the same with the church. A proper church is one with the proper ground. Therefore, in determining whether or not a church is proper, our only basis should be its ground.

Thus, regarding the knowledge of the church, the primary thing is to know the ground of the church. Once we are clear concerning the ground, we can pay attention to condition. Whereas the ground is a matter of being proper or improper, the condition is a matter of good or bad. Today many people focus only on the condition of the church and neglect the ground of the church. Those who pay attention to the condition and neglect the ground cannot discern whether a church is proper or not. They will also be unable to stand the test of time even if they happen to be meeting on the proper ground. Experience proves that all those who take this way because of the good condition of the church are eventually unable to stand the test of time. They may stay for ten years, but in the eleventh year they will leave if they think that our condition is no longer good. Only those who recognize the ground will never sway or change. We must take this way when the condition is good, and we must take this way when the condition is bad, because this is the proper way. Although our condition may not be good, our way is proper.

I thank the Lord that I have met many faithful companions over the past thirty years. Throughout these years, we have passed through many difficulties. Sometimes the condition of the church was not so good, and the meetings were not so enjoyable, but the brothers and sisters who knew the ground nevertheless walked on this way even with tears of inward pain. They knew that although the condition was poor, this was still their home. When the condition is good, it is their home, and when the condition is bad, it is still their home. Hence, they cannot deny, leave, or forsake this home. On the contrary, by the grace of God, they strive and struggle to turn the abnormal condition around.

Hence, new believers must see that we take the way of the church not because of a good condition but because the ground of the church is proper. Only this can prevent us from being shaken and enable us to walk this way our entire life.

I was in northern China in 1935 when a missionary spoke with me concerning the ground of the church. I told her that all of God's people should leave Babylon and come back to Jerusalem. She asked me, "Where is Jerusalem today?" I replied, "Jerusalem is where the temple is built. Although the temple was torn down, its base, the site, is still there. Although today the church is desolate, the ground that the church has had from the beginning is still present. We should come back to this ground." Several years later I heard that after returning to her country, she left the mission. She left organized Christianity and went to many places preaching and teaching people. She did a great amount of work. However, a person who does not recognize the ground of the church is not secure in his path. After laboring in this way for approximately twenty years, she returned to the Anglican Church, went through a reconfirmation ceremony administered by the clergy, and was accepted to take Holy Communion. This is strong proof that those who have not seen the ground of the church are not stable and that the path they take is not secure. The condition of our meetings may be good today but poor tomorrow. The messages we give today may help and supply people, but they may not be helpful and supplying tomorrow. Choosing a church based on condition is unwise. The church has a ground, and its ground is definite. For example, although the temple was destroyed and not one stone was left on top of another, the site of the temple is still there. The site cannot be changed. Whether a certain place is Jerusalem does not depend on whether a temple is there but on whether the site for the temple is there. When the temple is there and the glory of God fills it, it is Jerusalem. However, even if the temple becomes desolate and is destroyed, the place is still Jerusalem because the site of the temple has not changed. It is the same with the ground of the church.

In this desolate, confused, and unstable condition of the church today, our discernment of a "church" cannot be based on its spiritual condition or the so-called measure of the stature of Christ. These factors cause people to be unstable because they are changeable. Our discernment must be based on the ground. We should ask only whether a certain church is meeting on the ground of the local church and not concerning its condition. This does not mean that we should not pay attention to the condition of the church. The condition of the church should be good, spiritual, and full of the stature of Christ. It is best if the ground of the church is proper, and the condition is good, spiritual, and full of the stature of Christ. However, whether a church is proper does not depend on its condition but on its ground. Hence, our basis for determining whether a church is proper must be the ground. We should inquire only concerning the ground, not the condition. When determining whether a certain place is Jerusalem, we should not consider the condition of the temple. There may be temples being built in Babylon, but we must reject them because their ground is wrong. Even though the temple in Jerusalem has been completely destroyed, we still go to Jerusalem because this is where God's people should be, and this is the proper ground. May the Lord have mercy on us that we would have the ability to discern the confusing situation of the church today.

THE FORMATION OF A DIVISION

In order to discern, we must know how a division is formed, because once a division is formed, the ground of the church is lost, and it becomes a condemnable sect. Therefore, to discern whether a church is proper, we must know how divisions in the church are formed, which is also how sects are constituted.

There are six conditions involved in the formation of a division. This does not mean that all six conditions must be present in order for a division or sect to be constituted. Any one of these six conditions will result in a division or a sect.

Having a Special Name

The church is something unique in the universe. The name of the church is the church. Hence, when a church is expressed in a certain locality, it is called the church in that place, such as the church in Jerusalem (Acts 8:1), the church in Antioch (13:1), and the church in Corinth (1 Cor. 1:2). There can be no other name for the church. However, many Protestant groups today have special names. Some are named after people, such as the Lutheran Church and the Wesleyan Church; some are named after nations, such as the Anglican Church and the Chinese Church of Christ; some are named after an item of the truth, such as the Church of Justification by Faith and the Holiness Church; some are named after a system, such as the Presbyterian Church (a system of elders administrating the church) and the Congregational Church (a system advocating rules by a governing body of the congregation); and some are named after a ritual, such as the Baptist Church. There are many other names, such as the Charismatic Church, the Church of the Apostolic Faith, and the Pentecostal Church. Whenever specific names are used, small circles are drawn within the boundary of a locality. These small circles become different grounds. Once a Christian group has this kind of ground, it loses the ground of the church and thus becomes a sect, a denomination. Hence, these Christians are not building up the church in their locality. They are building up their denominations, their sects. When those from the Baptist Church come to Taipei, they do not come to build up the church in Taipei but to build a Baptist Church. When those from the Lutheran Church come to Taipei, they also do not come to build up the church in Taipei but to build a Lutheran Church. This is mainly because they have special names. Their special names are their ground, making them sects or denominations.

We should never think that having a special name is a small matter. This is something that greatly offends the Lord. Names are a serious matter. All that we have is in the Lord's name. We are saved in the Lord's name (Acts 4:12), we are baptized into His name and called by His name (19:5; Matt 28:19; Acts 15:17), we meet in His name (Matt. 18:20), and we pray in His name (John 14:14). The apostle beseeched us to be one through the name of the Lord (1 Cor. 1:10). The Lord praised the church in Philadelphia for not denying His name (Rev. 3:8). The matter of a name definitely touches the Lord's heart. According to church history, the Lord's word of praise to the church in Philadelphia was practically and richly fulfilled when the Brethren were raised up approximately one hundred years ago. They put away all names other than the

Lord's. This is proper. We should take only the name of Jesus Christ, not any other name. We should be only of Christ, not of Luther, Wesley, or England. We should not take any name other than the name of the Lord. As soon as a Christian group takes a special name other than the Lord's name, divisions, that is, sects, will be formed.

Having Special Articles of Belief

In the lesson on the oneness of the church, we saw that only the seven ones in Ephesians 4—one Body, one Spirit, one hope, one Lord, one faith, one baptism, and one God—are our basic faith. Apart from this basic faith, we should not have any other special beliefs or creeds. Today, however, every denomination has its own creed. In the Apostles' Creed of the Episcopalian Church one of the lines reads, "I believe in the Holy Catholic Church." One may believe in the Holy Catholic Church, but another may not. Believing in the Holy Catholic Church does not add to salvation, and not believing does not take away from salvation. The Seventh-day Adventists' Church has a statement in their creed that says that they believe the seventh day is the Sabbath. If a person does not believe in that statement, he will not be accepted as their church member. These are examples of special creeds. Once there are special beliefs, there is division, and a sect is formed.

Some people are careless and have misrepresented us, thinking that baptism by immersion is an item of our creed. They tell people that anyone who comes to break the bread with us must be baptized by immersion. However, I am happy to say that some brothers who have been breaking the bread with us have not yet been baptized by immersion. Some sisters who do not have an adequate understanding say that head covering is part of our creed, and that if a sister does not cover her head, she cannot break bread with us. However, we thank the Lord that there are sisters who do not cover their head yet still meet with us. Baptism by immersion is not our creed and neither is head covering. We do not have a creed; we only have the faith. Our faith is the seven ones in Ephesians 4. Whoever holds these seven ones, whether he is baptized by immersion or sprinkling, practices head covering, or has left his denomination or still remains in it, may break the bread with us if he so desires. We are willing to have fellowship with him at the Lord's table. Besides these seven ones of the fundamental faith, we do not have any creed. If there is a creed, there is division, which results in a sect.

Having a Special Fellowship

Many denominations have a special fellowship. When I was young, before every Holy Communion in the Baptist Church, the pastor would stand up and announce, "Those who are not our church members, please leave." This is a special fellowship. Whenever there is a special fellowship, there is division, which results in a sect.

I knew a German brother in Beijing and a British brother in Shanghai who both belonged to the Brethren Assembly, but they did not break the bread or fellowship together. I found out that they did not fellowship with each other because they had different views concerning the truth. Any fellowship that requires the same view concerning different items of the truth is a special fellowship. We should be able to fellowship even though there are different views concerning the truth. Are we not in Christ? Do we not have Christ as life? Are we not redeemed by the precious blood of the Lord? Since we are the same in these matters, we should be able to fellowship. Being the same in these items and still needing to share the same views concerning items of the truth before we can fellowship is to have a special fellowship. Consequently, division and sects will be formed.

Having a Fellowship That Is Isolated and Not Universal

Some people say that they do not have any of the above conditions and that they are non-sectarian and non-denominational. They do not have a special name, a set of special beliefs, or a special fellowship. However, we still need to know whether their fellowship is isolated rather than universal. Over the past thirty years, quite a number of people have seen the error of sects and left the denominations.

Because they do not have a special name, a set of special beliefs, or a special fellowship, they think that they are non-sectarian and non-denominational. But there may still be a problem. Although they do not have a special name, a set of special beliefs, or a special fellowship, they have an isolated local fellowship, not a universal fellowship. They do not fellowship with all the saints on the earth. As a result, they become a local sect. According to lesson 14, even though the churches are expressed in different localities, they are still the Body of Christ, and their fellowship is universal. Therefore, if a Christian fellowship is limited to its locality and has lost its universality and the nature of the Body of Christ, it will be a local sect and will result in a division in the church.

Having a Separate Administration in the Same Locality

Acts 14:23 says, "Appointed elders for them in every church," and Titus 1:5 says, "Appoint elders in every city." This proves that an elder in a church is an elder in the city. This also proves that the church can have only one administration in a locality because there can be only one church and one group of elders in a locality. If there are separate administrations of the church in the same locality, this constitutes a division. For example, there is a group in Taipei standing on the ground of locality and meeting to serve the Lord. Later another group of believers rises up and claims that they have left the sects and have no special name, special beliefs, or special fellowship; however, they are unwilling to join with the first group. There may be fellowship between groups, but there are separate administrations. In this situation, the second group has produced a division and become a sect. Because there should be only one church in a locality, the ground and administration of the local church should also be one. Since the second group came out of a sect, they should join themselves to the brothers who left the sects earlier so that there will be only one administration. Having a separate administration from the first group proves that they are still a sect. This is very important, because only in this way can the principle of one church in one locality be preserved.

An Organizational Connection in the Background

Some groups seemingly do not have a special name, special belief, or special fellowship, and they present themselves as being non-denominational. However, upon further investigation, we find that they are actually still connected to a Christian organization. This can be compared to a kite that is flying freely in the air but still under the control of the person holding the string. The one holding the string may be in the United States or England; hence, if we are not careful, we will be deceived.

Therefore, even though a group may pass the above five points, we still need to examine whether there is an organizational connection behind the scenes. Special fellowship between a certain group in a locality and another group in another locality is not an organizational connection. However, if a group's connection to another group is organizational, it will eventually become a divisive sect because there is an organization in the background.

These six points are the basis for discerning whether a Christian group will become a sect and result in division. The first three points—having special names, special beliefs, and special fellowships—are obvious and easy to detect. The last three points—having an isolated local fellowship, having separate administrations in the same locality, and having an organizational connection—are rather hidden and not as easy to detect. If a group can pass all these six points without any problem, it is meeting on the local ground and is pure, without any factor of division or element of sectarianism. Only this kind of church, this way of meeting, can be considered proper. Hence, we can participate in the meetings of such a Christian group. Any other groups must be rejected. May the Lord bless us to have a clear understanding concerning this matter.

OUR PRACTICE AND ATTITUDE

In relation to knowing the church, we have covered five lessons on what the church is, the expression of the church, the oneness of the church, the ground of the church, and the division of the church. We have seen that the church is neither a lifeless building nor an organization of man's intention. Rather, the church is an assembly of the called-out ones, the Body of Christ, and the house of the living God. Contrary to what most people believe, the church's expression is not in heaven or in eternity. Undeniably, the nature of the church is heavenly and eternal, but its expression is on earth and today. The church is neither abstract nor suspended in the air; rather, it is practical, real, concrete, and substantial. We can touch the church.

The expression of the church on earth is according to the principle of "one city, one church." Just as there is one church in the universe, the expression of the church in a locality should also be one. The church is altogether a matter of oneness. The source, production, nature, principle, existence, administration, fellowship, and testimony of the church are all one. Through one faith and one baptism, the church received one Spirit, one Lord, and one God, and thus became one Body and has one hope. Everything pertaining to the church is one; therefore, the church should not be divided. Apart from the ground of locality, the church should not have any other ground. As long as believers keep the ground of locality, the church will be one in practicality and will never be divided. These few points are clearly revealed in the Scriptures and were manifested in the condition of the early church.

However, the church has become deformed. The church

today is in confusion. It is not in the condition that was initially expressed on earth. Since Christians cannot leave the church, what should our attitude be in the midst of this confusion? We must be clear that our taking the right way is not merely for us to grow in the Lord and to serve. It is also for those who come after us. We should clear a straight path so that those who come after us will have a way to go on. For this reason we will now consider our practice and attitude in relation to the church.

We must understand God's attitude toward Christianity. The light and prophecies in the New Testament show how God feels about today's Christianity. On the one hand, God is extremely dissatisfied with the desolate and deformed situation. Whether divisions, human organization, mixture with the world, or giving opportunity to Satan, all of these are condemned by God. On the other hand, although God condemns these things, He has no intention of eliminating or forbidding them; rather, He has an attitude of tolerance. Hence, today's confusion will not only continue; it will even worsen. There will be more divisions in Christianity, and the worldly condition of Christianity will worsen as well.

Since this is God's attitude, we should also adopt this attitude. We are merely a group of weak and feeble ones; thus, we do not have the strength to correct these many errors. However, we can love the Lord, follow Him, and be faithful in taking the way that pleases Him in the midst of such confusion. This should be our basic attitude. Now we will cover a few points concerning our practice that need our attention.

OUR PRACTICE

Abandoning All Other Grounds and Returning to the Ground of Locality

The foremost thing regarding our practice is to abandon every improper ground. Whether it is the Roman Catholic Church or the different denominations and sects of Protestantism, we do not want it. We do not want the ground of Roman Catholicism, nor do we want the ground of any Protestant denomination or sect. We must completely abandon, fully depart from, and have nothing to do with these grounds. We should simply return to the ground of locality.

In lesson 16 the ground of locality was clearly presented. The ground of locality is the ground of oneness. The church is divided because the saints have left the ground of locality. If the saints would keep the ground of locality, the oneness of the church would be spontaneously preserved. Therefore, wherever we go, we should simply be Christians in that locality. If there is a group of brothers and sisters who meet on only the ground of locality, we must put ourselves in their midst and serve the Lord together with them. We do not want a sectarian ground; we should simply return to the local ground of oneness.

It is a very serious matter that in both the Old Testament and New Testament, God never allowed His people to have two grounds of service, two grounds of worship. He ordained that the children of Israel worship Him in the place where He chose to put His name, His habitation (Deut. 12:5-14; 14:22-26; 16:2, 11, 15-16). They were told not to worship God "in every place that you see" (12:13). Even though they later became corrupted and divided into two kingdoms—the kingdom of Israel in the north and the kingdom of Judah in the south—the place of their worship of God remained one. It remained in Jerusalem. God never allowed them to have a separate place, a separate ground, of worship. Although Jeroboam did his best to set up a center of worship in the kingdom of Israel and wanted the people to worship at the altar in Bethel, God never approved of this (1 Kings 12:26—13:5). God allowed Jeroboam to establish another kingdom, but He forbade him to set up another center of worship. This offended God to the uttermost.

If we apply this example today, God may tolerate another work for a period of time, but He will never tolerate setting up another ground for worship. Under normal circumstances, even the work should not be divided. A person's preaching of the gospel in school originates from the church, and his laboring in the hospital also originates from the church. All the work should be one. There may be a time when the brothers are not one in the work because their condition is not good.

God seemingly is willing to bear and permit this. But He condemns and cannot tolerate someone setting up another center of worship, another ground of service.

God allowed the Israelites to have only one center of worship in order to prevent division. Although they were outwardly divided into two kingdoms, they were still one in reality as long as the center of their worship was not divided. Similarly, if the ground of the church is not divided, it is a relatively light matter if the outward activities are somewhat divided. Strictly speaking, they are not divided in reality. However, we do not want any other ground, and we cannot be on any other ground. We can only be on the ground of the church, which is the ground of oneness, the ground of the expression of one church in a locality.

Concerning the ground, we need to add two points of explanation.

First, we must not remain on the ground of a denomination, the ground of organized Christianity. In typology, this is to come out of Babylon. All those who know the Scriptures cannot deny that in the eyes of God, the Roman Catholic Church is Babylon, a place of confusion. Although Protestantism divided from Roman Catholicism many years ago, the poison of Roman Catholicism has not yet been fully purged. Moreover, it seems that Protestantism is increasingly inclining toward and following Roman Catholicism. Hence, in God's eyes, the Protestant churches are also Babylon. In the same way that Babylon was versus Jerusalem, the Catholic Church and the Protestant churches are versus the genuine church. Therefore, we cannot remain on any denominational ground, any ground of organized Christianity. This can be compared to the children of Israel in the Old Testament choosing to return from their captivity instead of remaining in Babylon. We must come out from Roman Catholicism as well as from Protestantism (Rev. 18:4). We should not remain in the organized Babylon of Roman Catholicism and Protestantism.

Second, we should not linger on small, scattered grounds. Today there are small, scattered grounds among Christians. Some are family groups, others are fellowship groups in schools, and still others are congregations or chapels on certain streets and alleys. There are meetings that are so-called non-denominational, and there are also meetings that are for free groups. In type, these small, scattered grounds are the scattered places between Babylon and Jerusalem. There was a significant distance between Babylon and Jerusalem. When Ezra and those with him returned to Jerusalem from Babylon, the means of transportation was bad, and the journey was very long (Ezra 7:6-9; 8:21-23, 31-32). This difficult journey aptly typifies the situation of those coming out of organized Roman Catholicism and Christianity to return to the ground of the church today. Their return is not instantaneous; rather, it requires journeying a significant distance.

There may have been some Israelites who left Babylon but lingered on the way and did not reach Jerusalem because the journey was long and difficult. Their forefather Abraham also came out of Babylon and went to Canaan. Abraham's coming out of Ur of the Chaldeans was equivalent to his descendants' coming out of Babylon. Ur of the Chaldeans is the same location as Babylon, and Jerusalem is in Canaan. Abraham did not arrive in Canaan immediately after departing from Ur of the Chaldeans; rather, he stopped midway at Haran and later continued on to Canaan. During the return from captivity, there may have been a good number of Israelites who lingered in some scattered places on the way and did not return to Jerusalem. According to typology, this signifies the many saints today who have seen the evil of denominations and abandoned them, not remaining in organized Christianity, but have not returned to the ground of oneness, that is, the ground of locality. They are groups that linger "halfway." Some form student fellowship groups, and others form family gatherings. They claim that they are non-denominational, having seen the error of denominations. Realizing that the Lord condemns denominations, they have rejected and abandoned them. There are also those in free groups who reject organization. This means that they do not want chapels for worship or anything that relates to organization. On the negative side, this is correct, but on the positive side, they have not arrived at the ground on which God desires the church to stand. In terms of the Old Testament type, they have left Babylon but have not yet returned to Jerusalem. This is not adequate. By the Lord's mercy we should not only leave the improper ground of the denominations, but we should also return to the proper ground of oneness. We are not on the ground of organized denominations, nor should we linger in any of the numerous scattered grounds in between. This is the first item of our practice.

Standing on the Ground of the Local Church according to the Principle of the Local Church and by Virtue of the Nature of the Local Church, Our Meeting Together and Serving in Coordination, and Thereby Living the Proper Life of the Body of Christ and Expressing the Life of Christ to Bear the Testimony of the Church, and Being Built Together to Be God's Dwelling Place for Expressing God Himself and Doing God's Will

There are twelve points included in this item of our practice.

First, we are standing on the ground of the local church. This is a strong statement. We do not stand on the ground of any creed; we stand on the ground of locality, the ground of oneness of the local church.

Second, we are according to the principle of the local church. The principle of the local church is that the churches carry out their administration separately according to their locality, each being responsible to the Lord. The churches cannot form federations or have headquarters.

Third, we have the nature of the local church. Although the church is expressed locally, it is universal. Hence, even though the administration of the church is local and independent, the fellowship of the church is universal. The local church has fellowship with all the local gatherings that stand on the ground of the church. Hence, the nature of the local church is universal and is of the Body.

Fourth, we meet together. Our meeting together is by virtue of the nature of the fellowship of the church; hence, we emphasize meetings. Our worship, service, and work are carried out through meetings. Meetings can be regarded as our collective move and corporate living.

Fifth, we serve in coordination. We also emphasize coordinated service. We do not merely listen to sermons or conduct Sunday services; we also learn to serve. In the matter of service, we do not approve of independence or agree with individualism. Since the church is an assembly, a Body, the saints should coordinate together and have a coordinated service, the service of the Body (Eph. 4:12, 16).

Sixth, we live the proper life of the Body of Christ. By the Lord's grace, we desire to live out the proper life of the Body of Christ on the ground of the church in order that the Body of Christ may be manifested as a reality among the churches in all the localities (Rom. 12:4-5; 1 Cor. 12:27).

Seventh, we express the life of Christ. When we live out the life of the Body of Christ, the life of Christ is spontaneously expressed and flows out. This not only causes Christ to be expressed but also causes man to receive the supply of life.

Eighth, we bear the testimony of the church. The totality of the preceding seven points is the testimony of the church. This testimony involves being a witness of Christ (Acts 1:8). The church is a vessel that bears the testimony of Christ. All our gatherings in various localities are vessels bearing the testimony of Christ. The testimony we bear is not of any particular truth but of the Christ who incorporates the truth.

Ninth, we are being built together. We do not only emphasize individual spirituality, but even more we emphasize the building of the church in life. We emphasize individual edification so that we can be built together (Eph. 2:22; 1 Pet. 2:5). We believe that what God needs today is not many spiritual individuals but a built-up church. Therefore, it is only by being built together that we can meet God's need.

Tenth, we are God's dwelling place. God desires to gain a house on earth to be His dwelling place (1 Tim. 3:15; Eph. 2:22) so that He and all those who belong to Him can dwell in it. We are being built together in order to become God's dwelling place so that God and His children can have a home, a dwelling place on earth.

Eleventh, we express God Himself. Our being built together in order to be God's dwelling place not only affords God a place to dwell but also enables Him to express Himself. Our gatherings in every locality should express God and cause people to sense that God is among us (1 Cor. 14:25).

Twelfth, we are doing God's will. We desire that God would grant us grace so that His will can be carried out in all the meetings of every locality (Matt. 6:10). We do not want human opinion to have any ground among us; our desire is to accomplish God's will (Heb. 13:21).

I believe that we are all clear concerning these twelve points. These points cover the ground, the principle, the nature, the meeting, the coordination, the Body life, the expression of the life of Christ, the testimony of the church, the building, God's dwelling place, God's expression, and God's will. We fully advocate these twelve points and emphasize them in a balanced way without bias or preference. Some in Christianity emphasize the matter of expressing Christ and living out the life of Christ but neglect the ground. Others emphasize the matter of the church having the Body life and the members not being independent or individualistic but neglect the principle and nature of the church. We do not want to be like this. The twelve points we have presented are comprehensive. We do not merely emphasize the ground while neglecting the expression of Christ, the testimony of the church, God's will, and so forth. We should not and will not neglect these matters. If we have the ground but do not have the expression of Christ or the practical testimony of the church, we are no longer God's dwelling place where He can be expressed and where His will can be accomplished. If this were so, our advocating would merely be empty, dead letters. Hence, we must have the Body life, the expression of Christ, and the testimony of the church. We must also be God's dwelling place for His expression and the accomplishing of His will.

However, if we have a practical and proper desire for the Body life, the expression of Christ, the testimony of the church, and God's dwelling place for His expression and the accomplishing of His will, the preceding points regarding the ground, the principle, the nature, the meeting, and the coordination of the church are indispensable. Without these preceding five points, it is difficult to have the subsequent seven points. We must have the proper ground upon which we gather; it must be in the principle of "one church, one city" with an independent, local administration; there must be the nature of the Body, the universal fellowship; and there must be the practice of meeting and coordination. When these five points are fulfilled, we can live the Body life by the Holy Spirit to express the life of Christ, bear the complete testimony of the church, and be God's dwelling place, expressing God Himself and accomplishing His will. Thus, in our practice we must pay equal attention to these twelve points. What we practice in every locality is only these twelve points.

Not Forming a Unique Sect and Establishing "Our Meetings" in Different Places

We will not form a unique sect. Although we differ from others, because of the ground we absolutely will not form a unique sect, establishing "our meetings" in different localities. Rather, we desire to meet and serve the Lord in various places on the ground of the oneness of the church, that is, the ground of locality, with all those who repudiate division and reject sectarianism.

Tolerating Different Doctrinal Views or Practices That Do Not Damage the Basic Faith

Today in Christianity, people have different views and interpretations of the Scriptures and hold different practices concerning the meetings and administration of the church. These can all be tolerated, provided that they do not damage the basic faith or the fundamental truth of salvation. Hence, although we practice baptism by immersion, if some want to be sprinkled because they feel at peace being sprinkled, we should tolerate it. Keeping the Lord's Day is according to the truth in the Bible, but if some brothers hold to keeping the Sabbath, we should not contend with them. As long as these understandings or views do not damage the basic, fundamental faith, we should tolerate them.

The fundamental faith of salvation is the one faith in Ephesians 4. This one faith can never be shaken, nor can anything be added to or subtracted from it. Different understandings and views on such things as head covering, baptism by immersion or sprinkling, breaking bread once a week or daily, and practicing embracing one another or foot-washing at the bread-breaking meeting do not damage the fundamental faith of salvation. We cannot say that a sister is saved if her head is covered and not saved if her head is not covered. Neither can we say that a person is saved if he is baptized by immersion but not saved if he is sprinkled. These matters do not affect a person's salvation; hence, we can tolerate them.

Brothers and sisters, we should not merely speak in this way, but we should have this attitude in our practice. If a brother is willing to return to the ground of oneness and meet with us but cannot drop the Sabbath and must break bread with a few brothers on the Sabbath, our attitude must be that we would not only let them break bread but would even break bread with them. Some may ask, "Would this not create disorder in the church and be improper?" We must bear in mind that being proper is a human concept. God sometimes tolerates things that are improper according to human concepts. In the New Testament the teaching of the apostles did not require the church to define each matter in a definite way. For example, concerning the matter of keeping days in Romans 14, the apostle did not mandate that a certain day must never be kept and another day must be kept. His attitude was that he who keeps that day, keeps it to the Lord, and he who does not keep that day, does not keep it to the Lord. The same also applies to eating. Paul did not mandate what we must eat and what we should not eat. Rather, he said, "He who eats, let him not despise him who does not eat; and he who does not eat, let him not judge him who eats" (v. 3). This shows that the apostle was general in his attitude toward these matters. Some may ask, "Is this not disorderly?" We must be assured that if we all learn to live before the Lord, any differences that we may initially have will gradually be eliminated.

Some brothers and sisters have truly misrepresented us in matters such as these. Someone once said that he wanted to break the bread with us, but another brother responded, "No, you may not break the bread with us because you were sprinkled and not baptized by immersion. The church will have baptisms a month from now. You can come and break the bread with us after you have been baptized." There was also a seeking sister who wanted to break bread with us. When she saw many sisters with their heads covered, she asked a sister, "Should I also cover my head when I come to break the bread?" The sister carelessly replied, "Yes, you should cover your head; otherwise, you may not break the bread with us." When things like these happen, they cause trouble. These misrepresentations give the impression that we are an "immersion sect" or a "head-covering sect." While some may wait to be baptized by immersion before they break the bread, others may object and say, "Have I not been baptized? If I am not baptized by immersion, does this mean that I am not saved? Sprinkling was good enough for me. Why must I be immersed?" When things like this happen, they cause trouble. Although we have never advocated this, the ones who spoke these things misrepresented us.

Recently I heard that on a Lord's Day evening four or five years ago, a believer came to a meeting hall of the church in Taipei to attend the bread-breaking meeting. When the ushering brother noticed that he did not have a nametag, he immediately stopped him and said, "You may not break the bread without a nametag." The believer replied, "I also am a saved brother." The ushering brother, however, would not permit him and eventually asked him to leave. Brothers and sisters, it would be awful if this had continued, for we would have become a strict "nametag-wearing sect." There are things to consider when receiving brothers, but when someone comes to break bread, we should not interfere too much and cause his spirit to be damaged. We can allow him to break the bread and then check concerning the condition of his salvation and take care of receiving him after the meeting. This may include giving him a nametag.

Hence, I hope the responsible brothers in all the churches

will be more cautious concerning these matters. Otherwise, a certain regulation may be established that would cause us to become a sect and thus damage the oneness of God's children. In fact, all God's children can break bread to remember the Lord with us as long as they are saved and they are touched by the Lord to do so. Wearing nametags is merely a convenience for fellowship and to know one another. There is no need to wear a nametag if we are familiar with one another. Our nametags do not guard the Lord's table. On the one hand, we should not casually allow people to break bread. We should know those who come to break bread with us. We should fellowship with them and introduce them. On the other hand, the nametag is not a checkpoint or a prerequisite; wearing a nametag is not a requirement. On these matters we must learn to be general and tolerant.

Suppose a sister does not feel to wear a black head covering but wants to wear a white head covering instead. We should be able to say, "I will wear a white head covering with you." When a brother says, "I must be sprinkled and not immersed," we should be able to say, "Thank the Lord. If you are sprinkled, we can still break bread together." Although his practice does not seem to be ideal, it is not necessarily a problem. The problem lies in whether or not we insist. If we do not insist, the Holy Spirit Himself will work and gradually bring the brothers and sisters into oneness. Our experience proves this. I hope we will all see that these kinds of things are tolerable.

Suppose someone thinks that only one cup should be used in the bread-breaking meeting, and another thinks that it is all right to use many cups. While using one cup is more scriptural, if some insist on having many cups, we should be general and not be divided over this. The few places I visited abroad all used many cups in the bread-breaking meeting. I did not lose the peace, and I enjoyed breaking the bread with them. In New York City the brothers were recovering the breaking of bread, and they were considering whether to use one large cup or many small cups. When they asked me concerning this, I said, "This is your church affair, and you should decide for yourselves. If you feel to use one large cup, then use one large cup, or if you feel to use many small cups, then use many small cups. You decide this matter by yourselves." Eventually, they decided to use one large cup.

These illustrations show that there are no criteria in these matters. Although there is a standard, we should not insist, for example, that the Sabbath is wrong and the Lord's Day is right. There is such a standard, but the apostle's attitude was general and tolerant. Some may feel that keeping the Sabbath is not right and want to keep the Lord's Day. Thank the Lord that they keep it to the Lord. Or they may feel that the Sabbath is right and keep the Sabbath. Thank the Lord that they keep it to the Lord. We should bear with all these and not criticize. Likewise, although baptism by immersion is scriptural, if someone wants to be sprinkled, he can be sprinkled. He can be saved without being immersed, and he can be spiritual without being immersed. We can tolerate all these things.

These words are not only for others but even more they are for us. We should never take these matters as our faith, our creed. We do not have a creed, and we have only the one faith spoken of in Ephesians 4. Only this one faith can never be shaken. One God, one Lord, one Spirit, one faith, one baptism, one Body, and one hope—these seven items are indispensable. This is the fundamental faith. Besides these, we may have some other things or we may not have them, and we may speak this way or we may speak that way. We should have a gracious heart and a non-contentious spirit to allow the Holy Spirit to work freely among us. If this is the case, the Holy Spirit will gradually bring us to a point where we are in one accord and practice according to the Lord's word.

Being Willing to Meet and Serve the Lord by Standing on the Ground of Oneness with All Christians of Orthodox Faith Despite Their Differing Opinions, as Long as They Are Willing to Not Be Divided and Are Willing to Abolish Any Existing Division

Although this is similar to the previous item, it means

that we are not afraid of people having opinions, but we are afraid of people being divisive. As long as they are willing to not be divisive and are willing to abolish any existing division, any opinion or view can be accepted. We do not require other believers to drop their views before meeting with us, but we require them to abolish their divisions. We can tolerate anything, but not division. Whether immersion or sprinkling, large cups or small cups, leavened bread or unleavened bread, head covering or no head covering—all these are not a problem. We can tolerate all such things. However, there is one thing we cannot tolerate; we can never tolerate division, because once there is division, the ground of the oneness of the church is lost.

Receiving All Believers with Different Views Except Those Who Meet the Conditions for Removal from Fellowship

We receive all believers, regardless of their views. As long as they are saved, we are willing to receive them. However, we cannot accept any believer who meets the conditions for removal from fellowship.

There are only two categories of believers that meet the conditions for removal from fellowship. In the first category, referred to in 1 Corinthians 5:11, are sinful men who are extremely filthy and who insult the Lord's name, such as fornicators, coveters, idolaters, revilers, drunkards, and the rapacious. In the second category, referred to in 2 John 7-11, are those who go beyond the teaching of Christ, speaking heresies that Christ is not God, that He did not become flesh, that His death did not bear our sins, that His blood cannot redeem us from our sins, and that He did not resurrect from the dead. Such heresies can be seen in today's so-called Modernism, which promotes the belief of the antichrists, who are an unbelieving sect. Those who accept this heresy claim that they believe in Christ but in fact resist Christ. This is a pernicious sin. We cannot receive anyone who is related to either of these two categories of sins, even if he is a Christian in name. If he has already been received, he must be removed. Apart from these, we would receive anyone who is saved, regardless of his views or opinions.

Desiring to Have Fellowship with All the Brothers and Sisters in the Denominations but Not Being Willing to Have Any Part in Their Denominations or Sects

We are willing to fellowship with all the brothers and sisters in the Lord, regardless of the sects they are in, even if they are in the Roman Catholic Church. We are willing to have fellowship with them, but we absolutely do not want to have a part in the denominations to which they belong. Brothers and sisters as individuals are one thing, but the denominations and sects that they are in are another. We must differentiate between the two. Sometimes when we forsake the denominations and sects, we forsake the brothers and sisters who are in them. At other times we do just the opposite. As we receive the brothers and sisters from the denominations, the denominations to which they belong are also brought with them. This is because we have not differentiated between individuals and organizations.

This can be compared to eating fish. When we eat the flesh, we must spew out the bones. We should not spew out the flesh because we do not want the bones, nor should we swallow the bones because we want to eat the flesh. We should be able to distinguish between the two: the brothers and sisters belong to us, and we want them, but the denominations and sects do not belong to us, and we refuse them. We want neither the Protestant churches nor the Roman Catholic Church. We want all the saved brothers and sisters in them. We should have fellowship and contact with them.

The degree of fellowship and contact we have with them depends on the relationship, effect, and consequence that this kind of fellowship brings to the denominations and sects. If the fellowship causes the denominations and sects to be built up or the testimony of the local church to suffer loss, it should not be carried out. Therefore, no one can predetermine the degree of contact and fellowship that should occur. It must be carefully considered before the Lord for the sake of the Lord.

Receiving but Not Committing Responsibilities in the Service to the Brothers and Sisters with Different Views

Although we receive brothers and sisters with different views, we cannot commit any responsibility in the service to them. This prevents problems in the service. Receiving is one thing, but bearing responsibility in the service is another.

We feel that in raising us up the Lord has commissioned us, and we should be faithful and responsible to His commission. Therefore, although the Lord's table is open to all God's children and every believer can partake of it, we cannot be so open related to responsibility in the service. Only brothers and sisters with the same view should join in and bear the burden together. If those who do not have the same view bear responsibilities, neither they nor we will profit from it. We should be able to make this distinction. Being unable to bear responsibility in the service should not prevent one from being received, nor does being received mean that he can bear responsibility in the service. This matter is not so simple.

For example, we should not refuse a brother who emphasizes sprinkling and wants to break bread with us, even though we practice immersion. We should still receive him. However, after receiving him, there will be problems if we ask him to immediately take up responsibility in the service. He will bring in his ideas and opinions and contend and argue with others. As a result, neither he nor others will benefit. Hence, we need to exercise wisdom in these matters. There is no problem with breaking bread and fellowshipping with this brother, but giving him responsibility in the service should not be done quickly. This does not mean that we will never give him responsibility but that this needs to be done slowly. We need to find opportunities to have thorough fellowship with him. Perhaps our views are wrong, and we should be adjusted; or his views are wrong, and he can be gradually subdued. In any case, we must have the same view in order to bear the same responsibility.

Some who are still not clear concerning this may think that we are being too narrow. I would simply ask, "Can every believer be an elder?" Of course not. Even though every saved person is a brother and can come to break bread, not everyone can come here and be an elder. This is because breaking bread is a matter of salvation, but the eldership involves a commission of responsibility that can be assumed only when a person arrives at a certain level in spiritual condition. Here is another illustration: While we all have equal opportunity to serve, not everyone can give a message. Everyone can break bread, but not everyone can stand up to minister the Word. This is because ministering the Word is a matter of commission, a matter of responsibility. It is impossible for an eighty-year-old grandfather, a fifty-year-old father, and an eight-year-old child to bear the same responsibility in a family. At mealtime there is no distinction between the three at the dinner table. However, in relation to bearing responsibility for the family, no responsibility would be given to an eight-year-old or even to someone who is eighteen years old. This is because they are not matured. Giving them responsibility for the family can only cause problems. It is all right to let the children do some daily, trivial tasks, but when weighty matters arise in the family, only the father, the mother, and the older brothers and sisters can participate.

We must see that although the Lord's table is open, responsibility in service is restricted. It is not wrong for brothers with different views to invite people and accompany them to gospel meetings, but the responsibilities of the church cannot be committed to them. Responsibility can be given only to those who are more experienced and mature. I hope that all the leading ones in the churches can understand this and will not give responsibility to someone simply because he has been received or not receive a person because he is unable to bear any responsibility. We must be able to discern between receiving someone and committing responsibilities to him.

Encouraging the Brothers and Sisters, Whenever They Arrive in a Locality, to First Look for a Meeting That Is on the Ground of the Church in Order to Meet and Serve Together with Such Saints; If No Meeting Is Found, Endeavoring to Preach the Gospel, Lead People to Salvation, and Lead the Believers to Know the Church, and Establishing a Meeting on the Ground of the Church with Them

Whenever we go to a place, we should first find out if there is a meeting that is on the ground of the church in that locality. If there is a meeting on the ground of the church that is proper in nature, not belonging to a sect or denomination, we must meet and serve with them, regardless of whether we knew of or fellowshipped with them previously. We must not set up another meeting. If we set up another meeting that is apart from them in that locality, we are creating a sect; we are dividing the church.

If such a meeting cannot be found, we need to be faithful and not fear the hardship. On one hand, we should not take part in a denomination that may be there, and on the other hand, we should endeavor to preach the gospel to lead people to be saved, to know the church, and to have a clear understanding of the ground and the way of the church so that a proper meeting on the ground of the church can be established with them.

OUR ATTITUDE

Now we come to our attitude, which is our declaration.

Our Not Being Either the Roman Catholic Church nor a Protestant Church, and Our Recognizing Neither the Roman Catholic Church nor the Protestant Churches

Just as we do not consider the Roman Catholic Church to be proper, we also do not consider the Protestant churches to be proper. They have both forsaken the proper ground of the church. Hence, we do not want to be in the Roman Catholic Church, nor do we want to be in the Protestant churches. We are neither the Roman Catholic Church nor a Protestant church. Just as we do not recognize the Roman Catholic Church, we also do not recognize the Protestant churches.

Our Not Being the So-called Brethren, Whether Exclusive or Open

The Brethren were raised up over the past one hundred years. We are not the Brethren. We are neither the exclusive Brethren nor the open Brethren.

Our Not Being the Small Free Groups That Have Left the Catholic Church or the Protestant Churches but Do Not Have a Definite Ground— Our Meetings Standing on the Definite Ground of the Church

We believe that it is not adequate to merely depart from the Catholic Church or the Protestant churches yet still not return to the ground of the church. Therefore, we are not small free groups that do not have a definite ground. Our meetings stand on the definite ground of the church, that is, the ground of locality.

Our Not Considering Only Ourselves to Be the Local Church in a Locality; Our Being Only a Part of the Local Church, Standing on the Ground of the Local Church in Every Place and Bearing the Testimony of the Church according to the Principle of the Local Church and by the Nature of the Local Church

Some brothers have said that only the saints meeting with us are the local church. This kind of speaking is too much. We should say only that the believers meeting with us are a part of the local church. Although according to the ground, principle, and nature there is no question that we are the local church, according to quantity we are only a part of the local church. For example, the local church in Taipei, in principle, includes all the believers in Taipei; however, because of the division of the church, many believers are segregated in denominations. They have departed from the ground of the local church and left us, the minority, to stand on the ground of the local church. Hence, in reality we are only part of the local church in Taipei. If all the believers would return to the local ground, the church in Taipei would include all the believers in the local church.

Our Acknowledging That Those Who Are Saved in the Denominations and Sects, Including the Catholic Church, Are Our Brothers and Sisters in the Lord and Members of Christ Even Though They Have Lost the Ground of the Church

Today there are saved ones in every sect and denomination, including the Catholic Church. We acknowledge that they are our brothers and sisters and are members of the Body of Christ, yet they have lost the ground of the church and no longer stand on the ground of the church. They can be compared to family members who have left home and have gone to other places.

According to the Revelation of the Scriptures, Our Believing That Both the Roman Catholic Church and the Protestant Churches Will Not Be Changed or Abolished, Thus Not Expecting Them to Change, but Hoping That People Will Depart from Them and Return to the Ground of the Church

When some brothers and sisters who love the Lord see that the denominations are wrong, they endeavor to change or eliminate them. However, the revelation in the Scriptures reveals that neither the Roman Catholic Church nor the Protestant denominations will be changed or abolished. Therefore, we should not expect them to change, because this expectation will never be realized. We can only hope that individuals will depart from them and return to the ground of the church (Rev. 18:4). For example, not one denomination in China has changed in the last thirty years. The Presbyterian Church has not changed, the Baptist Church has not changed, and the Methodist Church has not changed; no denomination has ever changed. Although some of them admit that they are wrong, they remain unchanged and have not been abolished. On the contrary, they have become stronger, and their condition has worsened. Thus, there is no need for us to hope that they will change. Frankly speaking, all such hopes are wild and false hopes that will only disappoint. All effort to change the denominations is a futile waste of energy. It is clearly shown in Revelation that the church in Thyatira (2:25), the church in Sardis (3:3), and the church in Laodicea will remain until the Lord comes. This means that the Roman Catholic Church, the Protestant denominations and sects, and even the lukewarm Brethren will remain until the Lord comes. They are all deeply rooted, and there is no way to change them. Hence, we can only hope that some, like Martin Luther, will come out of the Roman Catholic Church, and others, like the brothers and sisters throughout the generations, will come out of the various organizations of Protestantism and return to the ground of the oneness of the church.

Our Believing That Any Form of Union That Preserves the Ground of the Denominations and Is Reluctant to Forsake Such Ground Is Not Absolute, Is of No Value, and Is Unprofitable to the Testimony of the Church; Such a Unity Dividing While Uniting and Uniting While Dividing

In today's Christianity denominations and sects are reluctant to forsake their ground but desire to be united with one another. They either organize joint evangelistic meetings and joint choirs, or they exchange ideas concerning their work. The pastor of one congregation may preach in a second congregation, and the pastor of the second congregation may lead the first congregation. It seems as if everyone is united in the Lord and not divided, yet in fact, this is a kind of "shaking hands over the fence." Apparently, they are shaking hands and communicating, but in fact, there is a tall fence between them. Although they are standing on either side of the fence, they are joined by shaking hands over the fence. They are willing to shake hands, but they are not willing to tear down the fence. This kind of union that divides while uniting is totally unprofitable to the testimony of the church and is even harmful. This is not an absolute union. It seems to be a union, but it is not actually a union. We should not participate or approve of this kind of union; we should strictly condemn it.

This kind of union brings in confusion and damages the principle of being "according to their kind" as spoken of in the Bible (Gen. 1:11-12, 21, 24-25). This is an obscure situation, a condition of being divided yet united and united yet divided, a condition of being neither black nor white. They might as well be what they are—divided and not united. God's law ordains that everything should be according to its kind. If they are divided, they should be divided; if they are united, they should be united. Being divided while seeking unity and promoting unity when they are divided is confusion. This is sin upon sin. If unity is desired, why is there division? Unity should condemn the sin of division. If being divided is right, why is there a need for unity? The desire to unite after being divided proves that division is wrong. Since division is wrong, it should be dealt with thoroughly. However, having no desire to deal with it thoroughly, they attempt to be united. This can be compared to a woman who marries someone she should not have married and later wants to marry someone she should have married; yet she is reluctant to leave the first. On the one hand, she is reluctant to leave the first, and on the other hand, she wants to unite with the one she should have married. This is sin upon sin. But this is the situation in today's Christianity. The situation of being divided yet wanting to be united is a great confusion in God's eyes. We dare not have any part in it.

Our Believing That All the Work outside of the Church That Is Not for the Building Up of the Local Churches Should Not Exist; Thus, Not Being Willing to Have Any Part in It

In the sphere of today's Christianity much work is being done outside of the church that does not result in the building up of the local churches. Concerning God's plan for the church, we feel that this work is a contradiction and damage; hence, we do not wish to have any part in it.

Even with Such an Attitude, Our Still Confessing That Our Great God Has the Sovereign Authority to Use People Who Are Different from Us; His Being Able to Use Even Those in the Catholic Church, Which Is Condemned

We acknowledge that although there is much work that is not carried out in the church and is not for the building up of the local church, there are still some who have received some blessings from God. Because God is gracious and merciful in this age of grace, wherever there is an opening, an opportunity, God's grace will flow, just as water seeps through the cracks. We cannot, however, approve of such works based solely on this supply, concluding that God fully delights in such works and workers. In the book of Daniel, Nebuchadnezzar was a Gentile king who worshipped idols. We cannot say that God delighted in him, but God used him to accomplish His will. The book of Job shows that God can use even His enemy, Satan. Oh, the Lord is great! He can use all kinds of people, even those whom He dislikes quite much. Thus, it is one thing to be used by the Lord, and it is another thing to be well pleasing to and approved of by the Lord. We cannot approve of a work based on God's use of it. Nevertheless, because the Lord is great, even though we do not approve of these works or wish to take part in them, we should not interfere with them. We want only to serve the Lord in lowliness, with a pure conscience, and according to His shining and pleasure in order to bear the testimony that He has committed to us.

LESSON NINETEEN

SERVING THE LORD

THE STATUS FOR SERVICE

Once we are saved, our status is completely changed. After our salvation there are many aspects to our status. For example, we are children of God in His household and citizens in His kingdom (Eph. 2:19). We are also priests of God. Revelation 1:5-6 and 5:9-10 say that God saved us in order to make us not only His people but also His priests. The basis for our service after we are saved is our status as priests.

Priests are a group of "professionals," just as teachers, lawyers, doctors, and engineers specialize in a profession. Teachers specialize in teaching, doctors in healing the sick, lawyers in handling legal affairs, and engineers in construction work. Priests specialize in serving God. Serving God is the profession of priests.

In today's Catholicism and degraded Protestantism only a minority of people serves as priests. In Catholicism there is a group of people called priests, and in Protestantism there is a group of people called pastors. These people specialize in serving God, that is, in being priests, but the rest of the people are not priests. This condition is altogether unscriptural. God's speaking in the New Testament clearly unveils that every believer is a priest of God. God desires that all those who belong to Him would serve Him.

The Old Testament shows that God's original intention was for all the children of Israel to serve Him as priests. According to Exodus 19:6 God wanted them to be a kingdom of priests, a kingdom in which every Israelite would be a priest. However, because they worshipped the idol at the foot of Mount Sinai, they fell from God's goal, and God separated a group of people, the tribe of Levi, to be priests. As a result, there were two groups of people among the children of Israel—the priests and the congregation, the rest of the people.

In the New Testament, however, God no longer wants such an abnormal situation to exist. God has no intention of having a group of people who are priests and another group of people who are a congregation. Rather, God desires all the believers to be priests. Hence, in the New Testament, the saints are the priests, and the priests are saints. Nevertheless, the Roman Catholic Church brought the degraded condition and system of Judaism into the church and divided the saints into two classes—the clergy and the laity. This was a great mistake and heresy. It is sad that during the Reformation, Martin Luther did not completely purge out this evil influence of Roman Catholicism. Hence, in today's Protestantism there still remains the distinction between clergy and laity. Even to this day in the English-speaking world, the title of *Rev.,* meaning "Reverend," is added to the name of pastors. This is a confounding heresy. This does not come from the New Jerusalem but is a product of Babylon the Great. It is also a great offense to God. One who serves God in a proper way could never bear the title *Reverend.* Although there are some among us who serve full time, this refers only to a way of service. These ones are absolutely not clergy; hence, we should never add the title *Reverend* to their name or call them pastors. Every believer is a saint, a holy person, that is, one who serves God. We should never forget our status.

We are not saved to go to heaven but to be priests who serve God. When we were saved, we may not have been clear that God did not save us to go to heaven but to be priests to Him. Going to heaven may have been sufficient for us, but God wants us to be priests. Hence, not only do we have the status of priests (Rev. 1:6), but we are also a holy priesthood offering spiritual sacrifices acceptable to God (1 Pet. 2:5). All believers are priests.

The believers also have another status pertaining to service—they are slaves of God. We are not merely servants of

God; we are slaves of God. Being a servant is general, but being a slave is specific. When we speak of a slave, we are referring to a person who has sold himself to be a bondservant (Exo. 21:5-6). Romans 6:22 and 1 Corinthians 7:22-23 say that we are slaves whom God bought with a great price. God is not only our God but also our Master. As priests we must serve God devotedly, and as slaves we must serve Him faithfully.

We have yet another status related to service—we are members of the Body of Christ. Romans 12:4-5 says that we are members one of another. Since we are members of the Body, we have certain functions. Just as every member in our body carries out its function, so also every member in the Body of Christ has its function. This function is to serve.

Our statuses after salvation—a priest, a slave, and a member of the Body of Christ—speak forth our need to serve God. These are our statuses for service.

THE LIFE FOR SERVICE

Service is not only a matter of status but also a matter of life. In the universe every life bears a certain characteristic and does certain things. Plant life produces flowers and bears fruit. Animal life also has a particular behavior and living. This is an unalterable law. The life that we obtained through salvation is Christ Himself. This life also has its characteristics, one of which is holiness. For this reason, whenever we lead a holy life, the life within us feels at ease, but whenever we do not lead a holy life, this life feels uncomfortable. This is because the life within us has the characteristic of being holy. Another characteristic of the life of Christ is love. Whenever we love others, the life within us feels comfortable, but whenever we hate and envy others, this life feels uneasy and uncomfortable.

Another characteristic of the life of Christ is serving. The life of Christ is a serving life (Mark 10:45). If this serving life within us is not allowed to serve, we may feel like a bird that is locked in a cage and not allowed to fly. This is truly a suffering to the bird. A characteristic of the bird's life is to fly. If a bird is released from a cage and allowed to fly freely, it will surely enjoy flying and have a wonderful time. Likewise, the more a Christian serves, the more he feels released inwardly, because a characteristic of the life of Christ is to serve.

Acts 3:13 and 26 and 4:27 and 30 show that Christ is the Servant of God. Philippians 2:7 says that when the Lord became a man, He took the form of a slave. We often say that our Lord is the Lord of all, but we forget that He is also a Servant. When He was on earth, He was a Servant. Among the four Gospels, the Gospel of Mark speaks particularly of Him as a Servant. In 10:45 the Lord said clearly that He did not come to be served, but to serve. This shows a characteristic of His life. If we serve according to this characteristic, we will feel comfortable, free, released, and joyful within. On the contrary, if we do not allow this characteristic of serving to freely operate in us, we will definitely be unhappy.

Every believer has had this experience. If we do not serve the Lord, we have no inward joy. Serving the Lord is troublesome and may at times be burdensome, yet we inwardly feel joyful and comfortable because this is a matter of life. This can be compared to eating. Our need to eat adds many troubles to our human life. It would be wonderful if we did not need to eat. However, we must eat because it is a characteristic of life, a necessity of life. It is the same with serving the Lord. Although it is not simple or easy to serve the Lord, it is more of a suffering when we do not serve Him. This is because serving is a matter of life, a requirement of life, and a characteristic of life.

THE DESIRE TO SERVE

Serving the Lord is also a matter of the heart, a matter of desire. When we speak concerning the heart, the desire to serve the Lord, we must first speak of the Lord's love. One who is genuinely saved has tasted the Lord's love. Even an indifferent Christian, a backsliding believer, has been touched by the Lord's love. According to the Chinese Union Version, in 2 Corinthians 5:14-15 the apostle Paul says that as we consider how the Lord died for all, His love will motivate us and cause us to no longer live to ourselves but to Him. This story of love can never be quenched in a Christian, and it always stirs our heart, our desire, so that we cannot help but serve God.

Moreover, in Romans 12:1 the apostle Paul says, "I exhort you...through the compassions of God to present your bodies a living sacrifice...to God, which is your reasonable service." To serve God in this way is reasonable; it is logical and rational, because we are people saved by grace and loved by God. Who does not have a desire to repay God for the grace he has received? Who can withhold his response to being loved by God? Since we have received the Lord's grace and love, we spontaneously have a response of love in our heart and are willing to present ourselves to the Lord to serve Him.

For this reason, our serving the Lord is also a matter of our heart. Every believer has felt the Lord's love within him and has been motivated by this love. Therefore, there is a spontaneous response in us to want to serve God and live for Him. There is no reluctance to serve in this life, and there should not be any reluctance in us.

The Lord never forces or compels us to do anything. He asks us to serve Him by stirring our heart with His gentle love so that we would serve Him willingly. When the Lord appeared to Peter at the Sea of Tiberias and asked Peter to serve Him, He asked him three times, "Do you love Me?" (John 21:15-17). It was by this love that the Lord attracted and motivated Peter to rise up and serve Him by shepherding His sheep. The Lord did not come to force Peter to serve Him; rather, He motivated and attracted Peter inwardly with love. His love was the factor that made it impossible for Peter not to serve Him.

Therefore, serving the Lord involves our status, a requirement of life, and the desire of our heart. These three points show that it is perfectly right and reasonable for us to serve the Lord. As far as our status and position are concerned, we are priests. Our occupation should be to serve God. If we do not serve God, we have the wrong occupation. This is similar to a doctor who does not see patients but instead sweeps the streets. His occupation has completely changed. As far as the divine life within us is concerned, there is a characteristic of service. The more we live by this life, the more we will serve.

This is a wonderful matter. Furthermore, as the Lord's love motivates us, we have a heart for Him and we desire to serve Him. Hence, it is logical and reasonable from every aspect for us to serve the Lord.

THE PRACTICE OF SERVICE

There is also the practice of service. We now have the status, the standing, to serve, the life to serve, and the desire to serve because of the Lord's love. But how do we actually serve?

Serving in the Church

In whatever we do, we need a proper ground, a proper setting. For example, a school is the proper setting for a teacher, a courtroom is the proper setting for a lawyer, a hospital is the proper setting for a doctor, and a workplace is the proper setting for an engineer. Similarly, to serve God, we must be in the church. The church is the proper setting for us to serve God. Without the church and without being in the church, our service would have no setting and would be aimless. For example, without the church where can we take someone whom we have led to salvation? We cannot tell him to simply pray and read the Bible at home. This is inadequate. How can we shepherd a person and lead him to serve the Lord after he is saved? The church alone is the answer to this question. The church is the proper setting to render the proper service. Hence, our service must be in the church. If we desire to serve the Lord, we must resolve the matter of the church and be in the church.

It is pitiful, however, that the church as the setting for service has been damaged by Satan. The situation of the church today is confusing, making it difficult for those who have risen up to love and serve God to know where they should serve and where they should bring the fruit of their service. It seems that there is no place for them to give themselves to. This is today's pitiful condition. This is the reason we spoke concerning knowing the church in the previous lessons. According to what was spoken in those lessons, we must identify the proper church and be in such a church to serve

God. If there is not a proper church in the place where we are, we must be faithful so that through us the Lord can raise up a church in that place that is according to His heart's desire and on the proper ground. In this way there is the ground for us to serve, and a situation is opened up for all God's children to have a place where they can give themselves to serve.

Serving in the Body

In order to serve God, we also need to be in the Body. In fact, to be in the church is to be in the Body because the church is the Body of Christ. However, there is a slight difference. With respect to serving in the church, the emphasis is on the setting for service, but with respect to serving in the Body, the emphasis is on the coordination in service. If we have the setting, we will not be aimless, and if we have the coordination, we will not be individualistic. If we do not serve in the church, we are a person without a proper setting, serving aimlessly, and if we do not serve in the Body, we are a person who is without coordination, serving individualistically.

It is a suffering and even an abnormal and terrifying thing for a member of a body, be it a hand, a foot, an ear, or an eye, to be individualistic and detached from the body. If a detached hand were placed in front of us, we would be terrified. When we shake hands with others, however, we think that the hand we are holding is lovely. But if a detached hand was put in front of us, we would definitely be scared. When a hand is attached to the body, it is lovely, but when this hand is detached from the body, it is terrifying. Certain believers today are hands that are detached from the Body of Christ. Such ones are truly terrifying! The loveliest members can become the most terrifying ones if they are detached from the Body.

A member that is outside of the Body is not only terrifying but also useless. Any member that is detached has lost its function. Hence, if we desire to be useful persons and manifest our function in the church, we must be joined to the Body and coordinate with all the brothers and sisters. We must see that we are merely one of many members in the Body. Any function we may have depends upon the other members. Hence, no one can boast.

There is a story concerning the eyes boasting to the feet, saying, "If it were not for me, how could you see?" The feet on the ground refused to give in and said, "Do not boast. If it were not for my standing up, you would have already fallen down." Therefore, the eyes cannot boast to the feet, and neither can the feet boast to the eyes. Both must learn to be humble. Even though every member has something to boast of, the members actually have nothing to boast of, because they are all mutually dependent.

Twenty years ago in northern China I had some experiences regarding coordination. We were having intensive gospel activities during the Chinese New Year. Although it was not on a large scale, we truly had authority, power, and God's presence. I was responsible to speak in the meetings. Because of the heavy burden and solemnity of the occasion, my entire being was poured out for the speaking. After speaking twice a day, I was completely exhausted, not even having the strength to speak once I went home. Other than taking three meals, I could do nothing other than lie down. I did not even have the strength to pray. Although I could not pray myself, I did not feel any lack. My spirit felt that there was much prayer. I knew that many brothers and sisters were praying, and I stood on their prayers, applied their prayers, and relied on their prayers. I deeply felt that there was a prayer group upholding me with their prayers when I stood up to speak.

Anyone who attended those gospel meetings would admit that the gospel messages were not conveyed merely with words but with power and authority. The Holy Spirit was truly working, and there were many signs and wonders. Often people repented because their hidden sins were made manifest through the messages. This kind of power and authority came from the coordination of the Body. Although the burden of delivering the messages was heavy, the entire Body was in coordination, supplying and supporting the speaking one; hence, the speaking was altogether living and able to pierce into men's deepest part like a sword. Through those gospel activities I truly experienced the need and impact of the coordination of the Body. In serving the Lord, we need the proper setting, and we need to learn to coordinate. The setting is the church, and the coordination is in the Body. As soon as we coordinate with the members of the Body, our beauty and function will be manifested.

Serving according to the Spirit, Not according to the Letter

Our service must be fully according to the Spirit, not according to the letter (2 Cor. 3:6). This requires our utmost attention when we serve the Lord.

Serving according to the Spirit, not according to the letter, means to constantly live before the Lord in spirit. In whatever we do in our service, whether dusting the chairs or cleaning the windows, we must follow the Spirit and live before the Lord. We should not do it in a mechanical way, merely coming to the meeting hall every Lord's Day to clean chairs. We should touch the Spirit within even concerning the time we should go to clean. If we practice this, we will have many good experiences. For example, a brother may have the habit of cleaning chairs at seven thirty every Lord's Day morning but may sense in his spirit one day to go at seven o'clock. When he arrives at the meeting hall, he may see a brother who has been saved for one week and fellowship with him. Such fellowship will be a great help to the newly saved brother. Hence, this service is not merely the cleaning of chairs but a service according to the Spirit in the New Testament which issues from following the Spirit.

Although our service is in the church and in the Body, it is neither aimless nor individualistic. We should not serve according to dead letters and regulations, being bound by many rules and arrangements. Our service should be in the Spirit and should be living. However, this does not mean that as long as we are in the Spirit, we can violate the principles in the church. These two aspects are not contradictory. A genuine church will not add bondage to people. A local church that binds people and prevents them from having a living service according to the Spirit should be adjusted.

Seemingly, serving in the church and in the Body is a matter of regulation and is incompatible with and contrary to serving in the Spirit. When we actually serve, however, we will realize that there is nothing incompatible or contrary in this service. The more we serve by the Spirit, the more we are in the Body and the more we are in the church. On the contrary, if we do not care for the sense of the Spirit but serve merely by the letter, thinking that we are in the church and in the Body, we will become a most opinionated person and will be unable to get along with others. Therefore, we must learn to live in the Spirit and serve by the Spirit. The more we serve in this way, the more we are on the ground of the church and in the coordination of the Body. This is what the Lord desires. These three items work together without any conflict or contradiction.

Serving in the church, in the Body, according to the Spirit, and not according to the letter is the practice of service. If we pay attention to these three matters in our service, the practice of our service will be perfect. On the one hand, we have the status of a priest. We are persons who serve God, having a serving life and a heart to serve. On the other hand, in our practice we serve in the church, in the Body, and according to the sense in the Spirit and by the Spirit. These conditions make our service lovely and glorious.

THE LIVING OF SERVICE

Our service to God is not a performance but a living. Actors may have a life that is totally different from when they are performing. They may act humble on the stage but be proud in their living. They may act nice and kind on the stage but be ferocious in their living. Therefore, living and acting can be two entirely different matters. This should not apply to us who serve God. Our living should be consistent with our service. Our service should be our living, and our living should be our service. On the one hand, serving God should be our occupation; on the other hand, serving God should be our living. For example, one who serves God does not preach the gospel only when the church preaches the gospel; he preaches the gospel in his daily life. He is not affected even if the church is not preaching the gospel, because he preaches the gospel to everyone he meets.

Therefore, in principle, there are not some Christians who

are devoted to serving God and others who are not. There is no such distinction. The normal condition of a believer should be that he serves God every day. A brother who is a teacher should serve God when he is teaching, and a brother who is a doctor should serve God when he is attending his patients. The entire living of a normal Christian should be devoted to the service of God. Therefore, we should never say that only full-timers serve God. There is no such thing. All the brothers, whether they are teachers, doctors, laborers, servants, or rickshaw men, should devote themselves to serve God.

Hence, no one should consider preaching as an occupation by which one can earn a living. We do not earn our living by serving God; rather, we are living to serve God. If God takes care of our living, we do not need to set aside the time, strength, and energy to earn a living, but if God does not give us this kind of provision, we should set aside the time, strength, and energy to work in order to support our living according to His leading. However, even this kind of work is a part of our service. Therefore, among us there is no distinction between those who, so to speak, serve God with their full time and those who do not. We must all serve God with our time. Serving God is our living as well as our main occupation. Occupations for earning a living, such as being a teacher or a doctor, are only side jobs. Even sisters who do housework, being wives and mothers, should serve God and testify for Him.

When people say, "Brother Lee, you are serving God," I always reply, "If only I am serving God, then whom do you serve?" Dear brothers and sisters, we should not have a fallen and religious concept that some people should serve God but others do not need to serve God. We should all be devoted to the service of the Lord. Serving the Lord is our living and our main occupation.

THE GOALS OF SERVICE

The goals of our service are preaching the gospel to save sinners, ministering Christ, and building up the church. Whether we are cleaning the meeting hall, ushering, offering material riches, visiting gospel friends, or visiting the saints, the goals of these services are preaching the gospel to save sinners, ministering Christ, and building up the church. In serving the Lord, we should not seek our own gain or have any personal expectations. We should simply learn to preach the gospel so that sinners can be saved, and minister Christ to others so that the Body of Christ, which is the church of God, can be built up. We should respect and treasure everything that is profitable for these goals, and we should despise and reject anything that is contrary to them.

Our goals in serving the Lord consist of only these three points. We hope that the gospel of the Lord will be spread and that precious souls will be saved, that the glorious Christ will be ministered to people and become their riches, and that the church of God will be built up in every place. We do not have any other goals apart from these, and we are willing to give our all and pour out our all. If we can attain these goals, we will be joyful and glorious.

What can we give ourselves to other than preaching the gospel to save sinners, ministering the glorious Christ for others' enjoyment, and building up the Body of Christ? What is more worthy than this? These are the goals of our service. The whole world cannot be given in exchange for these goals, and the glory and riches of the world cannot be compared to them. The Lord Jesus said that it is not profitable for a man to gain the whole world but forfeit his soul-life (Mark 8:36). The world is not worth the value of one soul, yet the goal of our service is to save thousands of souls. Our service is much more glorious and worthwhile. Furthermore, we can also minister the glorious Christ to others and build up His mystical Body. This is glorious as well. This is worthy of our service. It is worthy of our paying the price. May we all bow down and say to the Lord, "Lord, allow us to serve. We kneel before You and implore You to let us serve, because this is a glorious and valuable matter, which will last for eternity!"

PREACHING THE GOSPEL

THE RESPONSIBILITY TO PREACH THE GOSPEL

The gospel preaching we refer to is not the preaching commonly referred to by others. Rather, we are referring to fruit-bearing. The preaching that others generally refer to is done by preachers. Fruit-bearing, however, is the responsibility of every believer. The Bible says that every believer is a branch in the true vine, which is the Lord Himself (John 15:1-2). The unique responsibility of a branch is to bear fruit. Since preaching the gospel is fruit-bearing, it is a responsibility. Therefore, gospel preaching is not a special profession carried out by specialists. It is the daily responsibility of every Christian. No one should regard gospel preaching as a profession. Every believer should regard gospel preaching as a responsibility of his daily life.

It is significant that the Bible uses a vine to describe our relationship with the Lord. There are various kinds of trees. Some, such as sweet osmanthus and cherry trees, are appreciated for their blossoms. Others, such as the pine and the juniper, can be used as raw material. Still others are not appreciated for their blossoms and cannot be used as raw material; they are solely for bearing fruit. Among this group of trees, the most obvious is the grapevine. The vine can never be used as raw material, and its branches are not even good for fuel. The flowers of the vine are almost non-existent because they are tiny and they only bloom for a short period. Hence, they are not worthy of any appreciation. Thus, grapevines are solely for fruit-bearing. Other fruit trees, such as the peach tree and the pear tree, have attractive flowers and can also be used for timber. However, the vine is neither good for flowers nor for timber; it is solely for bearing fruit.

The Bible uses numerous kinds of trees as types of the Lord Jesus. For example, in Song of Songs 2:3 the Lord is typified by the apple tree. This indicates that the Lord Himself bears fruit. However, the vine best portrays the relationship between the Lord and us. We are branches of the Lord Jesus who is the vine. The branches of the vine are for bearing fruit. Fruit-bearing is their sole responsibility. Aside from bearing fruit, there is nothing else that they do. Therefore, since we are branches of the Lord as the vine, our responsibility is to preach the gospel, save sinners, and bear fruit.

THE LIFE OF PREACHING THE GOSPEL

Gospel preaching is neither a profession nor an outward behavior. Gospel preaching is related to the life within us. Every kind of life has its own ability. Fish can swim in water, and birds can fly in the air. Swimming and flying are abilities of life. The fact that trees can bear fruit is also an ability of life. Trees do not bear fruit because of outward behavior but because of their inner life. Even though bearing fruit is an outward manifestation, it shows the ability of the life within a tree. Since gospel preaching is a kind of fruit-bearing, it is an ability of the divine life. We must see that the regenerated life is within every believer. This life has many abilities, that is, many characteristics and functions. One of these characteristics and functions is to preach the gospel, and not merely to preach the gospel but to preach the gospel under any circumstance. Believers have a special instinct—the urge to preach the gospel. This is not a hobby; rather, it is the life of a believer.

For example, cats cannot be forbidden from catching mice; neither can dogs be prohibited from barking. Catching mice and barking are characteristics of the cat and dog life. Similarly, Christians preach the gospel out of a characteristic of the life within them. This is the reason that the brothers and sisters respond enthusiastically whenever the church preaches the gospel. They willingly spend their energy and money because the life within them is a gospel-preaching life.

The life within us is not merely a holy life, a loving life, and a meek life; it is also a gospel-preaching life. If we try to not preach the gospel, we will feel uneasy and unhappy. On the contrary, when we preach the gospel, we feel joyful and at ease because we are following the nature of our inner life. If we want to grow, we must allow the inner life to develop so that the characteristics and functions of this life can be freely manifested. Once we allow this life to develop and be expressed, we cannot help but preach the gospel.

Therefore, we should not have the concept that since we have "joined" the church, we should encourage others to "join" the church. Neither should we think that since we are members of the church, we should preach the gospel only when the church is encouraging us to preach the gospel. Preaching the gospel under these circumstances is not a spontaneous expression of life. We must understand that gospel preaching is neither a religious activity nor a pious behavior for a believer. It is altogether a matter of life.

THE POWER OF PREACHING THE GOSPEL

There is a common belief in Christianity that the power of gospel preaching is the issue of sufficient prayer and the out-pouring of the Holy Spirit. There is no doubt that prayer and the outpouring of the Holy Spirit are needed in order to have power for preaching the gospel. However, a new believer does not rely that much on prayer or the outpouring of the Holy Spirit for power when he preaches the gospel. Rather, he preaches the gospel because he is a believer. This is his capital, his basic power, for preaching the gospel.

Another inaccurate concept we have is that only experienced believers have the power to preach the gospel. For example, one may think that the elders surely have the power to preach the gospel. However, the exact opposite may be true. A "mature and experienced" believer often has difficulty preaching the gospel because he has become old and cannot bear fruit. No grapes in a vineyard are brought forth by old branches; rather, they are brought forth by new branches. This is why old branches are pruned when winter comes, and then in the following spring, new branches grow and bring forth grapes. The power of fruit-bearing is with new branches. Similarly, every new believer is a new branch in the Lord as the vine. Their power for preaching the gospel lies in their being new believers. Hence, for the church to preach the gospel and save more people, new believers must be encouraged to preach the gospel. If a person is saved this year, he should preach the gospel this year. This is the power of the gospel.

Often, when I was invited by the saints to preach the gospel to their relatives and friends, I would encourage them to invite a new believer instead. It was often easier for him to lead others to salvation than it was for me. I am speaking the truth, although many do not quite accept or believe this because they have not changed their concept. They still think that in order to have power when preaching the gospel, they need maturity in life, sufficient prayer, and the outpouring of the Holy Spirit. This concept causes new believers to shrink back from preaching the gospel. They think that they need to equip themselves and practice before they can preach the gospel. This ruins many newly saved brothers and sisters.

Our concept must be changed to see that new believers do not need to have experience, much prayer, or even the outpouring of the Holy Spirit in order to preach the gospel. Their newly acquired salvation is their capital, their power. The underlying power for gospel preaching is an issue of being newly saved. On the contrary, an experienced apostle may need to pray for ten days, like Peter did, and receive the outpouring of the Holy Spirit in order to preach the gospel. But today a new believer can be a small disciple. Praise the Lord that he does not need to be an experienced believer to be qualified. As long as he is a new believer, he can preach the gospel. His new experience of salvation is his capital. Any other capital that preaching the gospel requires will come with time. But a new believer can utilize the capital of his new salvation. A new believer is a new branch.

I feel that this kind of encouragement is lacking among us. In particular, some churches that have been established for some time seldom give new believers the opportunity to participate in preaching the gospel. Instead, the preaching of the gospel is always carried out by the "older" believers. The older ones give the gospel message, and the older ones visit the gospel friends. But once a person is old, he may be ineffectual. The more recent a person's salvation, the fresher and the more effectual is his preaching. A person who was baptized last month and goes to invite his relatives and friends this month will surely be powerful, fresh, and living. He may not present the truth of the gospel accurately, but he can cause others to be saved.

Gospel preaching is different from any other work. Teaching the truth requires absolute accuracy, but preaching the gospel does not necessarily require accuracy. It only requires that people be saved. Some brothers are very accurate when they preach, but people are not saved. Others seem to speak nonsensically, yet people are saved. Brother John Sung, who was very much used by the Lord in China more than twenty years ago, was an excellent example. Some of his gospel preaching was actually not according to the truth. For example, he once said that the "flow of blood" spoken of in Mark 5 refers to the precious blood of the Lord Jesus. Nevertheless, large numbers of people were saved. I am not encouraging us to teach wrong doctrines, but I want us to see that leading people to salvation does not fully depend on our accurate preaching of the truth. The preaching may be good and correct, but people may not get saved. A newly saved brother may be unclear concerning the Bible and unable to give a message, but as long as he preaches, people will be saved. Therefore, we need to see that fruit-bearing depends on new branches, not on the correct preaching of the truth. Gospel preaching fully depends on the fact that we are believers. This is our power.

Some argue that a believer who does not have a proper appearance cannot preach the gospel. Once a person begins to preach the gospel, however, he will become proper. If we wait until believers are proper before encouraging them to preach the gospel, they will become more improper. But if they begin to preach the gospel just as they are, they will become proper. It is amazing that almost all of those who do not preach the gospel are improper, while almost all who preach the gospel are proper. If a person does not preach the gospel, he will gradually become improper. However, with those who are not proper, the more they preach, the more proper they will become. Therefore, as long as one is a believer, he must preach the gospel and not consider other things.

THE SKILLS FOR PREACHING THE GOSPEL

Skills are essential in whatever we do. Hence, skills need to be considered in preaching the gospel, but we should tell new believers that they should simply go and preach the gospel and not be concerned with other things. Our preaching is our skill. There are two things that newly saved brothers and sisters should pay attention to when preaching the gospel. First, they are believers, and this is their power. Second, their preaching is their skill. If they do not know how to preach, they will know how to preach when they preach. If they are unable to preach, they will be able to preach when they preach. They should not ask how they will know or how they will be able to preach, because the more they ask, the more unclear they will be.

Every law is spontaneous and has a natural outcome. Being a Christian is the power for preaching the gospel, and preaching itself is the skill. Both of these are natural. Therefore, we do not need to learn many methods. We should simply preach according to the natural law.

We often like to do everything in an orderly manner. We feel the same about our gospel preaching, but God may not like it this way. Gospel preaching was always disorderly in the Bible. After Philip met the Lord Jesus, he immediately went to preach the gospel (John 1:43-46). He even said the wrong thing, not caring for accuracy. As soon as he met Nathanael, he preached Jesus to him. Philip seemed to be saying, "Whether or not He is Jesus the Nazarene and the son of Joseph the carpenter does not matter. You must believe in Him. If you do not understand, just come and see." His preaching was a complete mess, but Nathanael was eventually saved through his preaching. Nathanael was not saved by an experienced, accurate, and skillful evangelist but by a new believer who was unclear, inaccurate, and ambiguous in his preaching. Therefore, new believers must go and preach the gospel. The skill for preaching the gospel is in their preaching. Being a believer is the power, and their preaching is their skill.

THE PRACTICE OF PREACHING THE GOSPEL

In the practice of gospel preaching, we should first make a list of our relatives, friends, colleagues, and schoolmates. We do not need to be concerned for those who are already saved, because those who are not saved are the objects of our gospel preaching. We should first preach to our relatives and friends. According to Exodus 12, if a household could not eat an entire lamb at the passover, the children of Israel were to share it with their neighbors (v. 4). Every local church should lead all the new believers to practice this. Acts 1:8 says that the gospel was to be preached "in Jerusalem and in all Judea and Samaria and unto the uttermost part of the earth." The principle in spreading the gospel is to spread from the center. Hence, we need to start with our closest relatives and friends and spread from there. After listing the names of our unsaved relatives and friends, we should try our best to contact them, not to befriend them or to socialize with them but to preach the gospel to them. In contacting them, we do not need to talk or argue much. This may hinder them and shut the door of salvation. When the church holds a gospel meeting, we should do our best to invite those on our list so that they can hear the gospel and receive the Lord.

Second, as the opportunity allows we should endeavor to preach the gospel to all men. A good way is to distribute gospel tracts whenever there is the opportunity. They can be distributed on buses and trains or even at bus stops and train stations. We can distribute them to people on our way to a meeting. Sometimes a team of two or three should distribute tracts at street intersections or important locations. We may even sing gospel hymns, post banners, or speak to people. These should be done without formality. We often did these things when we were in mainland China. It is regrettable that we seem to have neglected them. May we all pick these things up again and practice them diligently.

THE SPEAKING OF THE GOSPEL

In the preaching of the gospel, speaking is a must. This is a crucial point that is generally neglected by Christians. Many hold the concept that gospel preaching depends entirely on the testimony of the daily walk and not so much on speaking. This is the enemy's scheme. The more a brother or a sister speaks the gospel to others, the more their daily walk will be changed. Someone who does not preach the gospel may say, "How can I preach? Look at my daily walk. Since my conduct is poor, I should not speak. If I do speak, it will be useless and may even cause damage." In reality, however, his conduct will worsen if he does not speak. But if he rises up to preach the gospel, he will be more proper day by day. Brothers, the gospel is not preached by our conduct but by our words. Therefore, we should go and preach. We should go and speak. The more we preach, the better our conduct will be. The more we speak, the more proper our living will become. Our conduct is poor because we do not preach the gospel. One may have been saved for three years but still go to the movies because he does not preach the gospel. If he preached the gospel immediately after his salvation, saying, "I have believed in Jesus. You should believe. Jesus is the Savior of sinners. Jesus can save people from their sins and from their bad habits," he would be the first one to be delivered from his bad habits. He would never again go to the movies, and if he went, his own speaking would condemn him.

Ephesians 6:15 says that the gospel is a pair of shoes for our feet, which keep us away from the world's filth. The more we preach the gospel to others, the less they will ask us to join in their sinful activities. They will say, "Do not ask him. He just preached the gospel to us yesterday, so what is the use of asking him?" If we remain silent and never speak the gospel, but instead merely think of our good behavior as being a testimony, our colleagues who gamble and our classmates who watch movies will drag us along with them. There are many such cases. A person often does not have a good testimony before his neighbors because he has never spoken the gospel to them. Speaking the gospel once would preserve him from wrongdoings before his neighbors. Therefore, we should never say that in order to preach the gospel, we need to have good conduct. This word should be spoken to believers who have been saved for a long time. However, we should simply tell the new believers to go and speak. Gospel preaching requires speaking. This speaking is our safeguard.

When I was young, I also heard that it is better to preach the gospel by good conduct rather than by speaking. Later, a servant of God overthrew this teaching by asking, "What verse in the Bible says that the gospel is preached by conduct or that preaching is not by speaking but by conduct?" He pointed out that Acts 4:17-18 shows that Satan always wants to shut people's mouths and stop them from preaching. In order to preach, our mouth cannot be shut. We should not think that we cannot speak because we are weak; rather, we are weak because we do not speak. Once we speak, we will be strong. We should not think that since our living is abnormal, we should not speak. Our living is abnormal because we do not speak. Once we speak, we will be normal. We must overthrow the common concept in Christianity and not consider our own condition but simply go and speak. Gospel preaching is not simply taking people to a meeting but speaking to people. Even if we do not know how to speak, we must still speak. Even if we cannot speak well or our speaking is incomplete, we must still speak. Oh, I cannot stress this secret too much; I cannot exhaust this mystery. We will know how to speak as we practice. Because the God whom we serve is a speaking God, we should be a speaking people. Our God is not a dumb idol.

This treasure, which belongs to every believer, has been lost and even seized by the children of the devil. The most prosperous people in the world today are the most articulate ones, but they speak lies and deceit. The words that we speak are the truth, yet we do not speak. This is a huge mistake! We should speak constantly. When on the bus, we should stand up and speak as soon as the door closes. When we are in the barbershop for a haircut, we should speak. Whenever we have the chance, we should speak, regardless of whether people listen or whether they believe. Two months ago six hundred brothers and sisters were baptized in the church in Taipei. If, from the day they were baptized, everyone spoke daily, they would stir up Taipei. But the present situation is silent and dormant. This is abnormal. Although some say that gospel preaching causes trouble and brings unrest to society, actually, the gospel stabilizes society. In the newspapers we daily read of such things as murders, suicides, fornication, and robberies. This shows that society lacks the gospel. Therefore, we must go and speak. What the law cannot do, the gospel can; what man cannot restrain, God has the power to restrain. It is a pity that degraded Christianity has turned gospel preaching into a profession that can be used to make a living. Our concept must be changed. At the same time, we must not think that only those who are matured, grown, experienced, and know the truth can speak. Even those who were baptized yesterday should go and speak. We should not keep our mouths shut. A believer's mouth should not be shut. Believers must speak constantly. We should go and speak. Whether we speak correctly or incorrectly, we still need to speak. As long as we preach Jesus as the Savior, our preaching cannot be wrong. By this continuous speaking, the gospel will be spread.

THE RESULTS OF PREACHING THE GOSPEL

On the one hand, we should expect results, but on the other hand, we should not trust too much in the results. We should hope for results, expecting large numbers of people to be saved, even expecting people of fine character to be saved. However, we should not have confidence in results, saying, "It is so wonderful to have more than six hundred people baptized." We should realize that the best ones probably have not even been baptized and that those who have been baptized may not remain for long. Someone may say that a few of the ones who were baptized are very good but some who were baptized are not so good. However, the ones whom we think are not so good today may be very good five years from now, even becoming elders in the local churches. But those whom we think are very good today may not do so well later, and their condition may deteriorate. Hence, we cannot quickly evaluate the results of the gospel. We should not trust the immediate results. Neither should we comfort ourselves, saying, "Because we do not trust results, we do not care whether people are saved." On the one hand, we should always expect people to be richly and dynamically saved. But on the other hand, we should not put our confidence in the results.

OUR EYES BEING CLOSED IN PREACHING THE GOSPEL

When we preach the gospel, our eyes should be closed. We should be fervent in heart yet not so discerning in our mind. Our heart should be burning, but our mind should be "foolish" (1 Cor. 1:21, 23). We should speak concerning the Lord with whomever we meet, telling them that they will be saved simply by believing. Once a person believes, we should tell him that according to the Word of God, he is saved. We should never worry whether one has been genuinely saved and thus may be a tare and not wheat. If we think about discerning people in this way, we will be unable to preach the gospel. We should not be afraid of bringing "false ones" into the church. Discernment of this nature is a matter of church administration, not a matter of gospel preaching. Concerning church administration, everyone should have a clear and sober mind, but concerning gospel preaching, the more foolish we are, the better.

BEING THICK-SKINNED IN PREACHING THE GOSPEL

In preaching the gospel, our eyes should be closed, and we should have thick skin. Our skin needs to be thick. We should exercise to be totally oblivious to ourselves to the extent that when we are scolded, we would not realize it, and when we are laughed at, we would not feel it. Then we can preach the gospel. If we blush when others stare at us, our skin is thinner than paper, and we will have no way to preach the gospel. People with thin skin cannot preach the gospel. In order to preach the gospel, we should practice being thick-skinned.

About a hundred years ago, there was a preacher named Hunter Corbett who came to northern China from America to preach the gospel. He was thick-skinned and not self-conscious. When he passed through the villages, crowds of children would follow him, throwing dirt at him and mocking him. But he was conscious of nothing and kept walking. After a while, he would turn around and say with a smile, "Enough, enough." By being oblivious of his self, the gospel was eventually preached.

People who preach the gospel should not be sensitive. Sensitive people cannot preach the gospel. All those who are sensitive need to lose their sensitivity before they can preach the gospel. We are not speaking of being thick-skinned by nature. Only those who become thick-skinned and oblivious to the self for the Lord's sake are useful. This does not mean that we should not know shame and have a sense of shame. Shamefacedness is a protection for our conduct. Particularly with sisters, shamefacedness is a safeguard. But in the matter of gospel preaching, we should abandon this sense of shame and know no shame for the Lord's sake. Only then can we preach the gospel.

THE FAITH FOR PREACHING THE GOSPEL

Finally, we come to the faith for preaching the gospel. When preaching the gospel, regardless of the object, the time, or the place, we must possess faith. We must believe that the gospel is the power of God unto salvation to everyone who believes (Rom. 1:16). We should not look at the environment, at the contrary situation, or the existing condition. If we are easily discouraged by the slightest opposition, we cannot preach the gospel. Even if the opposition intensifies, we must still believe and continue to preach. Regardless of the situation, we should always believe that the gospel has the power to save people. We should believe that whomever we are speaking to will eventually be saved. This faith includes being unyielding, bold, and courageous. We should be able to say, "I do not care what kind of person you are, how much you oppose, or how difficult the situation is; I do not care about any of this. I care only for the gospel I preach, which is powerful. This is the reason I preach. Even if people are unsaved after three years of my preaching, I still believe that they will be saved. Even though my relatives have not repented after five years of my preaching, I still believe that one day they will repent." Faith is persistent. This is the faith for preaching the gospel, which is indispensable and requires exercise.

THE PRACTICE OF FELLOWSHIP

(1)

Experience shows that most of a believer's problems are related to fellowship. If a believer has normal fellowship, his life will be normal. Hence, new believers must have a good understanding of this lesson and practice it. Since this is a very broad topic, we will cover it in a few lessons.

THE MEANING OF FELLOWSHIP

Fellowship is the contact between God and man. This, however, is a shallow definition. Fellowship also includes the mutual contact among God's people. In a deeper sense, fellowship is a kind of mutual flow. The blending and flowing of two kinds of liquids is a mutual flow. In one sense, fellowship is a two-way contact, but in a deeper sense, it is a mutual flow. Something flows into us from God, and something flows from us to God. At the same time, as God's people, something flows mutually among us. This is what we call fellowship.

A LIFE OF FELLOWSHIP

The Christian life is a life of fellowship. A believer cannot be independent; neither can he be individualistic. Being independent is toward God, and being individualistic is toward other believers. No believer should be separated from God and live an independent life. Anyone who is separated from God and becomes independent from Him can no longer live a normal Christian life. A believer who is severed from God is a Christian in name only, but he is no longer a Christian in his practical living. We may be a Christian in name and in position and yet no longer be one in our practical living. Whether we live a Christian life in reality depends on whether we are living a life in fellowship with God or are independent from God. Being independent from God means that we have broken our relationship with Him and have lost the mutual flow with Him. Thus, God is separate from us, and we are separate from God. There is no flow joining us and God. We are separated from one another.

Man's eating of the tree of the knowledge of good and evil in Genesis 3 was according to the principle of independence from God. The principle of the tree of the knowledge of good and evil is that man lives and works apart from God. Man lives without God, without needing God, without having God, without depending on God, and without contacting God. This is the principle of independence, the principle of the tree of the knowledge of good and evil. The principle of the tree of life is the opposite. Its principle is dependence, not independence. In the universe anything dead is independent and unrelated to other things, but anything living is dependent. As long as a tree is living, it relies on soil, and as long as a fish is living, it relies on water. But once they die, soil and water mean nothing; the tree is independent from the soil, and the fish is independent from the water. The tree of the knowledge of good and evil results in death; therefore, its principle is independence. The tree of life results in man having life; therefore, its principle is a continual dependence on God. The entire Christian living should be of life. There should not be any trace of death. Nevertheless, whenever we are independent from God and live according to the principle of the tree of the knowledge of good and evil, we are living in death, not in life. Regardless of whether we are working, studying, taking care of our family, or doing other things, as long as we do these things on our own, apart from God, we are cut off from fellowship with God. This is abnormal. A normal Christian life is a life of fellowship. This means that we cannot be separated from God; we cannot be independent from God. From the day of our salvation we no longer exist as individuals, and we should no longer be independent.

Today people love to speak concerning freedom and independence. Although it may be right for human beings to speak in this way, it is abnormal for Christians to speak in this way, because Christians are the most dependent people. Whenever a believer becomes independent, he is no longer a believer in his living. Christians are people who depend entirely on God. Without God they do not have life, without God they cannot live, and without God they will fall into death.

Even if we do something very proper, we will be dead if we are independent from God, because the principle of independence is death. We usually pay attention to whether something is right or wrong or good or bad, but these are moral concepts. Being pious is a religious concept. Our concept in God's salvation should not be morality or religion; it should be fellowship. We may be right in doing something, but we should ask whether it was done in fellowship. We must ask whether we did it independently from God or in fellowship with God. Therefore, a life of fellowship means that we have fellowship with God, are connected to Him, and have a mutual flow with Him in everything. We should not focus on doing things that are right, good, or godly. Rather, we should focus on whether we are joined to God, connected to Him, and in a mutual flow with Him when doing things that are right, good, or godly. We should focus on not being separated from God.

Before a person is saved, he may be the most independent person on earth. He may be great, capable, and able to do everything by himself. But once this great and capable person is saved, he becomes a dependent person. Without God he cannot live, make decisions, or have an opinion. Previously he had his own point of view, method, and insight concerning everything. But from the day he becomes a Christian, he is changed and can no longer decide things on his own or be independent. He feels that he needs to contact and consult God related to every problem he encounters, that is, to bring every matter to the Lord and to consider, examine, and determine things before Him. This believer is the best type of Christian. In this respect, every Christian needs to be weak to the extent that he neither has his own ideas, makes his own decisions, or takes any action related to what he encounters without contacting the Lord and consulting with Him, allowing Him to make the decisions. This is the best and sweetest living of a Christian.

We need to realize that every descendant of Adam, every fallen man, is very strong and independent. This applies both to men and women and to the elderly and children. We can all find a way out of any situation and cope with problems on our own. We have all had this experience. Therefore, one of the consequences of being saved is that strong, independent persons such as ourselves become weak and are no longer strong or independent. We feel that we have no alternative but to fellowship with God in all things, discuss all things with Him, and allow Him to handle all things, speak in all things, and make every decision. Whenever we encounter something, our being is softened. We feel that we cannot do anything without Him. Therefore, we depend on Him and rely on Him. We are not independent persons, but we are dependent persons. Today it is shameful for someone to be referred to as a dependent person; rather, it is considered an honor to be self-supporting and independent. However, for a Christian to be self-supporting and independent is shameful, not glorious. It is glorious for a Christian to be dependent. No normal Christian can be independent. We depend on another One—God—at every moment and in every matter.

A life of fellowship not only has the aspect of not being independent but also has the aspect of not being individualistic. This means that we not only need God, but we also need other Christians, other brothers and sisters. On the one hand, we are not independent from God; on the other hand, we are not individualistic toward the brothers and sisters. We must all be very clear that the nature of Christians is that of a flock. In the Bible Christians are likened to sheep. Sheep are always in a flock. They always flock together. Individual sheep cannot survive very easily, but in a flock one can survive easily. Christians are not like butterflies flying around individually. Rather, we are like bees, which are always in a swarm. Hence, as Christians, our nature is altogether corporate and related to being in a flock.

If we desire to be a normal Christian, we must not be independent toward God and individualistic toward the brothers and sisters. We fellowship with God and with the brothers and sisters in all matters. We have God, and we have the brothers and sisters. Hence, in everything we can say, "I have consulted with God, and I have also conferred and considered it with my brothers and sisters." If we are like this, everything we do will be safe and secure, and it will definitely be full of light, peace, and sweetness. When we are living in this way, we are living in fellowship, and this kind of life is called the life of fellowship.

In this life of fellowship, we must constantly see that we not only have God but also have the brothers and sisters. It is true that as a Christian we should keep certain things to ourselves. But one thing is certain: the more we open to the brothers and sisters, the better Christians we will be. As long as we have thoroughly fellowshipped with at least two or three saints, we can be assured that it will not be easy for us to make a mistake; at least, we will not sin. There is hardly anything in our Christian life that does not require fellowship with the saints. There are bound to be risks and mistakes in anything we initiate, decide, and do on our own. Being individualistic, not fellowshipping, is a mistake in itself. The best way for us to keep from sinning and from making mistakes is to fellowship with the saints in everything. For example, if we want to watch a movie, we should first fellowship with the saints to see if we should watch the movie or if they would watch the movie with us. We will be clear once we fellowship. Another example is playing sports. We should fellowship with the saints concerning our being involved in certain kinds of sports. There is a greater likelihood that we are doing something right if a brother can go with us and fellowship with us. If what we do is in fellowship, there will not be much problem, and there will be a safeguard. On the contrary, anything that we cannot do in fellowship is dangerous and should not be done. Hence, we should not be independent toward God; moreover, we should not be individualistic toward the brothers and sisters. This kind of living, which is neither independent nor individualistic, is the normal life of a Christian. Our entire

Christian living should be one that depends on God and relies on the brothers and sisters.

FELLOWSHIP WITH GOD

Now we will focus on our fellowship with God. This is an extremely important topic. The more we can labor on this topic, the better. Hence, we will use several points to cover it.

God Being Spirit

First, we must be very clear that God is Spirit. It is very difficult to explain the statement that God is Spirit because it is difficult to explain the matter of Spirit. When the Bible refers to God as Spirit, using the term *Spirit* to refer to God, the emphasis is on God being the highest life, a life that is not physical and cannot be touched by man with the five senses used to contact the physical world. This means that God cannot be seen by eyes, heard by ears, smelled by noses, tasted by tongues, or touched by hands. These organs can be used to contact the physical world, but they are of no avail in contacting God, because God is Spirit. He is not physical.

In the original languages of the Bible, in both the Old Testament Hebrew and in the New Testament Greek, the word *Spirit* is the same word as *wind* or *breath*. We can see the manifestations of wind or breath, but we are unable to see either the wind or breath. It is the same with the Spirit. We can be assured that He is here, but we cannot see or touch Him. Furthermore, the Spirit is more mysterious than either wind or breath. Whereas wind and breath are lifeless and therefore not living, the Spirit has life. Although the Spirit does not have a physical form, He is life and even a strong life. The strongest and highest life in this universe is the Spirit of God. The God whom we contact is not physical. He has the strongest life. He is a person who is living and strong.

In almost every religion man outwardly worships a visible image with his body, and this image is an idol. Idolatry is present not only in pagan religions but also in so-called Christianity. The numerous images in Catholicism, such as the image of Jesus and the image of Mary, are in the principle of man worshipping a physical object with his physical body.

No matter what name man gives an image, be it Jesus or the Lord of heaven, it is in the principle of idols and offends God. The Bible shows that the God whom we contact and have fellowship with is Spirit. He is not physical. He is invisible and untouchable, yet He is full of life, very living, and strong.

Man Having a Spirit

Second, we must see that man has a spirit. In learning to fellowship with God, we not only need to realize that God is Spirit, but we must also know that we have a spirit. Shortly after I was saved, I read some publications concerning the difference between the spirit and soul and tried to apprehend the difference in my experience. However, for years I was unable to differentiate the spirit from the soul, much less speak clearly concerning them to others. But today I have no difficulty. In order to speak clearly on the subject of man having a spirit, we should consider it from the two aspects of feeling and need.

We will first speak concerning the aspect of feeling. Often we have the desire to do something and a willingness to do it; our heart desires and is inclined to do it. There also may be very good reasons to support it, with no logical reason against it. If we decide to do it, however, a feeling may spring up from the deepest part of our being to protest and disagree with that decision. This does not happen only to Christians; even unbelievers have this experience. The Chinese call this the operation of man's conscience. This is truly a function of the conscience, but the conscience is a large part of the spirit. Hence, the functioning of the conscience is also the functioning of the spirit, and the objection of the conscience is also the objection of the spirit. Our emotion may favor something, and our mind may approve it, but when we decide to do it, something in our innermost being rises up to object. The Bible refers to this part as the spirit of man. We always say that a person should be genuine when he speaks. Actually, being genuine when one speaks is to speak from the spirit. The spirit is the genuineness of man, the genuine self, the deepest part of man. Nothing can be deeper than man's innermost part. It is deeper than the sensation of the body, deeper than the emotion, deeper than the mind, and deeper than the will. This is what the Bible refers to as the human spirit.

In the Chinese Union Version of the Bible there are several places where the word *spirit* is translated accurately. For example, 1 Thessalonians 5:23 says, "May your spirit and soul and body be preserved..." Here it clearly distinguishes the three parts of man: spirit, soul, and body. Hebrews 4:12 says, "Piercing even to the dividing of soul and spirit..." Here it says that the spirit and soul can be divided. These passages were translated well. However, there are other portions that are ambiguous, because *spirit* and *soul* are mixed together. Moreover, in some places where the word *spirit* is not used in the original, the Chinese Union Version translates it as "spirit-soul." Then there are places that refer to the spirit that are not translated with the word *spirit*. The good thing is that the Chinese Union Version uses the word *spirit* to refer to the spirit and the word *soul* to refer to the soul, which is different from the spirit. The spirit is the deepest part of our being. We first know that there is such a spirit by its sense. The inward sense that is deeper than all other parts proves that we have a spirit.

There is also the aspect of need. We all know that we have different needs, such as food, clothing, housing, and transportation. These are physical needs of the body. In addition to physical needs, man needs comfort, music, art, friends to talk with, travel, exercise, and knowledge. These are psychological needs of man's soul. (Mentality, or psychology, refers to the soul.) Man usually realizes and takes care of the needs of the body and the soul. However, in reality, he has another need in addition to his physical and psychological needs. Many times when man obtains physical and psychological satisfaction, feeling complete and content, he discovers that he is still dissatisfied in the deepest part of his being and that he still has a feeling of need. His physical and psychological needs have been met, yet deep within there is still a lack. This lack comes from the need within the human spirit. Therefore, every one of us has three kinds of needs: physical, psychological, and spiritual. Spiritual needs show that we have a spirit. The sense that comes from the operation of the conscience and the needs of the human spirit enable us to have a definite realization that human beings have a spirit.

The Fellowship between the Two Spirits

Third, we must see that our fellowship with God is the fellowship between two spirits, that is, the mutual fellowship between the human spirit and the divine Spirit. God Himself is Spirit, and we have a spirit in the depths of our being. When these two spirits commune with each other, there is fellowship. Thus, the meaning of fellowship is that we use our spirit to fellowship with God, who is Spirit. If we cannot see this point, it will be difficult for us to practice fellowship with God.

In the beginning when God created all things, He created man with a spirit so that man would have an organ within to contact God, who is Spirit. God created the cattle, the sheep, the birds in the air, and the fish in the sea, but He did not give any of them a spirit because He did not intend for them to contact and receive Him. But when God created man, He wanted man to be a vessel so that He could enter into man. God wanted to be in man just as water is in a cup. In order for God to be in man, man must receive Him. In order for man to receive Him, man must have an organ; otherwise, it would be impossible for man to receive God even if he were willing. Therefore, when God created man, He formed a spirit within man as an organ for man to receive Him. This can be compared to God making man with a stomach because He wanted man to receive food. With a stomach, man can receive food. The stomach receives food, and the body receives the nutrients from the food. In this way the food also becomes the constituents of the body. In the same way, since God wanted man to receive Him as the constituents of his life, He created man with an organ, and this organ is the spirit. Just as the stomach within man is for receiving food, the spirit within man is for receiving God. Just as man needs to use his stomach to receive food, man also needs to use his spirit to receive God.

John 4:24 says, "God is Spirit, and those who worship Him must worship in spirit and truthfulness." To worship Him

means to contact Him and have fellowship with Him. Therefore, for man to contact God and fellowship with God, he must
be in spirit and exercise his spirit. We must worship God who
is Spirit in our spirit. We must use our spirit to contact God
who is Spirit. Only in this way can our spirit have genuine fellowship with Him.

The Condition of Fellowship
between the Two Spirits

What is the condition of fellowship between the Spirit
and our spirit? We must see this from the aspects of feeling and need. We will first speak concerning feeling. When a
person first hears the gospel, the speaker may say that everyone is sinful and give one illustration after another so that he
is without excuse. Being rational, he can only nod his head
and say, "This is right. Everyone is sinful, and I also am
sinful." However, the fact that he continues to sin without
losing any peace proves that the word of God has not touched
his spirit, though it may have convinced him in his mind.
Hence, there is no reaction in his spirit. As far as his spirit is
concerned, he is dead and has not touched the Spirit of God.
Therefore, although he confesses his sinfulness in his mind,
reasoning, and logic, he still sins as before. When he hears the
gospel again, and again hears that he is sinful, he may have a
sense that is deeper than merely an acknowledgment of being
sinful. Such a sense will cause him to feel regret, be sorrow-
ful, and repent bitterly. Then something deep inside him will
cause him to stay away from his former sins. This is God the
Spirit touching his spirit. When our spirit begins to contact
the Spirit, we will condemn ourselves and feel sorry about our
sins. We will be convicted of our sins and may even weep and
repent. This is the first condition of the contact between the
Spirit and our spirit.

Before our salvation we may have talked loosely. When
we wanted to rebuke others, we rebuked them, and when we
wanted to boast, we boasted. Moreover, we may have felt good
after rebuking others and been delighted after boasting. But
once we are saved, if we want to rebuke others or boast as in
the past, there is an inward sense that touches and restrains

us. Sometimes this sense is so strong that it seems as if it is an electric shock, and we can no longer rebuke others or boast. This is not the result of someone admonishing us to speak politely and no longer use filthy words, and it is not the result of being encouraged to be humble rather than proud. Instead, something has touched our deepest part; the divine Spirit has touched our human spirit. This is a condition of the contact between the divine Spirit and the human spirit.

Let us consider a more detailed example. Before we were saved, we may have bought whatever we wanted, because we were very free with our money. However, now that we are learning to live before God, we have another experience. When we are about to buy some nice clothes, an inward sense may forbid us, and we cannot purchase the clothes. This forbidding is the issue of God's Spirit touching our spirit. This is a condition in which the Spirit contacts our spirit. In the normal Christian life, this feeling is present whether we are working, studying, or having recreation. This condition shows that our spirit is touching the Spirit of God.

The aspect of need is also present within us from the time we are saved. Even though a person may be rich, educated, and have a good family life, he may still feel unhappy and dissatisfied. After listening to a gospel message, there is a sense of joy and sweetness within him. Furthermore, thinking of the Lord Jesus fills him with an inward sweetness. Whenever the Lord's name is mentioned, he senses its loveliness and preciousness, and deep within there is an indescribable satisfaction and pleasure. What is this? This is the Lord Jesus as the Spirit visiting him and touching his spirit. At this point it becomes impossible for him not to think of the Lord and impossible for him to forsake the Lord. This is because the Lord has reached him as the Spirit and visited him.

Although others may have a different experience, the principle is the same. A person may be encouraged and led by others to pray before being saved. Before he prayed, he was indifferent, but as soon as he prays, he feels inward satisfaction, joy, comfort, and support. He also senses that his problems are solved. This is not a psychological reaction or an illusion; it is the issue of the Spirit of reality entering into his spirit to touch his spirit. This also is the condition of the Spirit touching our spirit.

I have never heard of a religion that results in such a condition when one believes. No religion can produce this condition in man's spirit, because religions restrain people with regulations and cannot give people the salvation of the Spirit. The gospel we heard, however, does not restrain by regulations; rather, the living Spirit Himself becomes our salvation. This living Spirit is our Lord and our God. Whenever God visits us, reaches us, and touches us in our spirit, the joy, satisfaction, rest, and comfort within are unspeakable. The satisfaction of our needs is an indication that our spirit has touched God's Spirit and that the Spirit has contact and fellowship with our human spirit.

I believe that we now have some understanding of the matter of fellowship with God.

THE PRACTICE OF FELLOWSHIP

(2)

In the foregoing message we covered the meaning of fellowship, a life of fellowship, and fellowship with God. Now we come to the effect, time, place, and procedures of fellowship with God.

THE EFFECT OF FELLOWSHIP WITH GOD

What is the effect of our fellowship with God? According to the evidence in the Bible and our experience, the effect of fellowship has a negative and a positive aspect. On the negative side, fellowship with God continually removes the undesirable elements within us. One effect of our fellowship with God is the constant removal of things that should not be within us.

Every believer realizes that he is sinful. This is obvious, and many items are included in sin. All transgressions, unclean things, and unrighteous matters are sins. Besides sins, there are other less obvious things that should not be within us, such as the world. There are also other things that are less related to sins and the world within us. These are elements of the old creation, that is, the things of the flesh and the things of the self. The old creation, the flesh, and the self are of the same category. We may say that they are different expressions for saying the same thing. We can identify at least three categories of things that should not be in us—sins, the world, and the self.

Our fellowship with God has the function of gradually removing these three things from within us. The more we fellowship with God, the more they are exposed within us. This exposure requires us to deal with them. If our fellowship with God is deep and thorough, something will be constantly removed from us. Fellowship removes negative things from within us. Whether or not we have genuine fellowship with God can be seen by whether this function of removal is manifested in us. If it has been a long time since something has been removed from us, our fellowship with God has diminished or ceased. If we have fellowship with God, we can be certain that this fellowship will function to continually remove negative things from within us.

Being a Christian is absolutely not a matter of keeping regulations. We do not deal with certain matters because there are regulations that say, "This is a sin, so you must remove it"; "this is the world, so you need to remove it"; or "this is the self, so it must be removed." Dealing with sins, the world, and the self is not a matter of keeping regulations. It is impossible to deal with these by regulations. Although the principle of sin is defined, and the Bible explicitly says that all unrighteousness is sin (1 John 5:17), there is no rule for dealing with sins. At what point are dealings between human beings unrighteous? No one can set a standard for us. It all depends on the inner sense from our fellowship with God. Hence, there is no regulation related to our dealing with things; rather, this is an effect produced spontaneously through fellowship.

Any dealing produced through fellowship is not accomplished once for all. When we were newly saved, our fellowship with God caused us to sense that a few things within us were improper, and we confessed and dealt with these things before Him. Gradually, as we progressed, our fellowship with God increased, deepened, and strengthened. We began to realize that some things, which we had previously not considered as sinful, were sins, and we had further dealings. For example, a new brother feels that lying is a sin, and thus he deals with it. However, he may still gossip, spreading the affairs of others, without any feeling of being wrong. After six months or a year of deeper fellowship with God, he will realize that gossiping is also a sin in need of dealing. I believe that the saints have had this kind of experience. This gradual deepening of our fellowship is the way to thoroughly deal with the problem of sin. This process takes many years. It is not possible to thoroughly deal with the problem of sins in six months to a year after being saved. This is because our knowledge, condemnation, and dealing with sins absolutely depend on the deepening of our fellowship with God.

New believers may not have much feeling concerning these matters, but gradually they will realize that the intensified sense of the fellowship of life is restricting them. They might not have had the sense that something is sin, but after a period of fellowship, they will realize that this matter is sin and must be condemned. They may not have had the sense that gossiping and judging others are sinful, but gradually, as their fellowship with God deepens, they will sense through this fellowship that all their gossiping and judging should be condemned. The more they advance and grow in life, the more they will realize that there is a restraining function in their fellowship that rescues them from improper things.

A believer's strictness in dealing with sins to a large extent can be seen in his speaking. The more a brother or sister is restricted by fellowship with God, the stricter his speaking will be. It is easy for us to know if we have done something wrong in other matters, but it is not so easy to detect faults in our speaking and motives. These are exposed through the sense that comes from fellowship. Therefore, we always need to bring our motives and speaking into fellowship with God so that we can be examined. When we see that our motive is impure and our speaking is improper, we need to deal with them by the Lord. If we always have this kind of dealing in our fellowship with God, our intentions, motives, and speaking will increasingly be restricted by Him. This shows that the effect of fellowship, in the aspect of removing sins, is manifest in us.

The principle is the same concerning dealing with the world. It is even more difficult to define the world. Something that is not the world to one person may be the world to another, or it may not be the world to others, but it is to us. However, the more we live in fellowship, the more the fellowship will restrict us and require us to have deeper dealings, and the function of this fellowship will remove aspects of the world from us.

The same applies to dealing with the self. As we progress in the Lord, we will gradually see that a certain matter may be right and good and neither sinful nor of the world; however, it is full of the self. Our being right and good may not have God in it because it is of the self. This situation can be made known only through fellowship. It is difficult for us to know, let alone deal with, the self if we are not in fellowship with God. The deeper we fellowship with God and enter into Him, the more the things of the self can be gradually exposed. The self is in our contact with the brothers and sisters, in our spiritual preferences, in our desire to glorify ourselves, and even in our desire to be blameless. Only when we see the self through fellowship can we have proper dealings.

In conclusion, the more we live in fellowship, the more this fellowship will function to remove things from within us. There are many things that need to be removed from within us, not only sins, the world, and the self. Even things given to us by God must be removed. Just as God wanted Abraham to offer up the Isaac whom he had received from God, He will require us at a certain point to offer to Him all our spiritual experiences, our spiritual gifts, and the fruit of our work, that is, what we have received from Him. God requires that we let go of the things that we treasure from the past. Sometimes God will tear down those things that are perfect and praiseworthy. God's removing and stripping of us in our fellowshipping with Him are often quite detailed. After experiencing some dealing, we may think that we are all right. However, the more we fellowship, the more we will sense that other things also need to be removed. The removing function of fellowship is truly profound and continuous.

If we do not know this aspect of fellowship, we will be unable to understand a person who has deep fellowship with God. For example, we may not understand the Lord's word that John came neither eating nor drinking, and people said that he had a demon, and that the Son of Man came eating and drinking, and people said that He was a gluttonous man and a drunkard (Matt. 11:18-19). John's not eating or drinking was in fellowship, and the Lord Jesus' eating and drinking was also in fellowship. Those who live in fellowship do not uniformly express the same thing. Consequently, if we do not live in fellowship, we will be confused by these differences. Only by living in fellowship can we touch those who live in fellowship and understand their actions.

The effect of fellowship also has a positive aspect, which is the increase of the element of God. The more a person fellowships with God, the more the element of God will be increased within him. From the time we were saved, God's unique goal has been to work Himself into us abundantly and richly. God's work is not to make us good, whole, or spotless; rather, it is to work Himself into us. Hence, it often seems that the more we fellowship with God, the more God destroys our wholeness, goodness, and spotlessness so that He can add more of His element into us. This can be understood only in our experience, so I cannot speak concerning this aspect in a thorough way. Nevertheless, when we fellowship with God, we should sense that, on the negative side, God continually requires us to depart from the things that we should not have, and on the positive side, He wants His element to be continually added into us.

The increase of God's element can be compared to the process of metabolism in our body; in metabolism old elements are constantly replaced with new elements. This does not mean that God's element is added into us once for all. God is continually adding His new element into us in order to replace our old elements. From this we see that a spiritual person will not remain the same. A person who learns to live in fellowship is constantly undergoing a metabolic change. He may have had a certain condition last year, but he will have a different condition this year; he may have given people a certain feeling last year, but he will give people a different feeling this year. This was true even with the apostle Paul. We can tell from reading his Epistles that his early writings have a flavor that is different from his later writings because he was a person living in fellowship. He was constantly being changed and renewed. There is no outward standard for

Christians. Those in religion have a standard, but Christians do not. The only need of a Christian is to fellowship with God.

When I was newly saved, I set a certain standard for myself. Anyone who did not meet my standard was considered unspiritual, and I questioned his salvation, but gradually I began to see that this was absolutely not right. My standard was absolute; however, many of those who were genuinely spiritual and who lived in fellowship were not up to my "standard," whereas those who were up to my "standard" were apparently proper but not necessarily spiritual. Hence, we need to see that our genuine condition before the Lord does not depend on an outward standard but on inward fellowship. On one hand, this fellowship removes from us what we should not have; on the other hand, it continually adds the new element of God into us.

As an example, let us consider Bible reading. When I was young, I had the desire to buy sixty-six books of exposition on each of the sixty-six books of the Bible. I thought that this would give me a complete understanding of the Bible. However, gradually I saw that this was impossible. I needed to abandon the things I had received from others' expositions and even the things I received myself when I read the Bible in fellowship. By letting go of the things I received in the past, I could receive new light in fellowship. Perhaps when I read the Bible next year, I will need to let go of the light I saw in the past so that there will be new light. This shows that in fellowship something is constantly being discarded, and something is constantly being gained. The things that need to be discarded do not consist merely of sin, the world, and the self. Even things that were given by God but have become old must be discarded. Brothers and sisters, the true condition of a Christian is found only in fellowship. No one can measure himself according to an outward standard, and neither can anyone measure others according to an outward standard. Every person needs to live in fellowship.

The effect of fellowship has the two aspects of constantly causing us to lose something and to gain something. However, the very things that we gain today may be the very things that the fellowship will require us to lose tomorrow. This is truly amazing. The more we live in the fellowship, the more intensive the metabolic function will become. If this metabolism ceases, and nothing old is removed and nothing new is added, our condition will remain the same year after year; we will no longer be in fellowship, and our growth will stop. A certain brother may have been wonderful five years ago, and he may still be wonderful today; he may have been lovely five years ago, and he may still be lovely today. We may say that such a brother is stable, but according to our experience of fellowship, there might be a problem in the future. A Christian who is in fellowship should always be changing. Fellowship constantly changes a person; it continually discharges the old elements within him and replaces them with new elements. Hence, the entire Christian living should be in fellowship. If we truly live in fellowship, the things that should not be in us will be removed on the negative side, and God will be added into us on the positive side. More and more we will be delivered from the self, and God will increase within us. This is the effect of fellowship.

THE TIME TO FELLOWSHIP WITH GOD

Constantly

Practically speaking, fellowship with God, like breathing, should be constant and not limited by time. If we breathe in the morning, we still need to breathe in the evening. Likewise, our fellowship with God cannot be limited to only one time. We must fellowship with God moment by moment. This is what the Bible refers to as "unceasingly" praying (1 Thes. 5:17). Praying unceasingly is a kind of spiritual breathing; it is uninterrupted and carried out at every time and in every place. There should not be a time or a place in which we stop fellowshipping with God. We should constantly exercise concerning this matter. Some unbelievers rebuke us, saying, "You are captured and bewitched by God. From morning to evening and from evening to morning, you simply cannot forget Him." We should respond, "We are not only captivated by God; we are actually breathing Him." When we stop breathing God, we cease to live. We should not be separated from God at any moment. There should always be inward fellowship between God and us. Even while we are angry, we should be fellow-shipping with God; we should even fellowship with God when quarrelling with others. Some may say, "If we are in fellowship with God, we will not quarrel with others." It seems as if this should be the situation because the best way to avoid quarrel-ling is to fellowship with God, but this is not always the case. We should learn to fellowship to such an extent that even when we quarrel and are upset with others, speaking angry words to them, we would still be able to fellowship with God. There should not be one moment that we are not in fellowship with God. Constant fellowship with God is the first point related to the time to fellowship with God.

Setting Aside Fixed Times

Although we should be in constant fellowship with God, we still need to set aside some time each day for fellowship. A new believer especially should set aside time during which he can fellowship with God. Examples of this can be found in the Bible. Daniel 6:10 says that Daniel prayed before his God three times daily. Psalm 119:164 says that David praised God seven times a day. Psalm 55:17 says that he complained and moaned evening, morning, and noontime. He came before God three times a day. Acts 10:3 says that Cornelius prayed at the ninth hour of the day. He had a fixed time to fellowship with God. Even our Lord Jesus set aside a specific time to pray for needs that arose. During the two thousand years of church history, many spiritual men who were used by the Lord set aside a specific time every day to have deep fellow-ship with Him.

According to our experience, it is best to set aside a time in the morning, before the day dawns. This is the time when we are refreshed after a night of sleep; we have not had contact with any person or thing, and our outward environment and inner being are quieter. Therefore, it is the best and sweetest time to come before God to fellowship with Him.

It is also good to find another time in the evening to come before God. It would also be profitable to spend more time to fellowship at midmorning, noontime, or in the afternoon. If we cannot set aside three times a day, it would be good to set aside two times. If we cannot set aside two times, we should have at least one time. We should set aside a specific time every day to fellowship with God. If we have only one time, I would suggest that it be in the morning. If a Christian wants to learn to live before the Lord and have constant fellowship with Him, he needs to be one who touches God early in the morning. It is understandable if we cannot fellowship with God at midmorning, at noon, or in the afternoon and in the evening but it is not understandable if we cannot fellowship with Him early in the morning. Of course, it is more difficult for brothers who work night shifts, but they can sleep until noon and then fellowship with the Lord. Thus, their "early morning time" is in the afternoon. However, this is not as good as leading a normal life of sleeping at night and rising in the morning. Consequently, working night shifts creates difficulties. It is not easy for those who work night shifts to be good Christians. I hope the brothers and sisters will do their best not to work night shifts. Brother George Müller even said that it is not good to travel long distances at night, because it is not profitable for one's spirit and body. I fully agree with him. Night is the time for sleeping; this is God's arrangement. Traveling or working at night violates this natural law. Keeping a natural law is beneficial in every aspect.

We should learn to rise early in the morning. Those who want to rise early should learn the lesson of going to bed early. It is very interesting that the more fallen a person is, the more he likes to stay up late at night, and the more he loathes rising early. God ordained that man would go to bed when the sun goes down and rise when the sun comes up, yet the devil stimulates man to be active when the sun goes down and to sleep when the sun comes up. This can be seen in the bustling activities that occur late at night, such as gambling, drinking, movies, and dancing. When it is time for those who participate in these to rise in the morning, they are still asleep.

As believers, we should not be like this. We should work when the sun comes up, rest when the sun goes down, and rise early in the morning. In order to rise early, we must go to bed early. Any unwillingness to go to bed early comes from our fallen nature. Our fallen nature encourages us to stay awake, but the nature within a believer encourages him to go to bed early. Whenever we see a believer who always goes to bed late, we should be concerned because always going to bed late is an indication that one has no intention of rising early the next morning to draw near to God. Such a Christian will have problems. However, if a brother goes to bed early, we cannot say with confidence that he is spiritual. At the most we can be at least fifty percent assured that he is doing well. This is because going to bed early means that he is able to rise early, and if one can rise early to draw near to God, his Christian life is more or less on track. Therefore, under normal circumstances, we should not go to bed later than eleven o'clock. The best is to go to sleep around ten o'clock and rise up at six o'clock in the morning. This is the appropriate experience of many.

Immediately after we rise in the morning, we should fellowship with God. We should spend at least twenty minutes fellowshipping with Him every day. If we cannot afford to spend this much time, we should spend at least ten minutes, but this is quite poor. The best is to have at least half an hour to one hour every morning. Our coming before God in such a way to have a specific time to fellowship is profitable to our whole being. Not only our spirit will be strengthened, but even our physical life will be prolonged. Brother George Müller lived to be ninety-three years old. From his biography, we learn that he was not physically strong as a child. According to my impression from reading his biography, his longevity was very much related to his fellowship with God every morning. He would rise up very early every morning and read the Bible and pray while taking a walk outdoors. This was his morning watch. I believe this was most beneficial. Because he fellowshipped with God in such a way, he had joy and rest. Although there was much labor and work, not a single burden or anxiety could harass him; hence, he lived to such an advanced age.

Thus, drawing near to God in the morning and fellowshipping with Him not only causes our spirit to be fed and nourished but also causes our body to be healthy. At the same time, it renders much help to our mind, our train of thought, and our judgment. If we touch and absorb God every morning, we will have an intelligent mind, clear thinking, and sound judgment. Consequently, we will become those whose spirit, soul, and body are thriving and strong.

Therefore, we must learn to rise early and set aside a time to fellowship with God, to absorb Him. When we first start, it is not necessary to spend too much time; otherwise, it will become a burden that we will be unable to maintain. On average, it is sufficient to spend half an hour each day. It may also be necessary to make some resolution and determination and to find another brother or sister who has the heart to practice in order to remind and encourage one another.

THE PLACE TO FELLOWSHIP WITH GOD

Anytime and Anywhere

The principle related to the place to fellowship with God is the same as that for the time to fellowship. There is no place where we cannot fellowship with God. Whether we are traveling, working, taking a walk, or listening to a message, we can fellowship with God at all times and in all places. We can fellowship anytime and anywhere.

Setting Aside a Specific Place

We also need a specific place to fellowship with God. Personally, I feel that the devil has truly damaged Christians concerning this matter. Because both land and housing are expensive, people are always crowded together. Very few Christians have a room that is exclusively for prayer. We must admit that it is difficult to pray in crowded living quarters. In order to pray properly, however, a quiet place is needed. Therefore, we still need to try our best to find a suitable place.

Given this need, some people rise early in the morning to pray outside for half an hour while others are still asleep. This is one solution for the need of a place. There are some who go up to the mountains to pray since they live near the mountains. I have also lived in these conditions. In those days, a few of us would go up to the mountain every day, and we would each find a spot to fellowship with the Lord. The sweetness of this was beyond utterance.

We should not say that since fellowshipping with God is a matter in spirit, the outward environment does not matter. Even the Lord Jesus was not this spiritual. The Bible clearly says that He sometimes needed to go up to the mountain to pray. There is much to consider regarding the place for fellowshipping with God. We will learn more as we experience this ourselves.

THE PROCEDURES TO FELLOWSHIP WITH GOD

There are procedures for everything that is done. Fellowshipping with God also has procedures. Although these procedures are not rigid, we cannot deviate too much from them. We will reap the most benefit if we fellowship with God according to the best procedures. Of course, not all procedures are the same. Different people prefer different procedures; we can speak only in a general way.

Needing to Be Quiet

A person who fellowships with God must learn to be quiet. Being quiet is not merely to be freed from the entanglements of outward matters but also to let go of all the things that should not be in our mind, our thoughts. In other words, we need to quiet our mind.

The mind is the most difficult part of a person's inner being to quiet. The young ones and the older ones have many thoughts in the morning when they rise. When a Christian desires to learn to fellowship with God, Satan will work very hard to inject many thoughts into his mind. Sometimes Satan injects thoughts to bother his mind and disturb his inner being. Therefore, we must first learn the lesson of being quiet so that we can have good fellowship with God. Whenever we come before God, we should not immediately pray, read the Bible, or sing hymns. Rather, we need to settle our being both inwardly and outwardly. However, we cannot be quiet for too long; otherwise, many scattered thoughts will begin to come in. This will not produce the desired result. Doing anything prior to our time of fellowship will be a distraction, and also being quiet for too long will not be profitable; we need to be balanced.

Praying

After settling down, some people prefer to read the Bible first, but most people prefer to pray. We also feel that it is best to pray first. When we pray, however, we should not pray too long, we should not pray wordy prayers, and we should not pray concerning many different matters. Our prayer should be focused on touching God and contacting Him. Of course, this prayer should include confession and dealing. When we are calm in our to contact with God, we will spontaneously sense our mistakes and filthiness. Once we have this sense, we will spontaneously confess them and deal with them before God. However, we should be careful not to pour out all of our prayer burdens before God at this time. We should simply pray until we sense that we have contacted and touched God. Then we can stop.

Reading the Bible

Once we contact and touch God, we should turn to read the Lord's Word, the Bible. We should be careful not to exercise our mind merely to analyze while reading the Scriptures. This can be done at another time. This time is for eating. Studying about nutrition is one thing, whereas eating is another. Reading the Word in fellowship is not for studying God's Word but for eating it. When we come before the Lord and open His Word, we should spontaneously exercise our spirit to absorb His Word and thus eat spiritual food. It is good when we understand, but we do not need to strive to understand. The less we use the mind, the better. We will easily receive inspiration by reading in this way.

Reading and Praying

As soon as we receive inspiration, while reading the Bible, we should turn the inspiration into prayer. Then our reading of the Bible will be turned into prayer. As long as time allows, we can continue reading and praying, praying and reading, thereby turning the inspiration we receive into prayer. This is the central and primary section of fellowshipping with the Lord.

Praying for Matters

After our inner being is well fed through the fellowship, if there is still time and burden, we can pray for some matters and persons. However, such prayer should not drag out too long; otherwise, it will disrupt our fellowship with God. In fact, we should learn to set aside another time each day to labor in prayer for various matters. This is different from prayer for fellowship. This is to bear the burden before God and pray for certain matters, work, and people. This is prayer more than fellowship. However, many brothers and sisters may be unable to set aside another time. Hence, after their fellowship with the Lord, they may spend some time to pray, giving themselves, their families, their work, and other people to the Lord.

Worshipping

At the beginning of this type of fellowship, we are always quiet. Being quiet implies worship. But at the end, there should again be some worship, praise, and thanksgiving. Therefore, one of the procedures at the end of every fellowship is to worship with thanksgiving and praise.

If the above six procedures can be done in thirty minutes, they will be done in a good and proper way. Of course, we may not be very skillful when we begin to practice. Gradually, as we acquire the skill, we will gain the benefit. The experience of others confirms this. Therefore, new believers should try their best to have this kind of fellowship at least once a day, with the best time being in the morning.

In summary, this is the way to come before God. We should be quiet and prostrate ourselves to worship God and then pray to contact Him. When we sense that we have some wrongdoings or sins, we should confess them. After touching the Lord, we can read His Word, not exercising our mind more than our spirit to absorb the Word. When we receive inspiration, we should turn it into prayer. Then we should read and pray more as time allows. If there is still time and burden, we can pray for other matters before God, committing ourselves, our families, and our work into God's hand. At the end, we can offer some worship, praise, and thanksgiving before God. If a new believer practices this daily, his progress before the Lord will be fast, and the riches within him will increase.

THE PRACTICE OF FELLOWSHIP

(3)

We have covered seven main points concerning the practice of fellowship. We will now continue.

Although we divided the lessons on the practice of fellowship into different points and have covered each point, our intention is not to understand more doctrine but to enter into the reality of fellowship in our daily living. Therefore, the saints who participate in this training should not merely come to listen to doctrine or learn some truth; rather, they should practice according to our fellowship. As we listen to these lessons, we should make a resolution before God to set aside a specific time each day to practice this kind of fellowship. After scheduling a time, we should check with one another to see whether we are practicing according to our plan. We can also ask each other where we practiced this fellowship. In addition, many of those who are beginning to fellowship with us may not be clear regarding the procedures of fellowshipping with God and may have difficulty practicing certain points. Hence, these difficult points should be considered and resolved in the meeting for new believers. As we practice, we will learn.

The living of a Christian depends entirely on his fellowship with God. If we truly enter into and live in this fellowship, many problems will be resolved. The teachings we have received and the truth we have understood are merely outward. In order to receive real help and solve our problems, we need to enter into this kind of fellowship. The empowering, enlightening, enjoying of rest, rejoicing, believing, overcoming of trials, temptations, and hardships, and comforting for a Christian all depend on fellowship. All of a Christian's problems can be solved in fellowship. Therefore, our fellowshipping will bring in a great blessing. Of course, we cannot expect to succeed by practicing only two or three times. We should thank the Lord if we are able to practice for two or three months and learn the lessons of fellowship.

THE MEANS OF FELLOWSHIP WITH GOD

All orthodox Christians agree that there are two important means to fellowship with God—prayer and reading the Bible. In these lessons we are devoting one lesson specifically to prayer and another to reading the Bible, in order to consider these two from the standpoint of how a new believer can fellowship with God through prayer and reading the Bible.

Prayer

Prayer is for contacting God and having fellowship with Him. The emphasis here is not on asking God concerning different matters. Prayer is a means and a way of fellowship. Fellowship with God must be by prayer and through prayer. In the lesson on prayer we stressed that the real meaning of prayer is to contact God and absorb Him. Now in this lesson we want to see how we can practically contact God and fellowship with Him through prayer.

In whatever we do, we need to have ability as well as practice. For example, although man has the natural ability to ride a bicycle, this ability can be developed only through practice. In the same way, in terms of spiritual ability, every believer can pray and contact God. However, in terms of practice, many new believers have not yet learned and lack practice; hence, they do not have the skill and may not even know how to pray. I am speaking from my own experience. When I was newly saved, I knew I should pray, I desired to pray, and I wanted to pray. However, I did not know how to pray. Gradually, after practicing and learning from others' experiences, I came to the conclusion that there are actually some secrets and points to consider in the matter of prayer. I hope that you will practice these points properly.

Speaking Genuinely from the Heart

First, prayer that contacts God consists of words spoken genuinely from the heart. We must pray according to our inward feeling. We should not exercise our mind like a student taking an exam. Neither should we focus on the wording of prayer as if we are writing an essay. Such prayers are not very genuine; they are rather pretentious. When we come before God to pray, we should not be pretentious. We should speak what we feel within. When we are angry, we should voice our anger before God. When we are happy, we should voice our happiness before God. When we are sad, we should voice our sadness before God. When we are under pressure, we should speak of this pressure before God. When we sense that we are sinful, we should confess it before God. We should speak what we feel within, speaking genuine words from our heart. This can be likened to a young child who always speaks what is in his heart to his parents. The words of our children are always genuine.

There is the danger that new believers will not open their mouths in the meetings because they are influenced by the prayers of those who have been saved for a long time. The prayer of such saints often flows with well-thought-out words like a torrent of water. When new believers compare themselves with these saints, they hesitate to open their mouth. This is abnormal. The church is a family, not a court. In a court one needs to carefully choose each word because a slight mistake will have serious consequences, but in a family one does not need to be so accurate in his wording. Very often the youngest child, who least knows how to speak, speaks the most because he does not care whether his words are right or wrong. The result is that his speaking is genuine. This should be our practice; we should not make up anything but simply pray according to our inward feeling. We should not be afraid of not knowing how to pray. God never blames people for not knowing how to pray. There are many examples in the Bible that prove that even unlearned prayers can be accepted by God. We may pray such prayers, but He will understand. He knows what we mean; He always answers us according to what is right. We do not need to worry, and we do not need elaborate prayers when we fellowship with God. We must speak genuinely from our heart.

Not Being Influenced by Memory

Second, our prayer should not be influenced by the things in our memory. Many people have a difficult time praying because they are influenced by their memory. I have had this experience. When I rose in the morning, I would consider the things I needed to pray for in morning watch. Then when I knelt down to pray, I would spend much effort trying to remember what I should pray for, and as a result, I failed to contact God in spirit. This is wrong. We should never try to remember things to pray for when we fellowship with God. Even if we do remember something, we should let it go so that it does not interrupt our prayer.

Some people make a record of the various items they prayed for on Monday, what they prayed for on Tuesday, and so forth. This is a good practice. If a new believer can practice in this way, it will be beneficial. This type of prayer, however, is not focused on our fellowship with God. The prayer that we are speaking of is related to fellowship with God. In this kind of prayer we need to forget everything. We do not need to remember any prayer burdens, such as prayer requests that we have received or promised others. This is not necessary. We must view prayer in a very simple way. Whether or not we remember certain items for prayer is of no consequence. We need not focus on any items we may remember.

Not Paying Attention to Composing Sentences

Third, we should not compose sentences; that is, we should not focus on the wording of our prayer. It does not matter whether our words are disorderly, disconnected, or even incoherent. We should simply utter the words as they come. However, those who are learning to pray should learn how to speak before God. We will speak concerning this in the future. Presently, as we are learning to fellowship with God in prayer, we can ignore matters of wording and phrasing and simply speak spontaneously. It is not important whether our wording is accurate as long as we fellowship with God.

Relying upon the Blood

Fourth, we must rely upon the precious blood of the Lord Jesus and learn to apply the effectiveness of His blood. Experience shows that when we pray according to the above points—not being pretentious, not praying according to memory, not caring about the wording, but praying spontaneously before God—it will be easy for us to sense our sins. This is a certainty. If we are pretentious and try to remember the things that we need to pray for, the feeling of being sinful will dissipate. If we contact God in a simple and spontaneous way, we will definitely sense within that we are sinful and have problems and faults. When this sense comes, we should learn to rely upon the precious blood and ask for God's forgiveness based on the effectiveness of the Lord's shed blood.

Needing to Confess Our Sins

We must confess our sins in order to rely upon the precious blood for God's forgiveness. The more we confess, the more we will touch God, and the more thorough our confession, the deeper we can enter into God. However, we need to be careful not to ask, "Have I sinned? Did I sin yesterday, the day before yesterday, or this week?" This is introspection. Confession that comes out of introspection has no spiritual value.

Both in the East and in the West those in religion advise people to examine themselves. Chinese sages say that we should examine ourselves three times a day. Many revivalists and spiritual men in Christianity speak concerning introspection. They use the only verse in the Bible, Haggai 1:7, that speaks of considering one's ways, as the basis for advising people to examine themselves. However, experience has proven that introspection is harmful to a Christian's spirituality. When a person wants to draw near to God, introspection is an interruption, a hindrance. Confessing our sins during our fellowship with God does not depend on introspection; it is altogether a matter of a spontaneous feeling. If we do not feel that we have sinned, we do not need to examine ourselves.

When we feel that we have sinned, we should confess that sin before God and ask for His forgiveness through the precious blood. This point is very important.

When learning how to fellowship with God, many believers neglect confession and therefore never learn to fellowship in a proper way. In the so-called "Charismatic movement," those who were revived were blessed through confessing. They knew that confession could help them touch God. However, they did it excessively, and it became harmful. When we practice confession in our fellowship with God, we should neither neglect it nor be excessive. We should confess in a spontaneous way. This matter is truly important and profitable.

Because there was no one to lead us in these important points concerning fellowship, we groped for many years, going in circles and wasting much energy with no progress. Gradually, we began to consider this matter and learned from other people's experiences. We have spent twenty to thirty years thoroughly and accurately considering the matter of fellowship. I know the condition of fellowship. When we come before God without being pretentious or memorizing the things we need to pray for and we simply place ourselves before Him and let the Holy Spirit shine in us, He causes us to sense and see certain sins or mistakes that we have committed. At that time, we should confess the sin according to this sense. We should confess only as much as we sense. We do not need to take care of what we have not sensed. While confessing, we need to receive the precious blood, rely on the blood, and apply the effectiveness of the blood. If we continue praying in this way, we can be assured that we will touch God's presence and contact Him.

Not Worrying about Other Things

We should never be distracted and consider other things after we confess our sins. Once we are distracted, the Spirit will stop moving within us. For example, it is very good for a sister to sense the need to confess as she is fellowshipping with God. However, she may suddenly remember that her child needs to go to school and that breakfast is not ready. Once she begins to have such thoughts, the fellowship within will stop. Or she may remember a relative who is recovering from an illness and needs prayer. If she begins to pray for this one, the inward feeling will disappear, and it will be difficult for her to continue fellowshipping. Therefore, when we sense something in our fellowship with God, especially the need to confess, we should never think of other things or bring other things into our fellowship. Even though we are still praying, these things can become serious distractions, and we will have no way to touch God's presence. Instead, they will cause us to lose His presence.

Not Being Restrained

We should not feel restrained when we confess according to the inner feeling. If we feel like crying, we should cry. If we feel like laughing, we should laugh. If we feel sad, we should be sad. If we feel happy, we should rejoice. We should not be restrained in our inner feeling. There is, however, another side to this matter. As we become skillful in fellowshipping with God, we should learn to exercise self-control. Initially however, there is no need to exercise any restraint. For example, immediately after confessing their sins, some people become afraid and hesitant to confess further. As a result, the Spirit stops moving within them. This is a pity. The Holy Spirit is signified by a dove, which is very sensitive and gentle. If we limit Him or disagree with Him even a little, He will retreat. We must obey Him all the time. If He wants us to confess, we must not hesitate, no matter what the sin may be. This applies only to confession before God, not before men. In confessing before men, there are times when we should exercise restraint.

As humans, we are very complicated. According to our experience, even our prayers are complicated. Sometimes we are concerned for this, and at other times we are concerned for that. It is difficult for us to simply and closely follow the inner feeling and confess. But if we are willing to be simple and not be concerned with other things but follow the feeling to confess, our prayer will lead us deep into God. We may even have the experience of the outpouring and the filling of the Holy Spirit.

Praising and Giving Thanks

According to general experience, after we have a thorough confession, we can praise and give thanks. However, this is not a rule. This is not a procedure to memorize and follow. We should not think that we must always praise and give thanks after confessing. Rather, after thoroughly confessing, a spontaneous feeling to praise God and give Him thanks may arise within us. At this time, we must release our inner feeling of praise and thanks without any reservation. The more we release this feeling, the more we will touch God. If we withhold it, we will lose the feeling of God's presence. Therefore, we must convert a feeling of praise and thanks into words and fully release them. The more we praise and give thanks, the better; the more thorough this release is, the better.

Worshipping

Toward the end of our fellowship, if there is still time, we should also worship God. It is rather difficult to describe exactly what worship is and what our inner condition should be when we worship. We may say that worship is a lingering before God. We should not simply get up and leave as soon as we have finished praising and thanking God. No, we should linger before Him a little longer. This kind of lingering is the issue of our heart's desire for God. It involves beholding, waiting, and inquiring; we behold God's glory, lingering before Him to wait on Him and inquire of Him. This is not an inquiring related to specific things. Instead, it is a waiting out of a desire to know His will. All these things are included in worshipping.

Praying for Practical Affairs

At this point some people spontaneously receive the burden to pray for certain practical affairs or to intercede, but this is not required. We should not expect that there will always be a need to intercede for practical affairs each time we fellowship with God. If our time and energy do not allow us to do this, we should not take up this burden. Our God is not a hard master. He never requests us to do what exceeds our limits. Therefore, we should not force ourselves to pick up the burden to pray for practical affairs. We do not need to do this every time we fellowship. However, the first nine points that we have spoken of should be considered as principles to be followed each time.

HOW TO LEAD THE PRACTICE OF FELLOWSHIP

Let us speak briefly to the leading ones concerning how to lead the meeting for the practice of fellowship.

If we want to lead new believers into this kind of fellowship, we must first tell them all the main points. We should not speak too much at one time. We should save considerable time to allow them to ask questions. Sometimes we can ask them to repeat what has been spoken to be sure they understand and are clear concerning those points. Each point should be discussed in detail so that everyone can understand.

After they are clear concerning the main points, we should ask them to commit to begin practicing. We should ask, "Brother So-and-so, how many minutes do you plan to use each day to practice, ten minutes or fifteen?" We should discuss their schedule with them and give them suggestions, helping them to set aside a suitable time. The time should not be too early or too late, nor too long or too short. This is a good way to fellowship with them. We may ask, "Brother, what time do you go to work? What are the things you need to do at home?" He may respond, "I am a teacher. I go to work at eight o'clock every morning. Since there are things to be done at home in the morning, I cannot set aside a time in the morning. There is no way." In that case, we must help him find another time. We must lead him in this way and help others one by one. However, we should not get into unnecessary details or be too rigid. Once we get into unnecessary details in the meeting or we are too rigid, everyone will lose interest. We must do this in a lively way, helping them one by one to set aside a time and promise to practice.

We should help them in this way. We should reserve eight to ten minutes before the end of the meeting to ask them to

pray for the Lord's blessing to carry out what they have pur-
posed to do in order that they can learn to pray and
fellowship with the Lord from that day onward.

There is still a need at the beginning of the next meeting
to ask them about the main points spoken in the previous
meeting. Then we need to ask them whether they have practiced according to their schedule. If they are practicing, we
should ask them to give a testimony to see if they have
encountered any difficulties or problems. There may not be
the opportunity to cover more items in this second meeting.
We can review what was spoken in the first meeting concerning fellowship, make adjustments, give explanations and a
supplementary word, and answer some questions. After speaking, we need to ask them to continue practicing.

I believe it is relatively easy to lead new believers into
practical experiences in this way. This will help them sense
that they have a way to go on and a place to bring their questions and receive answers. In this way, the new believers and
those answering questions will benefit, and we can research
and pursue our growth together. Moreover, this meeting will
serve the purposes of speaking messages, fellowshipping, and
praying. The entire meeting will be living and have God's
blessing and presence. People will also be able to touch something and learn something. Everyone will have a good taste
and will thus be willing to come to the meetings.

Whereas the first points concerning the practice of fellowship are theory, the last points concerning the time, place, and
procedures of fellowship require our practice. In particular, the
point concerning prayer being the means of fellowship requires
us to lead the brothers and sisters into a practice. It would be
good to help the saints to be clear concerning these points
over a period of five weeks. Only if the new believers are
brought into such a living will the messages that they hear in
the future have any effect on them. If they do not enter into
such a living, we cannot say that the messages they hear will
be of no benefit to them, but they must be in fellowship with
God in order for the word to have a definite effect on them.
Therefore, we must concentrate our efforts to bring the brothers
and sisters into fellowship, teaching them how to pray.

Perhaps not many of the seven or eight thousand brothers and sisters in the church in Taipei live in fellowship with God. There may not be even three to five hundred saints who fellowship with God daily. It would be a great thing if we could lead the saints to practice fellowshipping with God so that after a period of time there would be two to three thousand brothers and sisters who daily fellowship with God. The result of this slow, fine work would be great and unlimited. If we want to be quick and use other means, any useful results will come even slower.

Therefore, it is worthwhile for the responsible brothers in every local church to pay full attention to this matter. On the one hand, we ourselves need to live in fellowship with more learning and practice. On the other hand, we need to try our best to help and lead others. It does not matter if there are only a few brothers and sisters initially. A large number is not necessary. As long as we lead the saints in a living, practical, and enjoyable way, the number of saints will increase spontaneously. The church will also be greatly blessed.

THE PRACTICE OF FELLOWSHIP

(4)

In the previous lesson, we covered the first means of fellowship with God, which is prayer. Now we come to the second means, which is reading the Bible.

Bible Reading

We do not need doctrines concerning reading the Bible. Rather, I want to point out a practical method for us to practice so that we can fellowship with God through Bible reading. Therefore, this kind of reading of the Bible is different from a common way of reading it. Whenever we speak of reading the Bible, our natural concept is that it refers to understanding the Bible and knowing the contents of the Bible. However, reading the Bible as a means to fellowship with God is neither for understanding the Bible nor for knowing the contents of the Bible; rather, it is entirely for fellowshipping with God and contacting Him. When we read the Bible in this way, we need to remember the following points.

Not Having the Intention of Seeking Understanding

When we read the Bible for the purpose of fellowship, we should not read for the purpose of seeking to understand it. This seems to be a contradictory statement. If we do not seek to understand the Bible, why should we still read it? Apparently, everyone who reads the Bible seeks to understand it, but reading the Bible for fellowship is different from a common reading of the Bible. This kind of reading is absolutely not for knowing the Bible but for contacting God Himself and having fellowship with Him. If we read the Bible with the intention of understanding it, it will be difficult for us to enter into fellowship. Therefore, we need to resolve the matter that in reading the Bible to fellowship with God, we should not intend to seek an understanding of it. Even if we do not seek to understand the Bible, we will still understand a little as a result of reading in this way. This will be spontaneous. But before we begin to read, we should not have the intention to try to understand and know it.

If we come to the Bible with such an intention, we will encounter a great hindrance, a distraction, in our fellowship with God. An intention to understand the Bible in our fellowship with God makes it difficult for many of us to have good fellowship with God. Therefore, we must give up this intention whenever we come to God for fellowship through reading the Bible; we should simply come to fellowship with God through His Word without caring whether or not we understand it.

It is not easy to let go of this intention; it requires much consideration and practice. However, only when we learn to be delivered from this intention to understand the Bible can we properly learn to fellowship with God. In addition, only through reading the Bible in this way can we truly understand the Bible. Only those who do not seek a hasty understanding of the Bible will eventually know the Bible well. This is amazing. Many people can confirm this through their experience.

Not Studying or Researching

When reading the Bible to fellowship with God, we need to avoid study and research. We should not study, nor should we research; we simply need to read it. We still need to study and research the Bible, but this should be done at another time when we can use reference books, such as concordances and Bible dictionaries, in order to study the Bible in a detailed way. This is called studying the Bible, not reading the Bible for fellowship with God. We should never study the Bible when fellowshipping with God. This also requires much practice. Although I have been practicing this for a long time, I am still often tempted to study the Bible when fellowshipping with the Lord. At times I consulted a concordance, and at other times I referred to footnotes. As a result, even though I was studying the Bible with my mind, there was no fellowship with the Lord in my spirit, and thus, the fellowship with the Lord that morning was ruined.

Hence, we must avoid studying during this kind of reading of the Bible. If we understand the Bible when we are reading it, this is fine, and if we do not understand it, we should not be concerned. Some may ask, "What if I cannot correctly pronounce the words?" If you cannot pronounce the words correctly, just pronounce the words incorrectly. This is not a problem. We must absolutely, completely, and wholly let go of studying and researching. The less effort we exert in reading the Bible, the better and the more spontaneous our reading will be. Do not seek to understand, study, or research. The more spontaneous we are, the better will be our fellowship with God. We need to put all our efforts, energy, and intention into fellowshipping with God rather than studying the words of the Bible. If we read a portion of the Bible in a spontaneous way, we will definitely touch God in our fellowship.

Not Reading Fast or Too Much

We also should not read the Bible too fast, and neither should we read it too slowly. We should read as much as we can, without intending to read too much. There is what I would call a temptation to read the Bible too fast. Everyone who reads the Bible is tempted to read fast. After reading the first verse, we are tempted to quickly go on to the second verse, or we are tempted to quickly finish reading one portion in order to read the next portion. When we read concerning the death of Nadab and Abihu (Lev. 10), we are tempted to read faster in order to know what their father said concerning their death. When we read Numbers 17 where God told Moses to put twelve rods before Him, we are tempted to learn the result related to these twelve rods. This kind of fast and quick reading is common, but it is a great interruption to our fellowship with God. Therefore, we must practice to be calm, spontaneous, and not hasty when we read the Bible to fellowship with God. We should simply read according to the time we have available, not intending to read fast or to read too much. We may read one chapter, one paragraph, one verse, one sentence, or even a few words. What matters is that we touch God in fellowship.

Not Pondering

To ponder is another temptation when reading the Bible. It is strange that when we read fast, we cannot stop our mind, but when we read slowly, we often ponder. For example, when we read, "In the beginning, God created the heavens and the earth," we begin to consider what *the beginning* refers to and how many places *the heavens and the earth* include. We may consider different things and draw analogies. This is a great hindrance to our fellowship. Therefore, we should exercise not to ponder. Does this sound strange? We do not need to understand, research, study, read fast, read much, or ponder in order to fellowship through reading the Bible.

On one hand, reading the Bible in this way is spontaneous, but on the other hand, it may not be so easy. Can we come to the Bible without intending to understand or to research and study? Can we come without haste or the desire to read too much or too little? Can we instead read spontaneously and not ponder over the word? If we practice these things over a period of time, we will find that it is not easy. I do not believe that out of one hundred believers, three know how to fellowship with God in this way. Someone may occasionally touch God in fellowship through reading the Bible, but he cannot constantly and confidently have good fellowship with God whenever he reads the Bible. This inadequacy shows that there is a need for more practice.

When I was young, I was taught an ancient Chinese exercise called the "eight-section medley," which is a kind of calisthenics. When I was first shown how to do it, I thought that it was easy. But when I began to practice, I found that it was not easy. A few years ago, when I was in a workers' home in Manila, a young brother saw me practicing the eight-section medley. He also thought that it was easy and asked me to teach him. But as I taught him the exercise, he realized that it was not so easy or simple to learn. The exercise is a spontaneous and slow-motion type of calisthenics, but it requires much practice. In the same way, we should not think that it is easy to read the Bible in the way of fellowship. It may be easy to read a newspaper, but it is not easy to read the Bible. There are two difficulties in reading the Bible. First, it is not easy to understand the Bible and receive something from it. Second, it is not easy to fellowship with God through reading the Bible. These points are not related to reading the Bible for understanding but to reading the Bible for fellowship with God. Both ways of reading the Bible require practice. It would be very good for a believer to practice both aspects of reading the Bible.

We sincerely hope that every new believer will learn how to fellowship with God through reading the Bible. Every time they sit down to read God's word, they should consider the four "nots," that is, *not* trying to understand, *not* studying or researching, *not* reading too fast or too much, and *not* pondering. It is not necessary to understand, to study, to read fast, to read much, or to ponder. We should let go of these things and only fellowship with God in a simple and spontaneous way through reading the Bible. I say once again that this is not easy, and it requires much practice.

The previous four points are things that we should not do; now we must consider things that we should do.

Having the Intention to Seek the Lord

We need to have the intention to seek the Lord and contact Him. Our intention is not to understand the Bible but to seek and contact the Lord. We come to the Bible in order to contact the living God, not read dead letters.

The Lord is in His Word, and the Lord Himself is the Word. A person can touch the Lord in two places—the Word and the Spirit. The Lord is in the Word, and the Lord is the Word. The Lord is also in the Spirit, and He is the Spirit. We thank Him that we have the Word outside of us and the Spirit inside of us. We have the Lord's Word in our hand, and we have the Lord's Spirit in our spirit. These are the two places where we can contact the Lord. Even though the Lord is omnipresent, invisible, and intangible, we can surely locate Him in these two places. We can say that the Lord is in His Word and that the Lord is in the Spirit. We can also say that the Lord is the Word and that the Lord is the Spirit. We can contact Him only in these two places. On the one hand, we come to His Word, and on the other hand, we come to the Spirit. Therefore, when we read the Bible for fellowship, our concept should never be that we are merely reading a book or some words. Our concept should be that we are contacting the Lord Himself, because we know that the Lord is in the Word and also that He is the Word.

Contacting the Words in the Bible with Our Spirit

We should read the Bible slowly in order to give our spirit the opportunity to contact the words in the Bible. This is related to the earlier entreaty to not study, not research, not read fast, and not ponder so that we can touch the words in the Bible with our spirit.

New believers may ask, "What does it mean to use our spirit?" Let me explain with an example. When conversing with those close to us, whether our parents, children, husbands, or wives, what the mind understands is not as important as how much the emotion functions and is contacted. We speak with our emotion; we touch and contact the words with our emotion. In the same principle, when fellowshipping with God through reading His Word, it is not important to understand, study, or ponder with our mind but to contact and touch God with our spirit.

Reading with our spirit does not necessarily mean that we read only a short portion. It is possible to read three chapters in fifteen minutes without being too fast or too slow and without pondering over the contents. Sometimes after reading in this way, it seems as if I am not very clear about what I have read, but I feel as if I have taken a bath. Although no water remains on our body after we take a bath, there is a difference between taking a bath and not taking one. In the same way, if we contact the Lord's Word with our spirit, though it may seem as if nothing remains in our mind, the feeling in the spirit is very different.

We fellowship with God with our inner man, not with our outer man. The outer man is in the mind, but the inner man is in the spirit. When we fellowship with God and contact His Word in this way, we should read the letter with our mind outwardly, but we should contact the Lord's Word with our spirit. We should always have the intention to touch God Himself and not care for understanding or retention. Only in this way can we have good fellowship with God.

Therefore, I recommend that we have two ways of reading the Bible—one for fellowship and one for understanding. When reading for understanding, we need to exercise our mind. Although our mental capacity may not be large, the more our capacity, the better. It would be best if our capacity was greater than Solomon's and larger than the ocean. We also need to have a good collection of reference books. The more reference books we use in our time of study, the better. This is the way to read the Bible for understanding. The way to read the Bible for fellowship, however, is different because we do not understand the Word with our mind but contact the Word with our spirit. Whether or not we understand is not the point, neither is whether or not we remember. We should simply exercise our spirit to have good contact with God in His Word. This is to contact the Bible with the spirit.

Maintaining Constant Contact with the Lord

When reading the Bible in this way, we also need to pay attention to maintaining constant contact with the Lord and not being distracted by the outward letters. We should not pay attention only to reading but forget to contact the Lord. It is not easy to maintain our fellowship with the Lord when reading the Bible for ten to twenty minutes in this way. Some people can contact the Lord without reading the Bible, but once they start reading the Bible, their contact with the Lord is interrupted. Thus, to read the Word and still be able to maintain contact with the Lord is a spiritual skill that requires much practice. We need to practice reading while contacting the Lord and contacting the Lord while reading so that our contact with the Lord is not interrupted by our reading. In our reading, we need to maintain and remain in fellowship with the Lord. If we read the Bible in this way for twenty minutes, we will have contact and fellowship with the Lord for twenty minutes. This will be a great benefit.

Having a Feeling of Being Bathed, Warmed, Refreshed, Moistened, and Supplied by the Word in the Bible

When we touch the Lord's Word with our spirit and remain in continual fellowship with Him, our spirit should have a feeling of being bathed, as if our whole being were taking a bath in the Bible. This is refreshing, comfortable, and joyful. We should have this kind of feeling when we fellowship with God through reading the Word. If we do not have such a feeling, our fellowship with the Lord has ceased; otherwise, we would certainly have such a feeling. When we pass through God's word, we should be like a person who has taken a bath, a person who has been soaked in water.

Not only so, we should feel warm, as if we were sitting under the sun, and we should also be inwardly refreshed. The more we read, the more we should be refreshed. If we read for five minutes, we should be even more refreshed. Some may ask us to describe this freshness. Although it is difficult to fully describe this freshness, it is like the freshness of the morning dew. Consequently, we will also be moistened. We may not know what has touched us, what has enlightened us, or what we have learned, but we will be moistened. As we read verse by verse, we become moist and we will be full of an inward sweetness. In addition, we will sense a supply. The more we read, the more we will be inwardly satisfied, filled, empowered, and strengthened. There will also be light. But I am not stressing light because light implies understanding, and we have said that seeking to understand often becomes a hindrance to our fellowship.

This is the way we should read the Bible for thirty minutes in the morning. Although we may not understand anything, we will take a bath in God's Word and feel warm in our spirit. We will not have the sense of being hot, scorched, or burned, but we will have an indescribably warm feeling and be refreshed, moistened, supplied, and satisfied. This is good Bible reading.

This can be compared to eating a rich breakfast. We may not remember exactly what we ate, but we will feel full and energized. We will be satisfied without any hunger or thirst. This is an indescribable feeling. The more we read the Lord's Word and fellowship with Him in this way, the more we will know how real and sweet it is to read the Bible.

Receiving Inspiration

We will then receive inspiration. Inspiration is not understanding. Understanding comes from the mind, but inspiration is a feeling in the spirit. For example, when we read 1 Peter 5:5, which says, "God resists the proud but gives grace to the humble," we may receive inspiration in our spirit that touches us deep within, causing us to see that we are proud and that we do not know the meaning of humility. We must accept this inspiration and remain in this portion of the Word, without reading further. When we read Genesis 1:2, which says, "But the earth became waste and emptiness," we may receive the inspiration that there is just waste and emptiness within us. In this case, we must open to this inspiration and let it touch us even more deeply.

In addition to the functions of bathing, warming, moistening, refreshing, and supplying, reading the Bible to fellowship with God has a great function of giving inspiration. When we read the Bible to fellowship with God, it is easy to receive inspiration. In fact, we will receive much more inspiration when we read the Bible in this way than when we read it for understanding. This is because when we read the Bible for understanding, we mainly use our mind, but when we read the Bible for fellowship with God, we use our spirit to touch God's moving in our spirit. Once the Holy Spirit moves, there is inspiration. We should not regard the inspiration we receive lightly but should open to it in a deep way.

Meditating on the Inspiration
and Turning It into Prayer

We should meditate on the inspiration we receive. At this

stage of our fellowship with God through reading the Bible, we should not ponder, but we should meditate. Once we touch the inspiration, we need to meditate on it and then turn it into prayer. For example, if we receive inspiration and sense that we have lost the opportunity to be blessed because of our pride, we should immediately stop and meditate, saying, "Yes, I am self-satisfied in some aspects, and I am not humble enough." However, it is not good to meditate too long. Hence, we should turn the inspiration we receive into prayer and confess before the Lord, saying, "Please forgive me. There is pride within me. Have mercy on me and let me touch humility." This kind of prayer that comes out of inspiration and is through meditation is good fellowship. In this crucial stage, reading the Bible and prayer are now mingled together. Reading the Bible becomes our praying, and gradually, our praying becomes a reading of the Bible. We will cover this point in greater detail in the next lesson.

We need to receive inspiration, meditate on the inspiration, and then turn it into prayer. Sometimes this type of prayer is intercessory in nature; that is, we pray for others. Although we receive inspiration for ourselves, the prayer can result in intercession for others. This kind of intercessory prayer is often valuable, and God answers it.

Praying and Then Reading the Word

This type of prayer should not be long. After praying, if there is still time, we should read more from the Bible. We should never think that our fellowship with God is finished after we have read and prayed. In this type of fellowship, reading the Bible and prayer should continue side by side. We read and then we pray and then we read again. We do not need to be clear whether we are reading the Bible or praying because we are reading with prayer and praying with reading. We are not merely concluding our reading with prayer. This is not sufficient. Whenever we read, we should be ready to receive inspiration and then turn the inspiration into prayer and then continue to read after praying. However, this is not a law. Sometimes we may not be able to continue reading because the Holy Spirit touches us and asks us to pray.

Very often, however, we will first receive inspiration, meditate on the inspiration, and then turn it into prayer. After praying, we should continue to read. As long as time allows, we should simply continue to read and pray and to pray and read.

Remaining in the Feeling Received throughout the Day

Although this type of reading and praying and praying and reading will come to an end, the feeling that we receive from reading the Bible should not end. We may stop our reading of the Bible, but the feeling should not come to an end; we must keep this feeling in our heart. In other words, if we read the Bible in the morning, we should learn to abide throughout the day in the feeling we received. We should live in the feeling we receive through our fellowship with God in the morning. This is a precious and important matter.

THE PRACTICE OF FELLOWSHIP

(5)

PRAYING AND READING THE BIBLE COMPLEMENTING EACH OTHER

According to our experience, praying and reading the Bible always complement each other and cannot be separated when we truly fellowship with God. It is difficult for a man to walk with one leg. He can walk only if he uses both legs. Both legs function together to walk on the same path. In our fellowship with God it may seem as if praying and reading the Bible are separate matters, just like our right and left legs. If we only pray or only read the Bible, our fellowship will not be balanced and perfect. In order to have balanced and perfect fellowship, there must be praying with reading and reading with praying.

As we have seen, there are two types of prayer and two ways to read the Bible. One type of prayer is for fellowship, and the other is for asking related to matters and things. Similarly, one way to read the Bible is for fellowship, and the other is for understanding. We are not concerned with prayer that asks for things or with reading the Bible for understanding. Praying is for fellowship, and reading the Bible is also for fellowship. The emphasis in praying is not on asking for matters and things, and the focus of reading is not on understanding; rather, both emphasize fellowship. Praying is fellowship; reading is also fellowship. Praying for fellowship and reading for fellowship are two elements that are absolutely indispensable in our fellowship with God. Our fellowship with God is balanced and perfect when we have both praying and reading. Hence, we will now consider these two matters together. Otherwise, we may have an erroneous thought that we need a period of time for praying and a separate period of time for reading the Bible. Strictly speaking, these two matters should not be done at separate times. They need to complement each other, just as a man walks with both his right and left legs at the same time.

In order to understand the fundamental reasons for praying and reading the Bible together in our fellowship with God, there is a need for some basic explanation.

In the New Testament John gives the clearest explanation concerning God having a relationship with man, being man's life, and being experienced by man. John covers several matters related to these in his Gospel and Epistles.

God Being Spirit

In his Gospel John says, "God is Spirit, and those who worship Him must worship in spirit and truthfulness" (4:24). Here worship includes fellowship with God. This shows that if we want to fellowship with God, we must first be clear that God is Spirit. Since God is Spirit, He is in the Spirit. We should be clear concerning this first point. The first difficulty new believers encounter related to fellowship is that of wanting fellowship but not knowing where God is. This is a crucial point. John says that God is Spirit. Some other verses in the New Testament also tell us that God is in the Spirit. Hence, we should have this basic understanding of this point.

God Being the Word

Second, it still may be vague to us to say that God is Spirit because the Spirit is abstract and intangible. Thus, in his Gospel John also says, "In the beginning was the Word...and the Word was God" (1:1). In Revelation he also says that the Lord Jesus is the Word (19:13). In his writings John repeatedly speaks of God's being, saying that God is light, and God is love (1 John 1:5; 4:8). These two points are not directly related to our fellowship with God. But John also says that God is Spirit and that God is the Word, which directly relates to our fellowship with God. Fellowship refers to our contact with God. If we want to contact God, we must know that God is Spirit and that He is the Word.

We know that God is wonderful, hidden, and mysterious. He is invisible; we cannot see Him, much less locate Him. As a result, many people have the problem of not knowing how to touch God. They do not know how to contact and fellowship with Him. Because we are so used to hearing the expression *fellowship with God,* we may think that this is a simple matter. But if we consider this matter seriously, we will realize that this expression is very mysterious. It is easy to understand what it means to have fellowship with a brother, because we know where to find him. But when we say that we should fellowship with God, people ask, "Where is God? How can you touch Him?" These are difficult questions. But thank God that through John He said that He is Spirit and that He is the Word. He is Spirit, and He is in the Spirit; He is the Word, and He is in the Word. Therefore, to fellowship with God is to touch God in His Spirit and in His Word.

We may consider the Spirit to be abstract, but the Word is concrete. We all agree that the Word is something concrete. We may use ourselves as an example. Our thoughts are abstract, but when our abstract thoughts become words, they are concrete. Thank God that He is not only the Spirit, but He is also the Word. If God were only the Spirit and not the Word, we would have no way to touch Him or locate Him. Many of us have been saved for many years, but have we ever considered how difficult it would be for man to receive inspiration if God had not spoken, if He had not uttered one word? Without the Word of God, it would be difficult for man to receive any inspiration. We have the sense that we are touched by God because we have the Word of God. If God had never spoken, if He were merely God and merely the Spirit but not the Word, it would be difficult for us to be touched by Him. All the inspiration we receive is from His speaking, whether in a gospel meeting, an edification meeting, or in our personal meditation. When we say that the Spirit inspires us, it is actually the Word of God that has an effect on us. The moving of the Spirit within us is actually the moving of the Word. Someone may say that a person does not need the moving of the Spirit or the Word in order to know God because the eternal power and divine characteristics of God have been clearly seen since the creation of the world (Rom. 1:20). However, we would not have this realization without these words. If God were only the Spirit but not also the Word, He would be abstract to us; we would have no way to touch Him or to contact Him. But thank God that He is also the Word. We praise Him that He is the Word. Regrettably, not many children of God have realized the preciousness of God being the Word. We need to always remember that God is the Word. If He were merely the Spirit but not the Word, we would be in a helpless situation. As far as our feeling is concerned, we must have the Word. Otherwise, even if we receive inspiration, we may still not understand it. Although we cannot say that inspiration is not possible without the Word, we can say that without the Word we will not understand the inspiration we receive. We must have the Word in order to receive inspiration and understand it. Hence, we need to see clearly that God is not only the Spirit, but He is also the Word. God is not only in the Spirit, but He is also in the Word.

The Word Being the Spirit

Third, John says that the Word is the Spirit. This is wonderful. John writes in his Gospel that the Lord Jesus Himself said that His words are spirit (John 6:63). We need to see the preciousness of these three matters in the Gospel of John. First, God is Spirit (4:24). Second, God is the Word (1:1). Third, the Word is the Spirit (6:63). I hope that every brother and sister will remember these three matters: God is the Spirit, God is the Word, and the Word is the Spirit.

It is difficult to explain the Word being the Spirit. Simply speaking, the Lord speaks the Word, and the Word enters into us as the Spirit. His words remaining outside of us are merely words, but when they enter into us they become spirit. Hence, when we preach the gospel, we speak words, but when the words of the gospel enter into man, they become the Spirit.

After saying that His words are spirit, the Lord said that His words are life. When the words of the Lord enter into man and become spirit, they are life. A person who is saved after hearing the gospel is a person who has heard and received the words of the gospel into him. When the words of the gospel enter a person, they become spirit and life, and the person is regenerated and saved. A person who is not saved when he hears the gospel is one who does not allow the words to enter into him. He may even be able to clearly recite everything that was spoken. Thus, these words are not life to him. This applies not only to the gospel but also to the messages spoken in the meetings. For some brothers and sisters God's word is merely outside of them and has not entered into them. For other brothers and sisters God's word enters into them and becomes spirit in them, resulting in life. This also applies to reading the Bible. If the words of the Bible remain outside of us, they will be merely words. Even if we exercise our mind to memorize them, the words will still be words. However, sometimes when we read a verse or section of the Bible, this verse or section enters into us and becomes spirit, and as a result, we touch life. I do not know how to convey this mystery. I cannot explain this spiritual reality, but I do know it. When the words of the Bible enter into me and become spirit in me, they enable me to touch life within. This is practical and sweet.

Therefore, when these three facts are combined, they are meaningful and sweet. God is Spirit, and He is also the Word. If He were merely the Spirit but not the Word, we would have no way to contact Him. He must be the Word so that we can contact Him. When He comes to us as the Word and enters into us, He is the Spirit. God is Spirit. When He comes forth as the Spirit, He is the Word. When the Word enters into us, He becomes Spirit once again. As a result, we can touch Him. The coming out of the Spirit is the Word; the entering into us of the Word is the Spirit. In this way we can touch Him. If He did not come to us in this way, we would not be able to touch Him. If He were merely the Spirit, we would not be able to touch Him, and if He were merely the Word, we would also be unable to contact Him. However, He is the Spirit, He is also the Word, and the Word becomes the Spirit. In this way, the Spirit becomes the Word, and the Word becomes the Spirit; this way enables us to touch Him and to contact Him. These three verses in John are the key to touching God. Even if we cannot fully apprehend this, we need to remember it. Gradually, our realization that God is the Spirit as well as the Word will increase, and we will experience the Word entering into us as the Spirit. Then we will know the way for man to touch and contact God. We will know this secret.

The Spirit Needing Our Prayer

Now that we are clear concerning God, let us speak concerning ourselves. Since God is Spirit, we need to pray. From all that has been spoken in the training for the new believers, the messages given during regular meetings, and the publications, we should know that the emphasis in prayer is not on asking God for things but on contacting Him. God is the Spirit; hence, we need to contact Him through prayer. This is similar to contacting air by breathing, just as contacting water requires drinking, contacting food requires eating, and contacting clothes requires wearing them. In the same principle, contacting the Spirit requires prayer. God is Spirit, and contacting Him requires prayer. It is insufficient to merely meditate, and it is insufficient to merely study. Rather, we need to pray; we need to exercise our spirit to contact Him through prayer. We close our eyes when we pray to stop our entire outward being so that we can exercise our spirit to contact God who is Spirit. Only this is real prayer.

When people, believers and unbelievers, close their eyes, their outward man stops, and they can inwardly turn. When a believer turns, we immediately sense God. However, those who are proud are often unwilling to close their eyes, making it difficult for them to touch God. If we can lead a person to close his eyes when we preach the gospel to him, it will be easier for him to be saved. A willingness to close one's eyes is an indication that he truly desires to seek God and pray to God. Once he closes his eyes, stops his outward being, and turns to his spirit, he can immediately touch God. Sometimes even if a person in an extremely worldly situation closes his eyes, stops his outward being, and turns to his spirit, he will also touch God. This is truly wonderful.

Recently I read about a special name of God from the book of Numbers. Moses twice called God "the God of the spirits of all flesh." The first time is in 16:22 when the assembly of Israel rebelled against God, and God wanted to consume them. Moses immediately went to God and said, "O God, the God of the spirits of all flesh, will one man sin and You be angry with the whole assembly?" The second time is in chapter 27. After Moses went up to the mountain of Abarim and saw the land that God had given to the children of Israel, he was told that he would be gathered to his people and would not be able to lead the children of Israel any longer (cf. vv. 12-13). Thus, he uttered a prayer before God, saying, "Let Jehovah, the God of the spirits of all flesh, appoint a man over the assembly" (v. 16). In these two prayers Moses addressed God as the God of the spirits of all flesh. These words indicate that everyone has a spirit. God is the God of the spirit of man. God's relationship with man is altogether related to man's spirit. As the God of human beings, He is the God of the human spirit. God is not the God of man's mind; rather, He is the God of the spirit of man. He is the God of the spirits of all flesh. Therefore, there is no need to argue or reason with people concerning the existence of God. This only focuses people on gaining God through their mind, making God the God of man's mind. But God is not the God of man's mind; rather, He is the God of the spirits of all flesh. Hence, when we preach the gospel, the best way for our words to enter into man is to speak concerning sin, because this can touch man's conscience, which is a part of man's spirit.

Let me repeat: God is Spirit; hence, we need to pray to Him. We should always bear this word in mind. God being the Spirit requires us to pray, just as air requires our breathing and water requires our drinking. If we do not drink water, we have no way to contact and receive water; if we do not breathe, we have no way to receive air. Likewise, if we do not pray, we have no way to contact God who is Spirit. This is a universal law of God according to His creation and arrangement. We cannot understand and explain this law, just as we cannot understand and explain other universal laws. If we want to contact air in the universe, we must breathe, and if we want to contact food, we must eat. In the same principle, if we want to contact God who is Spirit, we must pray. Although we may not understand this, we have experienced it. If we turn to our spirit to come near to God and touch Him, disregarding our reasons, emotions, and outward environment, we will sense that God has touched us, because He is Spirit. We should not care whether we are happy, sad, rich, or poor, but we should simply stop our outward being. He requires us to exercise our spirit to pray to Him. Thus, the way to contact God is to pray. We need to pray so that we can contact and fellowship with Him. Thus, for us to fellowship with God, we must pray.

The Word Needing Our Reading

God as the Spirit needs our prayer, and God as the Word needs our reading. We pray in the Spirit, and we read the Word. We need to pray in order to fellowship with God because God is the Spirit. We need to read the Bible in order to fellowship with God because God is the Word. Because God is the Spirit and is in the Spirit, we need to exercise our spirit to pray in order to contact Him. Similarly, because God is the Word and is in the Word, we need to read the Word in order to contact Him. Everyone understands this principle.

As children of God, we may not have heard and understood much doctrine, but we do have some experience. This is the same with reading the Bible. We may not necessarily know how to read the Bible, but after we read and contact the Word of God and then are quiet and meditate, we sense that we have touched God Himself. As soon as we touch the Word of God, we sense that we have touched God. We have often had this experience. Even though I may forget what I read in the Bible, I feel that I have fellowshipped with God and contacted Him.

Having said this much, I believe that we should be clearer now. We pray because God is the Spirit, and therefore, He requires our prayer. We read the Bible because God is the Word, and therefore, He requires our reading. If we understand this, we will overthrow the erroneous concepts that we pray in order to ask God to give us something or to do something for us and that we read the Bible because we want to understand doctrine. We pray because God is Spirit, not to ask for things, and we read the Bible because God is the Word, not to understand doctrine. We pray to contact God, and we read the Word to contact God. We must change our concept. This will make us proper Christians who lead a normal Christian life. If we can enter into the fellowship of praying while reading and reading while praying, we will be able to avoid the mistaken teachings of Christianity. The new believers should understand that we pray because God is the Spirit, and we read the Bible because God is the Word. We need to contact God the Spirit by praying, and we also need to contact God the Word by reading the Bible. Only when we have such a concept can we enter into a good fellowship with God.

The Word Needing to Become the Spirit

Since we read the Bible to contact God, what we read needs to enter into us to become the Spirit. We should never think that this is difficult and time consuming. No, if we practice, the Word will easily become the Spirit whenever we read the Bible. If the words we read remain as words only, we have not practiced sufficiently and are overly relying on our mind. This is the reason I have repeatedly said that we should not intend to understand, to study, or to ponder. Once our mind is focused on studying and pondering, the words of the Bible will not enter us but will remain merely words. However, with sufficient practice, we can touch the Spirit whenever we read the Bible. When we touch the Spirit, the words will enter us and become the Spirit. When we read the Bible with our spirit, the words of the Bible will enter into us and become the Spirit. If we learn to read the Bible in this way, we will feel as if we have eaten a meal after reading. This is wonderful. Although we may read the Bible for half an hour and not remember much, we will feel as if we have eaten a full meal and taken a good bath in our spirit. Often I read the Bible with no intention to remember or ponder what I have read. Even though I do not remember what I read, my spirit is satisfied with food and drink. I feel refreshed within, as if I have just taken a deep breath of fresh air. The words of the Bible enter into me and become the Spirit.

It is wonderful that a word rises within us as a timely help in the midst of a particular need, even though we think that we do not remember much. This is the work of the Holy Spirit. We may not remember which verse, chapter, or even the book we read, but the word we contacted with our spirit entered into us and became the Spirit to be our inward help. Therefore, we need to continue to exercise to contact the Word of God with our spirit and allow the Word of God to enter into us and become the Spirit. This type of reading is different from reading for understanding. Although there is a need for that, it should be done at a different time.

The Spirit Needing to Become the Word

This point is the reverse of the previous point. When the Word enters into us, it becomes the Spirit; this is a matter of entrance. However, the Spirit becoming the Word is a matter of operation. This operation is similar to the moving of the Holy Spirit that we usually refer to. Once the Word enters into us, it becomes the Spirit, and once the Spirit operates in us, He becomes the Word. This is a sure principle.

We need to learn to contact the words of the Bible with our spirit. When we have the inspiration of the Spirit, we need to allow the inspiration within us to become the Word. At this juncture, our mind needs to be spiritual, and our thoughts need to be trained spiritually so that we are able to interpret the inspiration of the Spirit. Our mind needs to cooperate with the Spirit so that we can interpret the meaning of the inspiration we receive. In this way, the Spirit can become the Word in us.

The Word becomes the Spirit when our reading of the Bible is turned into prayer. We should be able to understand the meaning of the Spirit and let the Spirit become the Word in our prayer. Hence, it is not good to put off our prayer until the end of our reading. When we contact the words of the Bible and the Word becomes the Spirit within us, we should pray. This prayer involves worship, thanksgiving, and praise. Whenever the Word becomes the Spirit as we read, we should pray; once the Spirit becomes the Word through our prayer, we should continue to read. As a result, the Word becomes the

Spirit, and the Spirit becomes the Word. We read awhile and then pray; we pray awhile and then read. This is a sweet fellowship. The word we contact becomes the Spirit in us, and the more we pray, the more inspiration of the Spirit we receive. Gradually, the inspiration of the Spirit becomes the Word, and we read God's Word again. As we continue reading, the Word becomes the Spirit, and we pray again. As we continue reading and praying, we will surely have good fellowship with God. We will enjoy the fellowship to such an extent that we forget our sickness, our poverty, and even the many problems in our locality. We will forget all of these things.

Some may still ask, "What about my sickness? What should I do about not having enough money?" We should not have so many questions. After this type of fellowship with the Lord, we should simply rise and say, "Lord, You know that I am still sick and that I have no money in my pocket." This one sentence is sufficient. We should mention our needs before God in a simple way. This is strong and effective prayer. The faith we need will come spontaneously. God will do something. When we enter into God through fellowship, it is easy for us to know whether or not God wants us to mention such matters. Sometimes our inner situation is similar to Moses' experience in his last days, when God said, "Enough! Speak no more to Me about this matter" (Deut. 3:26). We can know whether God wants us to pray about a certain matter. Then all of our prayers will hit the mark. We will be able to touch and understand God's will. This will keep us from being overly concerned with bearing the burdens of sickness, poverty, and other things rather than fellowshipping with God and touching Him.

If we consider Abraham, we will see that his intercession touched God. He was always in fellowship and contact with God; in the end, he uttered a prayer to intercede for the city of Sodom. This was a person who touched God in his fellowship; hence, his prayer could be precise and simple yet powerful and effective. His prayer could restrict and bind God so that God had to answer.

The biography of Brother George Müller shows that he rarely begged God for anything. He lived before God and

fellowshipped with Him continually. Hence, when he mentioned a certain matter to God, he first asked God whether
He would do it. After he sensed that a matter was of God's
will, he would say, "Since this is Your will, I ask You to accomplish it." His prayer was spontaneous, easy, and effortless
because he was a man who touched God in fellowship. Certain
matters do require us to pray with much effort, even to fast
and fight, but this is another aspect of prayer. Now we
need to see that prayer requires us to first touch God in
fellowship.

Preventing Interruptions

In this kind of fellowship of praying and reading, reading
and praying, a fellowship in which the Word becomes the
Spirit and the Spirit becomes the Word, we need to do our
best to prevent and guard against interruptions. Then we will
enjoy the fellowship to the uttermost. We need to put aside and
not pray for the many things that may require prayer. Truth-
fully, many things do not require our prayer. As long as these
matters are in our heart, God knows about them and remem-
bers them accordingly. He wants us to worship Him, fellowship
with Him, absorb Him, enjoy Him, and gain Him; this is the
most pleasing to Him. The Lord said that our heavenly Father
knows all we need (Matt. 6:8). Thus, we should leave all these
things to Him. He knows our sickness, our family problems,
our lack, and our needs. We do not need to beg before Him;
instead, we should be at peace and believe. The one thing,
the best thing, we should do is to touch Him, worship Him,
believe in Him, pursue Him, and gain Him. He will add all the
other things to us. Therefore, we should not let consideration
of these things interrupt us. We should try our best to stay in
fellowship. If we have ten minutes, we should spend ten minutes to fellowship with Him; if we have twenty minutes, we
should spend twenty minutes to fellowship with Him. We can
lift up our face at any time and at any place and speak to Him
of our practical needs. But when we are fellowshipping with
God, we should not bring in these matters.

It is useless to merely speak concerning these things. We
need to practice them diligently and help others practice

them. As we gradually become more adept in the matter of fellowship, we will taste the sweetness and enjoy the riches of fellowship in reality.

ABOUT THE AUTHOR

Witness Lee was born in 1905 in northern China and raised in a Christian family. At age 19 he was fully captured for Christ and immediately consecrated himself to preach the gospel for the rest of his life. Early in his service, he met Watchman Nee, a renowned preacher, teacher, and writer. Witness Lee labored together with Watchman Nee under his direction. In 1934 Watchman Nee entrusted Witness Lee with the responsibility for his publication operation, called the Shanghai Gospel Bookroom.

Prior to the Communist takeover in 1949, Witness Lee was sent by Watchman Nee and his other co-workers to Taiwan to ensure that the things delivered to them by the Lord would not be lost. Watchman Nee instructed Witness Lee to continue the former's publishing operation abroad as the Taiwan Gospel Bookroom, which has been publicly recognized as the publisher of Watchman Nee's works outside China. Witness Lee's work in Taiwan manifested the Lord's abundant blessing. From a mere 350 believers, newly fled from the mainland, the churches in Taiwan grew to 20,000 in five years.

In 1962 Witness Lee felt led of the Lord to come to the United States, and he began to minister in Los Angeles. During his 35 years of service in the U.S., he ministered in weekly meetings and weekend conferences, delivering several thousand spoken messages. Much of his speaking has since been published as over 400 titles. Many of these have been translated into over fourteen languages. He gave his last public conference in February 1997 at the age of 91.

He leaves behind a prolific presentation of the truth in the Bible. His major work, *Life-study of the Bible,* comprises over 25,000 pages of commentary on every book of the Bible from the perspective of the believers' enjoyment and experience of God's divine life in Christ through the Holy Spirit. Witness Lee was the chief editor of a new translation of the New Testament into Chinese called the Recovery Version and directed the translation of the same into English. The Recovery Version also appears in a number of other languages. He provided an extensive body of footnotes, outlines, and spiritual cross references. A radio broadcast of his messages can be heard on Christian radio stations in the United States. In 1965 Witness Lee founded Living Stream Ministry, a non-profit corporation, located in Anaheim, California, which officially presents his and Watchman Nee's ministry.

Witness Lee's ministry emphasizes the experience of Christ as life and the practical oneness of the believers as the Body of Christ. Stressing the importance of attending to both these matters, he led the churches under his care to grow in Christian life and function. He was unbending in his conviction that God's goal is not narrow sectarianism but the Body of Christ. In time, believers began to meet simply as the church in their localities in response to this conviction. In recent years a number of new churches have been raised up in Russia and in many European countries.